THE PARTY IS OVER

THE PARTY

THE NEW LOUISIANA POLITICS

IS OVER

EDITED BY PEARSON CROSS AND CHRISTIE L. MALOYED

Louisiana State University Press
Baton Rouge

Publication of this book is made possible in part by the support of
The Noland Fund.

Published by Louisiana State University Press
lsupress.org

Manufactured in the United States of America
First printing

DESIGNER: Michelle A. Neustrom
TYPEFACE: Minion Pro
PRINTER AND BINDER: Sheridan Books, Inc.

All graphs and the map were drawn by Mary Lee Eggart.

Jacket image: iStock.com/Antonbr Anton

LIBRARY OF CONGRESS CATALOGING-IN-PUBLICATION DATA

Names: Cross, Pearson, editor. | Maloyed, Christie L., editor.
Title: The party is over : the new Louisiana politics / edited by Pearson Cross and Christie L. Maloyed.
Description: Baton Rouge : Louisiana State University Press, 2022. | Includes bibliographical references and index.
Identifiers: LCCN 2021031472 (print) | LCCN 2021031473 (ebook) | ISBN 978-0-8071-7658-0 (cloth) | ISBN 978-0-8071-7698-6 (pdf) | ISBN 978-0-8071-7699-3 (epub)
Subjects: LCSH: Louisiana—Politics and government—21st century. | Political culture—Louisiana.
Classification: LCC JK4716 .P38 2022 (print) | LCC JK4716 (ebook) | DDC 320.9763—dc23
LC record available at https://lccn.loc.gov/2021031472
LC ebook record available at https://lccn.loc.gov/2021031473

CONTENTS

ACKNOWLEDGMENTS

Even in the best of times, compiling an edited volume can be a daunting task. To do so amid an unprecedented global pandemic might have been ill-advised. But the contributors to this volume persevered against formidable odds to make the project successful. We are grateful for their persistence and patience throughout this process. Our understanding of Louisiana politics—the progress made and the challenges ahead—are deeply enriched by their thoughtful and informative essays. Along the way, we also solicited research and technical help from Harlan Picht, graphical assistance from Anna Kate Barnes, and the design and cartographical skills of Mary Lee Eggart. We are thankful for their contributions. We also appreciate the work of our editor, Rand Dotson, for his enthusiastic support and guidance in the process and the team at LSU Press for seeing it to print.

THE PARTY IS OVER

AN INTRODUCTION TO THE STATE OF LOUISIANA POLITICS

PEARSON CROSS AND CHRISTIE L. MALOYED

Commentators on Louisiana politics have historically focused on the uniqueness of the state. Long before T. Harry Williams wrote his Pulitzer Prize-winning *Huey Long* in 1970, the charming eccentricity of Louisiana was fixed in the public's consciousness. Contrasting Louisiana politics with the politics of less exotic states is a trope developed in countless articles, books, reviews, and films. Most writers, struggling to capture what makes Louisiana politics so different, have reached outside the United States for analogs, suggesting a comparison with "banana republics." Others, despairing of capturing the essence of Louisiana's unique politics, have called it a gumbo, which, of course, explains everything and nothing at all.

Broadly speaking, Louisiana politics reflects unique historical, demographic, cultural, and economic influences that have combined to produce a political culture quite unlike that of other states. Some of these differences include the extra-constitutional power of Louisiana governors, the election system arising from Louisiana's history of one-party politics, the corrupting influence of oil money on political practice, and the populist impulse that periodically arrays the people against powerful insiders. Other differences include Louisiana's civil law tradition inherited from French and Spanish sources, the geographical division of faith between North Louisiana Baptists and South Louisiana Catholics, and the domination of local governments by the state government in Baton Rouge.

While these factors have been useful in explaining Louisiana politics in the past, they are rapidly losing their efficacy. Modern American politics and life are burying what once made Louisiana unique and different. Indeed, Louisiana today is a Deep South state quickly shedding the vibrant culture and distinct political practices that for three centuries have distinguished it from its southern neighbors. A common theme uniting the essays in *The Party Is Over: The New Louisiana Politics* is that Louisiana has finally forsaken its colorful past for a more prosaic future as a southern Republican stronghold.

This realignment of Louisiana's state and local politics has not received much attention. Publishers have continued to focus on what makes Louisiana special rather than alike. In addition, books addressing Louisiana politics as a whole are rare. While several monographs have focused on significant persons or major events, such as Hurricane Katrina, a comprehensive reappraisal of Louisiana politics has not been undertaken since 1982, when the LSU Press published *Louisiana Politics: Festival in a Labyrinth,* edited by James Bolner. Bolner's book featured twelve scholars who analyzed Louisiana's constitution, legislature, executive, judiciary, politics, and public policies. More recently, Wayne Parent's illuminating book, *Inside the Carnival: Unmasking Louisiana Politics* (2004), unpacked many of the distinctive elements of Louisiana politics and government, hinting at, making fun of, and illustrating the complex history that makes Louisiana politics fascinating.[1]

Bolner's and Parent's work educated two generations of Louisiana students, examining and explaining the most important characteristics of the state's politics, government, policy, and demography. While there are unique institutional and cultural elements that continue to distinguish Louisiana's political tradition from that of other states, the homogenizing effects of national partisan and policy trends call for a revaluation of Louisiana's political status.

What has changed? Perhaps the most dramatic change to note has been the Democratic Party's reversal of fortune. Led by Barry Goldwater and Richard Nixon, white southerners began to identify as Republicans in the late 1960s. However, for reasons sketched below, many Louisianans resisted this region-wide trend. Up until 2003, for example, most registered voters, city and parish elected officials, legislators in both houses, and all state-wide officials (with one exception) were Democrats (see table I.1).

While this preponderance of Democrats did not prevent occasional Republican successes at the gubernatorial level and in selected legislative districts, taken as a whole, Republicans constituted a distinct minority in Louisi-

TABLE I.1. Party Registration Percentages, Louisiana Gubernatorial Primary Elections, 1999–2019

	Democrat	*Republican*	*Other*
1999	61.4	21.6	17.0
2003	57.0	23.4	19.6
2007	53.0	24.7	22.3
2011	49.6	26.8	23.6
2015	46.0	28.1	25.9
2019	42.4	31.0	26.6

ana. Since 2003, however, Republicans have emerged as the strongest political party at all levels of government in Louisiana, excluding only those districts with large numbers of African Americans and urban areas. During the same period, Democratic Party registration has plummeted from 57.0 percent in 2003 to 42.4 percent today, leaving aside the large number of citizens registered as Democrats but casting votes for Republican candidates.[2] While this stark change of fortunes did not prevent Democrats from electing a governor in 2015 and 2019, winning a state-wide election required special circumstances to overcome rapidly multiplying disadvantages, one of which was their abandonment by French Catholics in Acadiana.[3] While this regional ethnic and linguistic group had maintained ties to the Democratic Party long after other white groups, by 2003 most South Louisiana Catholics followed their priests and bishops into the Republican Party on the overwhelming appeal of opposition to abortion.[4]

Meanwhile, the losses Democrats experienced in the electorate paled compared to their losses in the legislature. In 2004, Democrats held a nearly two-thirds majority of the seats in both the House (69 of 105 seats) and Senate (26 of 39 seats). However, the 2020 figures reflect a profound change of fortune, with Republicans holding a nearly two-thirds majority in the House (68 seats) and an absolute two-thirds majority (27 seats) in the Senate (see table I.2).

Partly because of Republican successes, Louisiana's House and Senate have begun to exercise the independence expected of coequal institutions.

TABLE I.2. Partisan Makeup of the Louisiana State Legislature, 2000–2020

	House of Representatives		*Senate*	
	Democrat	*Republican*	*Democrat*	*Republican*
2000	70	33	26	13
2004	69	36	26	13
2008	55	50	24	15
2012	45	58	20	18
2016	41	58	14	25
2020	35	68	12	27

Beginning with the 2016 legislative session, Republicans thwarted Governor John Bel Edwards's traditional and historic role in naming the speaker of the House and president of the Senate, along with the leadership of the most powerful committees in the legislature. This migration from Democratic to Republican control in the legislature and in state-wide office has been aided by the many elected officials who switched party registration, none more prominently than State Senator Noble Ellington, whose switch in 2010 brought the Louisiana House under Republican control for the first time since Reconstruction. Prominent Republicans who were once Democrats today include former governor Buddy Roemer, recent Senate president John Alario, US Senator John Kennedy, former House speaker Taylor Barras, and a multitude of others. Table I.3 illustrates the vast number of officeholders who switched parties.

The change of leadership from Republican to Democrat in the House and Senate has proved to be consequential for state affairs in the areas of health care, higher education, K–12 funding, business investment, transportation, and energy. Under the leadership of Republican governor Bobby Jindal, a new governing philosophy began to take sway in Louisiana. Always conservative in practice, local Louisiana issues began to be swamped by national preoccupations with taxes and growth, health care costs, welfare, prison reform, and social issues. The Louisiana legislature began to legislate aggressively on abortion and prayer in school, while expanding the role of private organiza-

TABLE I.3. Partisan Switching in Louisiana, 2001–2019

Name	*Office*	*Original Party*	*New Party*	*Year of Switch*
Hunt Downer	Speaker of the House	D	R	2001
Juba Diez	Rep.	D	R	2003
Melinda Schwegmann	Rep. and Lt. Gov	D	R	2003
Rodney Alexander	Rep.	D	R	2004
Dan Morrish	Sen.	D	R	2005
Ernest Wooton	Rep.	I	R	2005
Bill Cassidy	Rep. and Sen.	D	R	2006
Isabella de la Houssaye	Rep.	D	R	2007
Elbert Lee Guillory	Sen.	R	D	2007
John Kennedy	Sen.	D	R	2007
Walter Boasso	Sen.	R	D	2007
Kenneth Odinet Sr.	Rep.	D	R	2008
Nancy Landry	Rep.	I	R	2008
Gillis Pinac	Rep.	D	R	2009
John R. Smith	Sen.	D	R	2010
Ernest Wooton	Rep.	R	I	2010
Troy Hebert	Sen.	D	I	2010
Walker Hines	Rep.	D	R	2010
Noble Ellington	Rep.	D	R	2010
Simone Champagne	Rep.	D	R	2010
Scott Angelle	Lt. Gov	D	R	2010
John Alario	Sen.	D	R	2010
Fred Mills	Rep.	D	R	2010
Buddy Caldwell	La. Attorney General	D	R	2011
Norbert Chabert	Sen.	D	R	2011
Jody Amedee	Sen.	D	R	2011
Taylor Barras	Rep.	D	R	2011
Ronnie Johns	Sen.	D	R	2011
Joel Robideaux	Sen.	I	R	2011
Mike Huval	Rep.	D	R	2011
Charles Chaney	Rep.	D	R	2011
Billy Chandler	Rep.	D	R	2011
Terry Landry	Rep.	I	D	2011

(*continued on next page*)

TABLE I.3. Partisan Switching in Louisiana, 2001–2019 (*continued*)

Name	*Office*	*Original Party*	*New Party*	*Year of Switch*
Elbert Lee Guillory	Rep.	D	R	2013
Rick Ward	Sen.	D	R	2013
James Fannin	Rep.	D	R	2013
Jim Morris	Rep.	R	I	2018
Wayne McMahen	Rep.	D	R	2018
Roy Adams	Rep.	D	I	2019
Neil Abramson	Rep.	D	R	2019

tions in partnership with government through charter schools, vouchers, and public-private contracts.

Meanwhile, a "campaign style" of governing began to be the norm in Louisiana as entrepreneurial state officials used social media to reach supporters and sway public opinion. In turn, newspapers found their readership declining as readers deserted them for news sources that catered to their political predispositions. This led to consolidation in the press and a lack of reliable sources of local information for citizens. Electoral campaigns themselves changed dramatically as outside groups and political action committees poured money into races from the governor down to the parish president. Even contests for the Board of Elementary Education (BESE) and Supreme Court seats became sites of partisan struggle, as outside dollars flowed to these formerly sleepy races.

While the legislature passed bills promoting prayer in school and restricting LGBT rights, the after-effects of Hurricane Katrina shook Louisiana socially, politically, and economically. Led by big city mayors like Kip Holden and LaToya Cantrell, Black Louisianans exerted influence on several contested issues, including education, incarceration, and Confederate monuments. Challenging the reformist impulse was the continuing reluctance of Louisianans to elect women to political office compared with other states. The shrinking coastline, wounded by the 2010 BP Spill, presented further challenges. As the state grappled with the cleanup, the legislature debated the reality of climate change and where BP's windfall dollars should be spent. Few in government seemed willing to admit that the "sportsman's paradise" was facing an existential challenge, and even fewer evinced any willingness to take concrete steps to address the issue.

Louisiana's economy continued to underperform, trailing the rest of the country and the South by most measures. Despite the efforts of two Republican and two Democratic governors (Foster, Blanco, Jindal, Edwards), Louisiana remained deeply mired in an extractive economy that failed to produce wealth for most of its people. Suffering the vicissitudes of the oil economy, Louisiana experienced massive dislocation and economic upheaval following the 2014 oil price crisis. In response, and continuing a trend begun during a similar crisis in the 1980s, hundreds of thousands of Louisiana's most productive citizens decamped in search of greener pastures in Texas, Colorado, and California. Those remaining in Louisiana found themselves struggling with poverty, income inequality, and a frayed social safety net exacerbated by an antiquated tax collection system and a legislature too willing to sacrifice local tax revenue for meager employment gains.

OUTLINE OF THE BOOK

The Party Is Over: The New Louisiana Politics offers a comprehensive reassessment of Louisiana politics and political life, analyzing major shifts in political institutions, partisan competition, and policy. Taking change as their starting points, the fourteen essays address the areas that have experienced the most profound and significant change, analyzing and updating our understanding of Louisiana politics.

Part I, "Institutions," introduces the foundational elements of Louisiana's government, including the constitution, legislature, governor, and local government. In "Louisiana's Constitution: Bigger Is Not Always Better," Beverly Moore Haydel, Steven Procopio, and Robert Travis Scott examine the lengthy Louisiana constitution, noting parallels between the conditions prompting the last constitutional rewrite in 1973 and the calls for a constitutional convention today. In "Following Francis: Legislative Evolution, from Populist to Partisan (1975–2020)," Jeremy Alford investigates changes in the Louisiana legislature, noting the effect of term limits on legislative careers, the increased power of Republicans in the institution, and changes due to the increasing role of women and Black lawmakers. In "From Circus Master to Band Director: The Shrinking Louisiana Governor," Pearson Cross shows how the legislature's increasing ideological divide and the passage of ethics legislation has worked to limit many of the powers and abilities that previously made the Louisiana governor so powerful. This institutional decline is countered, however, by the increasing use of emergency powers exercised by the governor in response to ecological, meteorological, and fiscal crises. In "Louisiana's Local Politics: Institutional and Economic Tug of War," Christie L. Maloyed describes strains in the economic relationship between state and local governments as both wrestle with outdated tax programs and structures. These economic conflicts are particularly evident in Baton Rouge and Lafayette because of their consolidated system of government.

Part II, "Politics," focuses on political communication, elections, women in politics, public opinion, and the political and demographic effects of Hurricane Katrina. In "The Latest Last Hayride: Louisiana's Political Journalism in Transition," Robert Mann charts the loosening hold that local news sources have on readers, dollars, and influence as the industry is reshaped by social media, memes, and outside groups. This dramatic reshaping of media has contributed to a decline in coverage of state and local news, resulting in fewer well-informed voters. In "The New Politics of Louisiana's Elections," Joshua Stockley details the movement of African Americans into Louisiana's Democratic Party and the rise of the Republican Party to dominance, focusing on the changing nature of party competition in Louisiana in recent elections. In "Public Opinion in Louisiana: More Change, More of the Same," Michael Henderson explores the relationship between polarization and partisanship in the Louisiana electorate, finding that Louisiana has become more partisan while polarization has lagged, mirroring national trends. The alignment of conservatives with the Republican Party is further illustrated in "Gone with the Wind (and Water): Hurricane Katrina, the Great Recession, and the Death of Populism," where Albert Samuels examines how Hurricane Katrina and the Great Recession ended the populist tradition in Louisiana and led to a dramatically more conservative political environment, linking Louisiana more closely with other southern states. In "Women in Louisiana Politics:

Barriers and Opportunities," Mirya Holman and Anna Mitchell Mahoney's essay closing Part II, the authors explore the underrepresentation of women in Louisiana politics, asking whether it is a problem of supply or demand. Their analysis suggests that increased numbers of women in elected offices have shifted the policy conversation in several areas. As more groups support the recruitment and training of women candidates, they continue to take a greater role in future Louisiana politics.

"Policy," the third part of *The Party Is Over*, analyzes Louisiana's changing policy environment, focusing on the economy, the social safety net, criminal justice reform, coastal restoration, and racial reconciliation. In "The Economy of Louisiana," Gary Wagner and Stephen Barnes provide an overview of the Louisiana economy, focusing on the industries, events, and trends that will help determine the shape and development of the state's economy in the future. In "The Coast: Federal and State Relations in the Midst of a Crisis," Mark Davis focuses on how Louisiana's coast, economic development, waterways, levees, and oil industry have been shaped by politics and law, and what this has meant for the state's ecological present and future. Focusing on the widespread poverty that continues to affect the state's citizens, in "Poverty and the Louisiana Safety Net in the Twenty-First Century" Jan Moller describes recent changes to Louisiana's public safety net and the politics that drove these changes. Changes include a dismantling of the public hospital system and transition to a managed care system, an expansion of Medicaid, and an end to most cash assistance. In "Louisiana Crime and Justice in the Twenty-First Century," Chase Edwards, Michelle Jeanis, and David Khey examine Louisiana's long and painful history of crime, sentencing, and incarceration and recent coalition-building across deep partisan and racial divides to reduce the size of the carceral state. Rick Swanson's concluding essay, "The Politics of Racial Memory in Louisiana," examines Louisiana's lengthy history of racial oppression. Using the debate over Confederate moments, he shows how representations of racial history have become embedded in narratives of identity.

The essays gathered in *The Party Is Over* provide a necessary reappraisal of politics in Louisiana and a base from which to construct future accounts of the state's politics and policy. Louisiana's developing politics contain opportunities and perils. This book describes both and provides a way to think through the current state of affairs.

NOTES

1. Attention should also be paid to the excellent essay by Wayne Parent and Huey Perry in *The New Politics of the Old South: An Introduction to Southern Politics,* 6th ed., ed. Charles S. Bullock III and Mark J. Rozell (Lanham, Md.: Rowman and Littlefield, 2018). See the "Selected Bibliography on Louisiana Politics" for additional suggested readings.

2. See Michael Henderson's essay for additional information on registered Democrats who identify as Republicans. See also Joshua Stockley's essay for a detailed evolution of partisan realignment within the state.

3. That John Bel Edwards was able to secure victory in Louisiana in 2015 was more than just a long-shot, it was based on a unique confluence of factors which are unlikely to be repeated. Tyler Bridges and Jeremy Alford make this clear in *Long Shot: A Soldier, a Senator, a Serious Sin, an Epic Louisiana Election* (Baton Rouge, La.: Lisburn Press, 2016).

4. Evidence of this is provided by the loss of hometown favorite Kathleen Blanco in Lafayette Parish during the 2003 gubernatorial runoff, which she lost to Republican Bobby Jindal 52–48 percent. (Statewide, the margin was reversed.) Louisiana Secretary of State, https://www.sos.la.gov/ElectionsAndVoting/GetElectionInformation/Pages/default.aspx.

PART I
INSTITUTIONS

LOUISIANA'S CONSTITUTION

Bigger Is Not Always Better

BEVERLY MOORE HAYDEL
STEVEN PROCOPIO
AND ROBERT TRAVIS SCOTT

Louisiana is a rare bird. Both charmingly and frustratingly different, the Pelican State's unique ways begin with its legal system. As the only state heavily influenced by the Napoleonic Code, Louisiana rests on the word of law. Indeed, the words are copious, beginning with the foundational governmental document: the state constitution.

Since Louisiana joined the Union in 1812, it has been governed by eleven separate state constitutions—more than any other state. Louisiana's current constitution was written by a convention held in 1973 and 1974, was ratified by voters in 1974, and became effective on January 1, 1975. The events that brought about the 1973 convention were not dissimilar from the conditions prompting current discourse about the need for a major constitutional rewrite. In this essay, we discuss the origins of Louisiana's current constitution as well as how and why it has veered off course. We conclude by looking at what it will take to get the constitution back on track.

Louisiana's constitution of 1921 contained 48,378 words when it was adopted, but with 536 amendments in fifty-one years, the document grew to nearly 255,500 words. That's about the length of Shakespeare's eleven longest tragedies combined. Not even the most consummate attorney could have known all that was in it. In his pitch for reform, newly elected Governor Edwin Edwards appeared on television in 1972 decrying the expanding number of books needed to contain the state constitution. Louisiana's practice had become government by constitutional amendment.

In 1970, a package of amendments was proposed to address the criticisms, but voters rejected all fifty-three amendment proposals on the statewide ballot. In two subsequent elections held during 1972, voters again turned down thirty-six of forty-two proposed amendments. With a constitution so detailed that it placed restrictions on many key facets of governance and with no realistic prospect for continued use of the amendment process, the alternatives were either a constitutional convention or a revision commission followed by a convention.

With the newly inaugurated administration of Governor Edwards, the 1972 legislature passed Act 2 calling for a convention. There were 132 delegates in all, 105 of whom were elected from the corresponding number of single-member districts for the Louisiana House of Representatives, together with 27 delegates appointed by the governor. Fifteen of the appointments were from the public at large, and the rest were from various industry groups and unions.

Act 2 required the delegates to convene on January 5, 1973, to elect officers and organize committees and then recess until July 5. During those seven months, a research team worked with each of the committees to draft a preliminary constitution. At the same time, convention delegates held a series of public meetings throughout the state to gather input on what should or should not be included in a new constitution. When the delegates reconvened in July 1973, the majority of the document had been written, which meant the delegates spent their time debating and refining its particulars. The convention process was highly publicized statewide, aided by the Public Affairs Research Council of Louisiana (PAR), which published analyses and commentary on matters before the body. PAR, a nonpartisan good government watchdog and policy think tank, has been involved with fiscal issues and constitutional reform since its founding in 1950.

After more than a year of work, the convention produced a new constitution in January 1974. The proposed document was much shorter (36,252 words) and simpler than the unwieldy monster that the 1921 constitution had become. Portions of the 1921 constitution's fifteen articles were reenacted as statutes, and many other provisions were repealed altogether. Nonetheless, the new document, in the eyes of many, still was not perfect. Indeed, on January 10, 1974, Governor Edwards acknowledged the practical challenges of crafting an ideal constitution when he addressed the convention:

> Now, I must suggest to you . . . that what criticisms I have of the document . . . arise, very candidly, from your failure to recognize that you were here to write a constitution, rather than to serve as legislators. Had you stopped your work after completion of the Bill of Rights and the three Articles on the Executive, the Legislature, and the Judiciary, a beautiful, fantastically well-engineered and prepared document would have been your work product. Practical aspects of your job, however, required you to go further; and it is when you got into those provisions which are really legislative, and not constitutional matters, that the problems began to develop.

Despite these perceived shortcomings, the new 1974 constitution was ratified by voters in a statewide election on April 20, 1974. Although fewer than 40 percent of the electorate turned out and voters in thirty-six of sixty-four parishes rejected the convention's document, the new constitution was ratified by a statewide vote with 58 percent in favor.

THE LOUISIANA WAY

On the surface the Louisiana constitution seems typical. The articles cover subjects similar to those of the US Constitution, such as the three branches of government, the method for constitutional revision, and instructions for transitions (see table 1.1). Like a Bill of Rights, the Louisiana constitution's first article declares the rights of its citizens. Whereas the US Constitution lays out the relationship between the federal government and the states, Louisiana's constitution guides the relations between the state and local governments. Some sections reflect the nature of the state and its economy. Given Louisiana's historical reliance on oil, natural gas, and timber as economic engines and sources of government revenue, the state constitution's article on natural resources might seem appropriate.

Forty-five years later, that basic outline and those articles remain. But otherwise, the constitution looks much different. The first changes came in

TABLE 1.1. Outline of the Louisiana Constitution

Article I	Declaration of Rights
Article II	Distribution of Powers
Article III	Legislative Branch
Article IV	Executive Branch
Article V	Judicial Branch
Article VI	Local Government
Article VII	Revenue and Finance
Article VIII	Education
Article IX	Natural Resources
Article X	Public Officials and Employees
Article XI	Elections
Article XII	General Provisions
Article XIII	Constitution Revision
Article XIV	Transitional Provisions

1978, and nearly every year since. Up through the 2019 election, 285 constitutional amendments had been proposed, of which 197 were adopted. The fall 2020 ballot held seven more proposed amendments. That is an average of seven amendments per year placed before voters, who approve nearly five per year on average, for an approval rate of 69 percent. In 2006 alone, voters were asked to decide on twenty-one amendments, the largest number of proposed changes in a calendar year since the 1974 constitution was adopted. All were approved, with less than 30 percent voter turnout.

The result of this constant and frequent constitutional modification is a document that is now 72,272 words—twice as long as the original (see table 1.2). As of 2018, Louisiana had the fourth longest constitution in the country, lagging behind only Alabama (388,882), Texas (86,936), and Oklahoma (81,666). Louisiana's constitution is three times the length of the average state constitution (26,000 words) and nearly ten times longer than the US Constitution. What was once a reasonably short document has now morphed into something that would take perhaps days to read and even more time to absorb. Moreover, many provisions that were once simple and straightforward

TABLE 1.2. Word Counts and Amendments Passed, 1921 and 1974 Louisiana Constitutions

	1921 Constitution	*1974 Constitution*
Original Word Count	48,378 (unofficial)	36,252
Final/Current Word Count	255,500	72,272
Number of Amendments	536	195
Notable Details	In 1970 voters rejected 53 amendment proposals.	36,200 words added since January 1975; 24,221 words added to Article VII alone.

have now been amended into detailed and often confusing restrictions left mainly to attorneys and academics to comprehend.

As one constitutional scholar observed, "Some states have resorted to constitutional amendments for more than tuning up the machinery of government. California, Georgia, and Louisiana in particular have chosen to shift many ordinary political disputes to the constitutional realm, using constitutional amendment as legislation by other means."[1] Another remarked, "Constitutional revision in Louisiana, whether in conventions or by amendment, has been sufficiently continuous to justify including it with Mardi Gras, football and corruption as one of the premier components of state culture."[2]

THE FAULT IN OUR STARS

As a result of these revisions, the Louisiana constitution has become an unwieldy and restrictive document that governs through narrow rules and restrictions rather than broad grants of authority. Ninety-nine of the amendments through 2019 have been to Article VII, which covers revenue and finance matters, including the state budget process and taxation. Each change has occurred separately through the piecemeal amendment process provided for in Article XIII, which authorizes an amendment if approved by two-thirds of each legislative chamber and a majority vote in a statewide election.

More important than the length of the Louisiana constitution is its lack of effectiveness. As the number of constitutional funds and detailed restrictions in the Louisiana constitution has increased, so too has the inability of lawmakers to address current and pressing fiscal concerns. Nearly two-thirds of all state dollars are already committed to specific priorities and programs as a result of mandates and restrictions contained in the constitution, leaving the governor and legislature little flexibility to deploy funds on other pressing priorities.

These flaws are widely acknowledged. Still, giant political, substantive, and structural obstacles stand in the way of broadly revising the Louisiana constitution. Some of these erupted in 2018 when lawmakers proposed but failed to pass House and Senate bills calling for a constitutional convention. The concerns and opposition ran deep, especially among local government entities fearing a shift in power or in guaranteed funding streams. At the time, the consensus had not grown large enough to lead to action, and many policymakers were uncertain as to exactly what constitutional changes or impact should be sought.

To help resolve the impasse, the Public Affairs Research Council launched a project to reevaluate the state constitution and to make specific recommendations for improvement. Understanding the issues with the constitution requires reviewing the history of its creation and taking a deeper look into some of the key problem areas regarding taxes, state spending, and state-local relations. An advisory council oversaw the PAR project, which in 2019 presented a set of guiding principles.[3] In 2020, the PAR project published a thorough review with a detailed blueprint for moving forward.

CULTURE AND THE CONSTITUTION

Why is Louisiana's constitution so long? What makes it cumbersome? Some of the problems with the Louisiana constitution stem from disagreement over its purpose. Should the constitution be reserved only for fundamental provisions, or is there a need to detail the everyday operation of government? Is the primary objective of a constitution to enable the operation of government through broad grants of authority, or instead to prohibit or mandate certain types of legislative action? What is the role of a state constitution in dictating how local governments operate?

Without a common set of key principles to guide the development of a revised constitution, any attempt at reform is over before it begins. Scholars and researchers who study constitutions generally agree on several principles that should govern the construction and purpose of state constitutions. Having been amended only twenty-seven times since its adoption in 1789, the US Constitution satisfies most of the criteria for a sound constitutional document. It is a concise, 7,591-word document that outlines broad, basic principles of authority and governance. And while the US government of the twenty-first century is far different than that of the 1790s, the document is broad and flexible enough to remain both relevant and effective.

Throughout the twentieth century across America, the pace of state constitutional amendments quickened, as did the ratification rate for proposed amendments. State constitutional amendments are thus being proposed and adopted more frequently. The average state constitution length is 39,861 words, and this number drops to 32,783 if you omit the mammoth Alabama constitution.[4] The average state constitution has been amended 152 times.

Various theories exist as to why this is true. Some have argued that the trend simply reflects changing public opinion and attitudes toward specific policies. As public opinion changes, constitutions will change to reflect that. However, this theory is at least partially undermined by the fact that, despite the vast majority of proposed constitutional amendments being ratified, many are approved by only a small percentage of the electorate. Indeed, amendments just in the past few years have been ratified in Louisiana by as few as 14 percent of registered voters. This undercuts the idea that the changes in the constitution reflect some major shift in popular opinion.

Others attribute the increased frequency of constitutional revision to growing dissatisfaction and distrust of the institutions and individuals tasked with operating state government. Under this theory, constitutional revision is the inevitable response to a lack of confidence in state legislators, who are prone to short-sightedness and vulnerable to political pressures of the day. But it is informative to consider how state constitutions compare to the federal Constitution. This discrepancy in length and amendment is partly related to the underlying substance and structure of the two types of constitutions.

Article I of the US Constitution grants Congress a long list of specific powers, such as the right to borrow and coin money, regulate commerce, establish post offices, and define and punish "piracies." The Supreme Court has long held that the federal government can exercise only those legislative powers specifically enumerated or implied by the US Constitution. By contrast, state governments have historically been understood to possess plenary legislative powers, meaning they possess all legislative powers not otherwise ceded to the federal government or prohibited by the federal Constitution. Louisiana courts have repeatedly confirmed the legislature's plenary authority over state finances, which allows it to take any action relating to finances not expressly forbidden by the state constitution. For this reason, rather than granting state legislators specific powers, state constitutions tend to *restrict* legislative power by placing limitations on the legislature's ability to do things, such as enact local or special laws, create new taxes, increase existing taxes, authorize gambling, or regulate the business of local governments without voter approval.

The plenary character of state legislative power, however, does not, on its own, explain the growing length and detail of state constitutions. Professor Alan Tarr from Rutgers University, who has written extensively about state constitutions, believes that by limiting the power of elected officials, state constitutions also reflect "a tradition of being skeptical of the people we put into political office."[5] As a result, state constitution makers have deemed it necessary to detail every limitation they seek to impose on legislatures. Louisiana's constitution certainly reflects this desire to limit legislative power. Indeed, almost every provision of Article VII is designed to limit the legislature's power of the purse by requiring the appropriation of funds to dozens of specific purposes and programs.

REVENUE AND TAXATION

The basic structure and operation of Louisiana's tax and spending system is set forth in the state constitution's Article VI (Local Government) and Article VII (Revenue and Finance). Broadly speaking, the constitution authorizes both state and local governments to impose and collect certain categories of taxes, including income taxes, sales taxes, and property taxes. Yet, the constitution also imposes important limitations on government's ability to raise revenue, primarily through mechanisms like numerical caps on the level of taxation and mandatory exemptions, credits, and deductions that are available to many categories of individual and corporate taxpayers.

Louisiana's current tax system is complex and often hard to navigate because of the large number of exemptions and deductions allowed. Indeed, there are more than eighty individual income tax exemptions and about two hundred state sales tax exemptions (many are temporarily suspended). Most are authorized by statute, but others, including many of the high-value exemptions and deductions, are mandated by the constitution. In addition to their complexity, exemptions and deductions cost Louisiana a significant amount of either foregone tax revenue or the opportunity for lower tax rates. In some cases, they result in a more unpredictable and volatile revenue source for the state. The long list of deductions and exemptions embedded within our current tax structure necessitates higher overall tax rates to raise the revenue needed to provide services to citizens.

Thus, the Public Affairs Research Council and many other tax analysts have been calling for an elimination of some exemptions and deductions and lower tax rates across the board. For such changes to have a meaningful fiscal impact, a revision of some portions of the constitution would be necessary. Regardless of whether there is consensus on the continued value of each of Louisiana's many tax exemptions and deductions, there is a benefit to providing the legislature with more flexibility to adjust Louisiana's tax system to respond to changing fiscal circumstances. Less detail in the constitution, not more, will help achieve greater fiscal flexibility and limit the need for continuous constitutional amendments to achieve minor policy changes. This focus on flexibility is imbedded in PAR's principles regarding revenue and taxation.

STATE SPENDING MECHANISMS AND REVENUE FUNDS

As noted earlier, Article VII of the Louisiana constitution is the article most amended, having been amended nearly one hundred times since 1974. Article VII of the original 1974 constitution was a mere 6,125 words and contained few dedications. Since then, it has grown by nearly 25,000 words (see figure

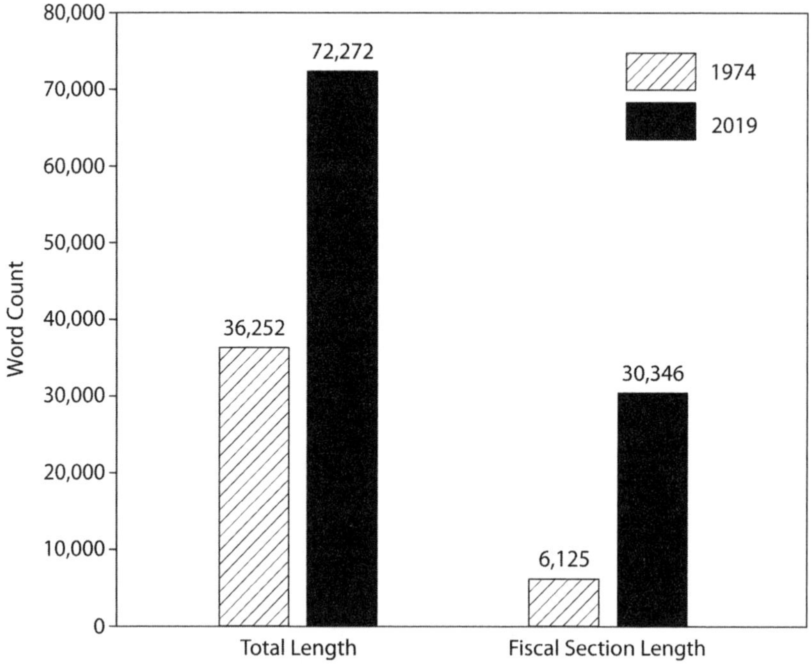

FIGURE 1.1. Length of Louisiana's Constitution.

1.1). It has become a fiscal mishmash. None of those amendments removed provisions from the constitution. Instead, each amendment has added new fiscal constraints—in most cases, new budget rules or dedicated funds—to the constitution.

Article VII is now nearly as long as the entirety of the original 1974 constitution and has become a complex set of rules and restrictions that govern how state revenues are appropriated and spent. The original constitution adopted in 1974 protected only a few specific funds; today's constitution protects thirty-three and references even more. With each new fund granted constitutional protection, it has become more difficult for our lawmakers to develop a budget that is both balanced and fulfills the state's current priorities and needs. The result is a budget that is, to a large extent, self-executing, leaving legislators with very little flexibility.

To put this challenge into perspective, the total state budget for the 2018–2019 fiscal year was roughly $34 billion, of which $9.5 billion was state general fund dollars derived in large part from all tax collections. According to the state's budget office, approximately $4.3 billion of spending was mandated by the constitution. This mandated spending, which the state has termed "unavoidable" or "nondiscretionary spending," includes items such as K–12 education funding through the Minimum Foundation Program, debt payments, and supplemental pay for local law enforcement officers. On top of the nondiscretionary spending mandated by the constitution, the document also siphons off approximately $2.7 billion of revenues that would otherwise flow into the state general fund. This leaves only $3–4 billion that the state legislators have discretion over out of the $10 billion general fund budget. Restrictions of this level magnify the impact of budget shortfalls, so they fall disproportionally on less protected areas, like universities and health care.

These "constitutional dedications" are spread across each of the thirty-three separate constitutional funds and even more subfunds. For each fund, the constitution defines specific requirements for what type of revenue flows into the fund, as well as how and for what purposes the legislature may appropriate monies from the fund. Some of these fund dedications are flowing to priorities that otherwise would be supported by the state general fund; therefore, it should be kept in mind that sometimes revenue that is "freed up" from a dedication does not usually count as "new money" to spend.

Some of the funds and related budget rules contained in our constitution are common among state constitutions and are clearly designed to protect the basic fiscal integrity of our state. The Bond Security and Redemption Fund, for example, was established to ensure that the state satisfies the principal and interest requirements of its bond indebtedness without the uncertainty of the legislative appropriation process. Similarly, the Budget Stabilization Fund, also known as the "Rainy Day Fund," is designed to prevent sudden and volatile budget inflation and to provide funding during economic downturns and budget shortfalls. PAR's review of other state constitutions revealed that almost every state has a Rainy Day Fund, and most are protected in the states' constitutions.

However, other funds in the Louisiana constitution are designed to protect much narrower interests or sources of revenue that certain interest groups, but not necessarily a statewide constituency, consider fundamental to our state government. Despite consistent growth in the number of new constitutional funds and therefore the number of restrictions facing the yearly budget process, the legislature has not engaged in a strong effort to determine which funds still reflect the current priorities and needs of the state.

Once a special interest group is successful at gaining favored status in the constitution for a particular priority, history has revealed there is little chance the legislature will have the political will to reevaluate or remove the protection, even in the face of serious fiscal challenges. Louisiana has been caught in a vicious cycle that is doomed to repeat itself without real and broad reform to our governing document.

THE RELATIONSHIP BETWEEN THE STATE AND LOCAL GOVERNMENTS

Louisiana's structure of government is highly centralized, particularly when it comes to decisions regarding raising and spending revenue. The state's dominance over local governments in fiscal issues is characterized by a complicated system under which state funds are used to pay for many functions that are local in nature. Local governments have come to rely on this funding, while at the same time the state has found it increasingly difficult to develop a workable budget that satisfies both the state's most pressing needs and local government obligations.

The constitution allows local governments to raise their own revenues, primarily through sales and property taxes, but also contains several important restrictions and limitations that affect local governments' ability to manage their own fiscal affairs. The most significant of these restrictions is the homestead exemption, which requires local governments to exempt the first $7,500 of assessed value of a resident's home from property taxes—or, practically speaking, the first $75,000 of the total assumed home value.[6] The homestead exemption was protected in the 1974 constitution, and the current value of $7,500 was set in 1982. Other constitutionally imposed restrictions on local government finances include a cap on local sales taxes, which can only be increased through a vote of the legislature, and a list of nearly two dozen separate categories of property that local governments must exempt from taxation.

At least some state programs and spending requirements are intended to offset the restrictions the state has placed on local governments' ability to raise and manage revenue. The Revenue Sharing Fund, for example, requires the legislature to appropriate to parishes and school districts $90 million from the state general fund each year through a formula based on population and homesteads. The money is spent on local priorities, not state ones. The fund was established specifically to offset the effect of the homestead exemption on local budgets. Other funding mandates from the state, such as the requirement to fund supplemental pay for local law enforcement officers, are not tied to a specific limitation on local revenue but are simply meant to help local governments fund services. Louisiana local governments also are reliant on the state for funding and operation of community colleges, charity and rural hospitals, and road work that in many other states are regional responsibilities.

This complex relationship between the state and local governments, in which the state has limited the flexibility of local governments while continuing to transfer large sums of money to local governments, creates incentives for local governments to rely on state rather than local funding sources. Just as important, constitutional requirements that transfer state dollars to local governments have the effect of further tying the hands of the legislature as they work to develop a budget that funds leading state priorities, such as higher education and health care, with limited state general fund dollars.

WAYS TO CHANGE THE CONSTITUTION

Article XIII of the Louisiana constitution, which addresses constitutional revision, lays out both the requirements for amending the constitution as well as the requirements for calling a constitutional convention and approving a new constitution. An in-depth analysis of state constitution data reveals that the frequency with which state constitutions are amended is correlated with their length and with their ease of amendment. As to the former, the most likely explanation is that longer state constitutions tend to include more detailed prescriptions and proscriptions, which build rigidities into the document, thereby limiting the state's ability to adapt to changing situations and necessitating constitutional change simply to govern. This is often the case with specific parts of state constitutions that have been amended over and over only to solve immediate or short-term problems without addressing the underlying larger problem. As scholars Frank Grad and Robert Williams have noted, "Every detailed constitution thus develops certain sore points, which become the foci for veritable clusters of constitutional amendments."[7] In this regard, it is safe to say that Article VII is the "sore point" of the current Louisiana constitution. The scholars have a term for it: "an amendment breeder."

As to the ease with which state constitutions can be amended, Louisiana's requirement of a two-thirds vote from each legislative chamber and a majority of statewide voters is similar to that of many other states. A few states, however, have made it considerably harder to change their constitutions. Tennessee's, for example, requires a majority vote from each legislative chamber, followed by a two-thirds vote from each chamber in the next legislative session, plus approval from a majority of statewide voters. This three-step standard for constitutional revision is reflected in Tennessee's current constitution, which is a short 13,960 words and has been in place since 1870. Vermont's constitution, which imposes a similar standard, is only 8,565 words and has been around since 1793.

To help achieve a more stable Louisiana constitution, revisers should seek to impose a more demanding standard for constitutional change. Changes in our state constitution should promote stability so that we do not once again find ourselves wishing for a new, simpler, and more effective constitution in the future. One way to achieve this is to adopt a system like Tennessee's that requires a lengthier approval process.

THE CHALLENGE AHEAD

The Louisiana constitution does not fit the ideal of what a constitution should be. It is long, unwieldy, and inflexible. It holds the state back from pursuing reforms and breaking from unhealthy traditions. Yet, reform would involve real challenges. No one can say what the outcome of a reform process would be. Whenever a long-established pattern of spending and governing is considered for change, opposition will arise.

The legislature is authorized by the constitution to make sweeping constitutional changes. For example, with a two-thirds vote of both chambers, it can rewrite an entire article and submit the proposal to voters statewide as a single amendment. It might also offer voters a package of constitutional amendments meant to accomplish much of what would be desired by reformers. Or it might call for a convention and determine how the delegates would be chosen.[8] A convention, some believe, creates the greatest possibility for grand changes because delegates may have more appetite for change than the legislature. And whatever new document the convention creates, it must meet voter approval before being adopted.

Those wishing to redesign the constitution should consider creating a more foundational document that loosens constraints on potential reforms rather than writing a new document with new constraints that further tie the hands of legislators and local governments. There is a significant difference between an enduring document that *allows* fiscal reforms to take place versus a constitutional storage box that *enshrines* a detailed set of reforms that are different but no less flexible than before.

Louisiana should be able to create a new constitution that is a true foundational document that allows elected officials to pursue broad reforms and to budget with more flexibility within the same means. Citizens, through their elected representatives, should be able to reexamine the spending priorities locked into the constitution in the 1980s and 1990s and determine if they truly reflect today's evolving needs and values. The constitution should have greater permanence that changes less with time. Ultimately, citizens should one day hold in their hands a constitution that they can read and understand, and that legislators and governors can more readily uphold.[9]

NOTES

1. Alan G. Tarr, *Understanding State Constitutions* (Princeton, N.J.: Princeton Univ. Press, 1998).

2. Mark Carleton, "Elitism Sustained: The Louisiana Constitution of 1974," *Tulane Law Review* 54 (1980): 560–588.

3. The Public Affairs Research Council offers a list of key principles to follow in redrafting the state's constitution in *Louisiana Constitutional Reform, Part I: Getting the Foundation*

Right, August 2, 2019, http://parlouisiana.org/wp-content/uploads/2019/09/PAR-Guide-2019-Amendments-Web.pdf.

4. Council of State Governments, *Book of the States 2018* (Lexington, Ky.: The Council of State Governments, 2018).

5. Jennie Drage Bowser, "Constitutions: Amend with Care," *State Legislatures Magazine* (September 2015), 16, https://www.ncsl.org/research/elections-and-campaigns/constitution-amend-with-care.aspx.

6. Since the assessed value of a home in Louisiana is set at 10 percent of the market value, practically speaking, the homestead exemption applies to the first $75,000 of the total assessed home value.

7. Frank P. Grad and Robert F. Williams, *State Constitutions for the Twenty-First Century,* vol. 2, *Drafting State Constitutions, Revisions, and Amendments* (Albany, N.Y.: SUNY Press, 2006).

8. The composition of the delegation is often a source of conflict, not just between parties but also between various interest groups that want to ensure their representation in any convention.

9. This essay is drawn from the constitution project publications of PAR, which retains the rights to the content and form of its work.

FOLLOWING FRANCIS

Legislative Evolution, from Populist to Partisan (1975–2020)

JEREMY ALFORD

The Louisiana House of Representatives was filled to capacity on January 13, 2020, when newly elected members comprising nearly half the body were simultaneously sworn into office. Family and friends joined reporters and others to witness the sea change in Baton Rouge, in which fifty of the chamber's 105 representatives made way for first-term replacements. Applause erupted after the shared oath, which some legislators live-streamed on their social media platforms. Handshakes and hugs could be seen clear across the floor, all the way to the front row, where Representative Francis Thompson clapped his own hands and raised them shoulder high. "I'm back!" he exclaimed with a widening grin.

Thompson, a freshman in name only, was first seated in the House in 1975, before being elected to the state Senate in 2007. Forced out of the Senate by term limits after twelve years there, and just three years away from being the longest-serving legislator in Louisiana history, Thompson was back in the House for more. A native of Delhi in Northeast Louisiana, Thompson was known for his country twang, fun-loving demeanor, and pragmatic approach to politics. "I can't support any deal," he often said, "that I'm not a part of." Over his long career, Thompson had carved out a policy niche on agriculture issues and could turn serious in an instant when it came to his district's farmers. Otherwise, Thompson was always in on the joke. During a particularly tough debate in 1996, he told his fellow representatives, "I know you're worried about being a hypocrite for voting for this, but that's our job."

When he began his legislative career some four and a half decades earlier, Thompson was representative of the legislature as a whole: He was a white

Democrat, pro-union lawmaker for whom local politics mattered more than anything else. He was part of a generational swap in the 1970s that replaced aging legislators with younger, more progressive ones. By 2020 Thompson was among the oldest members in a legislature trending younger, and he was one of the few white Democrats serving in the now Republican-controlled chamber. His new colleagues were attuned to national politics and were overwhelmingly pro-business. If you wanted to understand just how much the legislature had changed over the past forty-five years, there was no better case study than Thompson.

Much had changed since Thompson was first sworn into the House. From 1975 to 2020 he served under seven different governors during eleven terms of state government, legislating through a new constitution (ratified in 1974), numerous hurricanes, recessions, a gas shortage, an oil bust, outmigration, and a global pandemic. As a true freshman in 1975, Thompson saw the early partisan, racial, and gender trends that would one day alter the composition and complexion of the Louisiana legislature. As a returning freshman in the twenty-first century, Thompson bore witness to those composition and complexion changes.

Over the past four and a half decades, term limits transformed the culture of the legislature more than anything else. Prior to term limits, turnover was rare. It was not unusual for lawmakers to serve most of their adult lives in the legislature. By 2000, the House and Senate had begun its transformation from being mostly Democratic to predominantly Republican, which was a Deep South trend arriving late in Louisiana. The prolonged D-to-R shift was fueled in part by the rise of outside spending by political action committees. Back at the capitol, this influx of conservative influence polarized moderates by moving certain issues further to the right, such as enhanced tax incentives for businesses and fiscal accountability (like the use of one-time revenue only for one-time expenses). The increasingly sharp partisan divide influenced morale and, along with the inevitability of term limits, prompted record-setting midterm special elections.

The twenty-first century found more women and people of color serving in the legislature and in leadership positions. The average age of lawmakers was trending younger, but those gains were slow to develop.[1] By the time

Thompson returned as a seventy-eight-year-old freshman in 2020 there was more focus, albeit with limited success, on electing more women to office and correcting racial inequities. There were also intensifying efforts by lawmakers to expand the authority of the legislative branch at the expense of the executive branch.

In the following sections, I will show how term limits have transformed the nature of serving as a legislator and working as a lobbyist. I will also describe how slow and steady gains by Republicans, set against the backdrop of increased representation for women and Black lawmakers, have changed the legislature and its members' interest in national politics.

OFFICE SEEKERS AND JOB HUNTERS

Since 1970 there have been only four state legislators in the United States who served as both House speaker and Senate president.[2] Two of the four were from Louisiana. John Hainkel of New Orleans was the second to claim the dual honor in 2000, when he was elected as Senate president after a thirty-six-year stint in the House. John Alario of Westwego became American's fourth politician to do the same when he moved from the House and was elected Senate president in 2012.

Hainkel and Alario shared another distinction: They were the only two state legislators in the entire nation to serve as speaker and president while representing different parties, as both were Democratic speakers before they were Republican presidents. Hainkel and Alario were seated in the House in 1968 and 1972, respectively, just prior to the 1975 arrival of Francis Thompson to the legislature.

Most representatives and senators wanted to keep their jobs in Baton Rouge—a sentiment no less prevalent in 2000, when former state representative Ron Gomez of Lafayette likened legislative service to an addiction, publishing *My Name Is Ron, and I'm a Recovering Legislator: Memoirs of a Louisiana State Representative.* At the turn of the century, though, norms were changing as state legislatures nationwide adopted legislative term limits.

In 1995, voters endorsed a constitutional amendment that limited each member to three successive four-year terms in either the House or Senate

TABLE 2.1. Number of Terms Served by Legislators, 2020–2024

	House	*Senate*
First Term	55%	54%
Second Term	30%	20%
Third Term	15%	26%

(see table 2.1). The cycle of departures started with the 2008–2012 term, when thirty-one of 105 representatives were forced to leave, alongside sixteen of thirty-nine senators. While representatives often ran for Senate seats like Alario and Thompson did that term, a new trend, senators running for the House, was born of term limits. This was a trend Thompson would follow in 2020 when Alario decided to retire.

With the imposition of term limits, a new rhythm developed in the legislature as the time spent in office decreased and lawmakers became more eager than ever to hunt for new jobs. The proponents of term limits had argued it would limit corruption and the stagnation of ideas. However, the increasingly partisan atmosphere, hyper fundraising schedules, and policy gridlock, discussed below, were helping nudge lawmakers out of Baton Rouge as well. In the years following the implementation of term limits, lawmakers frequently complained on the House and Senate floors about name-calling, cyber-bullying, and the fraying social fabric of the legislature. The proof was in the numbers: from 2016 to 2019 there were an unprecedented nineteen special legislative elections. The general mood inside of the capitol during this period was unmistakably grim. In an interview following the 2018 regular session, Representative Julie Emerson, a white Republican from Carencro, noted that partisan divides were taking their toll. "It's the first session where everything seems very personal," said Emerson, "and the first session where we haven't been able to walk out and be as friendly."

Representative Cedric Glover, a Shreveport Democrat who served in the House from 1996 to 2006 before reclaiming his seat in 2016, described the mood of the legislature during this time as "difficult." Term limits created a "disconnectedness" in the legislature, he said, eroding the deep and lasting relationships that used to smooth the process. "The ability to be able to develop the kind of relationships that I observed in those veteran members that were here when I got here is not possible from 1996 going forward," said Glover. "You don't have the kind of dynamic that encourages that kind of connection and camaraderie."[3]

Glover's tone was matched by Representative Barry Ivey, a Central Republican. "It is embarrassing a lot of the time to be a part of this process," Ivey told senators during a summer 2020 committee meeting. "Politics are a distraction. I have no time for them. I don't know how much longer I will be able to stomach this job. Because I have better things to do."[4]

PICK A SIDE: LEFT OR RIGHT

While Alario and Hainkel switched political parties from Democratic to Republican when moving from the House to the Senate, Thompson remained a Democrat. Thompson said in later interviews that he never contemplated a party switch because he was a Democrat through and through. Unlike Hainkel, Alario, and others, though, Thompson did not represent an area that was a part of the conservative wave that swept through Louisiana in the new century.

Between 2004 and 2015, white voters fled the Louisiana Democratic Party at a shocking clip, with more than 225,000 altering their registrations, primarily to the Republican Party but also to independent. In 1978, not long after Thompson was seated in the House, 90 percent of Louisiana's voters were registered as Democrats. By the end of 2015, which marked the start of Thompson's final term in the Senate, Democrats comprised 46 percent of the electorate, compared to the GOP's 28 percent. In addition, the Bayou State also had a massive hidden electorate—Democrats who voted Republican without officially switching parties.[5]

For generations, Louisiana Democrats were not just the dominant force in politics, they were the only force. For longtime politicos the rise of the Republicans was jarring. In 2003, Democrats controlled six of Louisiana's seven statewide elected seats. Four years later, Democrats captured only two of those offices, and that figure was cut in half when former attorney general

Buddy Caldwell switched to Republican. In the following years through 2020, one statewide office was all Democrats could achieve, and party-switches like Caldwell's helped Republicans build their numbers on other elected fronts. The force behind the Republican wave in the legislature was led by former US senator David Vitter, who teamed up with a group of wealthy donors in 2007 to form the Louisiana Committee for a Republican Majority. The goal of this organization was to engineer the GOP conquest of the state legislature, starting with the House.

More than $2 million was spent to recruit Republican candidates to run in Democratic districts. Several Democratic districts were flipped in time for the 2008–2012 term, and Vitter and his allies were even able to convince a few elected Democrats to change party labels. By 2010, Republicans had fifty-three votes in the 105-member House, enough to control the flow of action and claim a majority. The edge was just as slight in the Senate, where Republicans held a 20–19 margin. Still, that was a far cry from the 1980 term of the legislature when there were only ten Republicans, all in the House. Seats and party labels continued to be flipped in subsequent years as the Louisiana Committee for a Republican Majority became the Louisiana Committee for a Conservative Majority and Vitter was replaced by Attorney General Jeff Landry.

By 2020, Republicans had a supermajority in the Senate (twenty-seven out of thirty-nine seats) and a near supermajority in the House (sixty-eight out of 105 seats). Oddly, this milestone coincided with the reelection of Democratic governor John Bel Edwards. The ongoing struggle between the legislature and executive had produced unprecedented levels of gridlock and dysfunction in Edwards's previous term, leading to stalled budget bills, numerous special sessions, repeated vetoes by the governor, and threats of veto overrides by the legislature.

If there were any doubts as to just how far to the right the legislature was leaning at the start of the most recent term, the conservative Louisiana Association of Business and Industry's (LABI) 2020 scorecard painted an unmistakably fire engine red portrait. That was the year a record ninety-seven lawmakers, or nearly 70 percent of the entire House, scored above 80 percent on bills LABI identified as "important to Louisiana businesses." By comparison, in 2019 only sixty-seven representatives scored the same.

Those who say you cannot take it with you clearly have not met Francis Thompson, the last serving legislator grandfathered into a law regarding how candidates can spend—and personally keep—certain campaign dollars. The quick-witted legislator has been fundraising or campaigning since he was seated in 1975, adopting a slow and steady philosophy over the decades for what would become his campaign finance account.

When he ran for the House again in 2019, Thompson had nearly $900,000 in his state campaign finance account, of which $660,000 was held in investments that garnered an annual return of $8,000. Thompson also had more than $16,250 sitting in a separate leadership committee account. To no one's surprise, he was a master of the capitol's longstanding fundraising circuit, which consisted of events hosted at the nearby facilities owned by Haynie and Associates, the Southern Strategy Group, the Beer Industry League of Louisiana, the Mid-Continent Oil and Gas Association, the Louisiana Oil and Gas Association, and the Louisiana Restaurant Association, among others.

"Real slow, with a little bit here and a little bit there. That's how I've done it," Thompson said of his fundraising style. "I raise it that way and I spend it that way. Plus, I don't live out of my account." (Based on his regular campaign finance filings, Thompson averaged about $32,000 in expenditures each non-election year—a relatively small amount, which may indicate the dearth of serious challengers for his seat.)

What truly set Thompson apart, however, was the $120,000 or so that he raised prior to July 15, 1988. That same year, Thompson joined other lawmakers in passing a state law that stipulated any money raised before the date would not be subject to future campaign finance regulations.[6] That meant Thompson, along with anyone else who raised money pre-1988, could treat it however they chose. At the time, in the late 1980s, the policy proposal did not raise many eyebrows because reporters and good government hawks were not yet in heavy pursuit of campaign finance reform, although they would be soon.

Thompson's introduction to Louisiana politics came during the early- to mid-1970s, which represented a transitional time. A new governor, Edwin W.

Edwards, was redefining the Bayou State's style of populism in the modern age of mass media. Meanwhile, some of the state's most storied and infamous political dynasties, such as the Long and Perez families, were fading. New lawmakers were only somewhat willing to embrace the "go-along-to-get-along" ethos cultivated by their predecessors. Most noticeably, a younger generation in the state House, dubbed the "Young Turks," wanted to govern with ethics in mind and show more accountability to voters. They declared independence from heavy-handed lobbyists who had previously controlled the legislature through their lobbying and money by restricting floor access for anyone who was not employed by the state and fortifying the body's voting procedures by scheduling votes and conducting committee meetings that were open to the public.

Although the legislature had been flirting with campaign finance reform and higher ethics standards for years, it was not until the election of Governor Bobby Jindal that true ethics reforms were passed. Calling a special session of the legislature, Jindal proposed a package of bills in 2008 that he called the "gold standard for ethics reform" in the nation, most of which Thompson and the rest of the legislature supported with gusto. Those gold standards included a ban on fundraising during regular sessions, restrictions on who could become lobbyists, expenditure limits for meals and entertaining, and reporting guidelines for almost anything related to government relations, among other requirements.[7]

In the years that followed Jindal's ethics reform, the planning and plotting over steak dinners in Baton Rouge changed as fewer lawmakers wanted to end up listed on lobbying reports that were accessible via the Internet. Events and fundraisers became carefully orchestrated by campaigns and lobbyists and closely monitored by the state. Tyron Picard, a Lafayette lobbyist who founded the Picard Group and whose father was a state legislator, predicted in 2020 that even more changes were to come.

"You think back to the old Ruth's Chris way of doing things," said Picard, "and I think that era is gone. There's a new breed of legislator, many of whom have residences in Spanish Town, and they prefer to be in shorts and flip flops sitting on a porch and not at these high-dollar functions and committee dinners. We're going to continue to see more informal settings, through a combination of this being generational and just the time we're living in due to COVID."[8]

DIVERSIFICATION IN SLOW MOTION

While Francis Thompson was considered by many in the legislature to be a grandfatherly figure with a wealth of institutional knowledge, by the time he moved back to the House, special interests, editorial writers, donors, and the public were also eager to see a broader spectrum of elected officials in the capitol.

Term limits, in part, helped address the generational gap that developed between the 1970s and 1990s. From the time Thompson was elected to the state Senate in 2007 to the start of his final term in the chamber in 2015, the average age of a Louisiana legislator dropped a staggering eleven years—with sixty-four being the average age of lawmakers elected in the 2007 election cycle, followed by fifty-eight in 2011, and then fifty-three in 2015.[9] That drop in age coincided with a wave of progress on several issues that were previously unable to gain passage in the legislature, such as acts related to criminal justice reform, medical marijuana, and resolutions regarding diversity and technology.

A major milestone in diversifying the legislature came in 1977 with the formation of the Legislative Black Caucus, which sought to strengthen Black voices in the House and Senate and elect more members to each chamber. Sidney Barthelemy of New Orleans, the Senate's first Black member, was elected the year prior and became the first chairman of the Black Caucus. Members focused initially on supporting each other's bills and ensuring minority voices were included in as many policy debates as possible. But caucus members also found success in the redistricting process during the 1980s and 1990s by participating in the redrawing of election lines that resulted in more Black representation not only in the legislature, but in other offices as well. Instead of recruiting Black candidates to run in racially mixed districts against white incumbents, Black legislators figured they could have a larger impact by instead drawing districts with Black majorities.

Significant gains were earned through the Black Caucus's redistricting efforts. From 1972 through 1976, thirteen Black men and women were elected

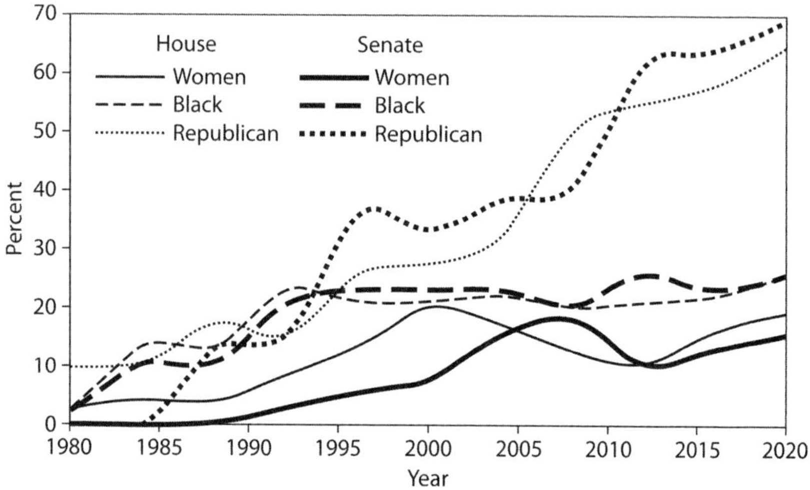

FIGURE 2.1. Gender, Race, and Partisanship in the Louisiana House and Senate, 1980–2020.

to the legislature, with Barthelemy winning a Senate seat and the rest gaining seats in the House. The number continued to climb; from 1988 to 1992, Black members of the House went from fourteen to twenty-four, and from four to eight in the Senate. In 2020, there were twenty-seven Black members in the House and ten in the Senate, far closer to the proportion of Blacks in the population (32 percent) than in times past. Although their growth slowed by 2020, the Black Caucus has an aggressive agenda for change. Motivated by the Black Lives Matter movement, members spent the first sessions of the term writing legislation connected to improving criminal justice and police practices.

The election cycle leading up to the 2020–2024 legislative term was billed as the "Year of the Woman" in Louisiana politics.[10] There were training sessions organized by groups like the left-leaning Emerge Louisiana to get more women interested in public service, women-led political action committees to underwrite campaigns sponsored by Les Femmes PAC, and even intense recruitment efforts by the state Republican Party. More female candidates than ever before pursued office, and the declaration of a year just for women made sense in reality as well as on paper. Hearing the call, Black female voters arrived at the polls with the highest propensity of any demographic. Yet, as the 2019 primary season came to a close, it became clear that 2019 would not be the breakout year for women. Six women were elected to the Senate, an increase of only one from the 2016–2020 term, and twenty women were seated in the House, a gain of three, leaving Louisiana with one of the lowest female representation rates in the country, according to the Center for American Women and Politics (see figure 2.1).[11]

Women, however, were moving into key leadership roles in the legislature by 2020, filling the roles of Senate president pro tempore and as chairs of a handful of committees, such as the Senate and Governmental Affairs Committee and the House Commerce Committee. Lobbyist and advocate Renee Amar created Louisiana Women Lead, or LEAD for short, to inspire more women to enter public office and to equip them with the tools they needed to win. This drive attracted national attention supporting LEAD's mission of serving as a new pipeline for "center-right, business-minded women." In a unique twist, the group planned to not only offer in-person training and mentor support, but also daycare services for its recruits.[12]

SEPARATION OF POWERS

The COVID-19 pandemic in 2020 quickly overshadowed the promise of a new term and Representative Thompson's return to the House. A newly elected House member, Reggie Bagala of Terrebonne Parish, died from the virus, and several other members tested positive. Policymaking, as Thompson and others had come to know it, was upended as public access was restricted. Social distancing required more space, such as using the House floor instead of a committee room, and temperatures were checked to gain entrance to the capitol.

Also new was a developing effort by conservative lawmakers to give more control and authority to the legislative branch at the cost of the executive branch. Thompson had spent most of his time as a legislator navigating a political environment where lawmakers followed the lead of governors on matters ranging from leadership votes to budget crafting. But the Republican takeover of the legislature during the terms of Democratic governor John Bel Edwards created an acrimonious relationship between the legislative and executive branches. While Edwards's partisan affiliation helped fuel the conflict between the branches, the power struggle was also the direct result of anxiety over COVID-19 and the exercise of the governor's emergency powers. Still, this battle had been in the making for years.

House members serving in the 2020–2024 term were no doubt empowered by their predecessors, who in 2016 for the first time in modern history had bucked the wishes of the governor on the selection of the next speaker, opting for Speaker Taylor Barras over Edwards's choice, Representative Walt Leger. Supporting the governor's choice for legislative leadership was a longstanding Louisiana tradition. Conservative legislators during the time of COVID-19 saw things differently and called themselves into special sessions, rather than waiting on the governor. They also spent considerable time attempting to gather enough signatures from the House and Senate to overturn Edwards's executive orders and threatening to override his high-profile vetoes.

An example of the legislature exerting its newfound independence came in the 2020 regular session. Representative Barry Ivey passed a bill to allow the legislature to call itself into an emergency session—without notice—during times of attack, disaster, or public health emergency, an authority previously held only by the governor. This may be the most significant change proposed to Louisiana's continuity of government laws in more than five decades. "The executive branch has very broad authority in regard to emergency powers and the Legislature does not," Ivey told his colleagues during the floor debate. "We are very limited in what are able to do," implying to those listening that they should be able to do more.[13]

Currently the law allows legislators to create a list of emergency interim successors (at least three, but no more than seven) to serve in their place during such times, should the elected representatives and senators not be able to serve due to death or failing health.[14] The relevant statutes, however, have not been updated since the late 1960s. If for some reason a disaster strikes and takes the lives of lawmakers with it, and no successors have been named, the governor is charged with making those interim appointments. Ivey's legislation would have stripped the governor of that authority and given it to the House speaker and Senate president. It would likewise charge lawmakers with submitting their lists of interim appointments, with names of individuals from their districts, during the organizational sessions held at the beginning of each term.

Ultimately the bill was stalled in the Senate, but it was passed by a 71–11 margin in the House, with Thompson opposing this change to Louisiana's system of checks and balances. Thompson liked the system the way it was, even if he recognized that the legislature should be a coequal branch. The 2020 regular session adjourned with lawmakers promising to revisit the matter. Change was in the air, much like it was in 1975 when Thompson was first seated in the House as part of a younger generation of lawmakers hellbent on upending the political norms of the day. But just like then, fundraising still mattered in 2020, as did local politics and ideology. All of it just looked and sounded a little different. After all, as any Cajun French legislator would have told you at the time, *plus ça change, plus c'est la même chose.*

The more things change, the more they stay the same.

NOTES

1. *Louisiana Legislature 2016–2020: Grass-Roots Guide* (Baton Rouge, La.: Louisiana Governmental Studies, 2016).

2. Karl Kurtz, "Legislators Who Have Served as Speaker and Top Senate Leader," National Conference of State Legislatures, October 27, 2011, https://ncsl.typepad.com/the_thicket/2011/10/legislators-who-have-served-as-speaker-and-top-senate-leader.html.

3. Jeremy Alford, "It's Personal: Nasty Insults, Attacks from the Mic and Short Tempers," *LaPolitics Weekly*, May 4, 2018.

4. Jeremy Alford, "Brought to Tears: Emergency Election Plan Gets Emotional," *LaPolitics Weekly*, August 21, 2020.

5. *Louisiana Legislature 2016–2020: Grass-Roots Guide.*

6. Louisiana Rev Stat § 18:1505.2.

7. Adam Nossiter, "New Louisiana Governor Pierces Brazen Style of Business as Usual," *New York Times*, February 28, 2008, https://www.nytimes.com/2008/02/28/us/28jindal.html.

8. Jeremy Alford, "Lobbying during COVID: From Beltway to Bayou, Everything Has Changed," *LaPolitics Weekly*, August 7, 2020.

9. *Louisiana Legislature 2016–2020: Grass-Roots Guide.*

10. Mark Ballard, "Increasing the Number of Women in the Louisiana Legislature Depends on the Nov. 16 Runoff," *The Advocate*, October 24, 2019, https://www.theadvocate.com/baton_rouge/news/politics/elections/article_88545db2-f6b3-11e9-90cb-7379d4bd4647.html.

11. Center for American Women and Politics, "Women in State Legislatures 2020," Rutgers Eaglton Institute of Politics, October 17, 2020, https://cawp.rutgers.edu/women-state-legislature-2020.

12. Jeremy Alford, "Center-Right Group Eyes More Elected Women," *LaPolitics Weekly*, August 21, 2020.

13. Jeremy Alford, "Expanding the Legislative Footprint," *The Tracker*, May 27, 2020.

14. Louisiana Rev Stat § 24:64.

FROM CIRCUS MASTER TO BAND DIRECTOR

The Shrinking Louisiana Governor

PEARSON CROSS

The unusual power of Louisiana's governors is undoubtedly related to historical trends and cultural attitudes peculiar to Louisiana, but in the exercise of his formal constitutional powers and his role as popular leader and chief administrator, the governor is in debt more to his own ability, to the evolution of American democracy, and to social and economic changes than to legal precedents. . . .

—**EDWIN EDWARDS,** "The Role of the Governor in Louisiana Politics: An Historical Analysis," *Louisiana History* (Spring 1974): 116

There have been growing concerns that we're not an independent, co-equal branch of government.

—**JOHN BEL EDWARDS,** Louisiana legislator and future governor, quoted in Tyler Bridges, "Once Called Governor's 'Lap Dog,' House Speaker Yanks on His Leash," *The Lens,* April 5, 2013

The governor of Louisiana is the most powerful politician in the state, regardless of personal characteristics, the era, the party, or the circumstances of his or her ascension to the office. This heightened sense of the governor's predominance, documented by commentators from John Maginnis to Wayne Parent, is not a chimera.[1] The legendary ability of governors like Huey Long and Edwin Edwards to command and dominate Louisiana politics still reverberates in the legacies, traditions, and institutions they left behind.

While this essay pays homage to the enormous power that Louisiana governors have historically wielded, my primary focus is the exercise of gubernatorial power today. To illustrate, I review the politics of Bobby Jindal's historic education legislation in 2012, showing how both formal and informal powers were integral to its passage. Notwithstanding Jindal's impressive display of gubernatorial power in 2012, the informal powers of Louisiana governors have weakened. Factors include the increasing transparency of the state's business and financial practices, the public's declining tolerance of corruption along with the passage of ethics legislation, the increasingly ideological character of partisan politics, and the emergence of competitors for power, both inside and outside government.

Despite losing power in some areas, the Louisiana governor often exercises extraordinary powers dealing with the budgetary, environmental, and social crises that regularly imperil life in Louisiana. A secondary theme of this essay is the expansion of the governor's powers during times of crisis.[2] Finally, this essay assesses the impact of gubernatorial leadership on the quality of life for the people of Louisiana, which, although difficult to measure, must comprise the ultimate proof of effective leadership in any state.

THE MULTIFACETED EXERCISE OF POWER

Governors have formal powers inherent to their office that are exercised by all governors, as well as informal powers exercised by individual governors as a result of their unique abilities and tradition. Assessing a governor's power requires asking several interrelated questions: What powers do governors exercise in performing their function in the political sphere? Are a governor's powers static, or do they rise and fall depending on circumstances? And finally, on whose behalf is gubernatorial power exercised?[3]

The Louisiana constitution, last revised in 1974, outlines the governor's role and formal powers in Article IV.[4] In addition to delineating the other executive officers (for example, the secretary of state and attorney general), Article IV lists the qualifications needed to run for executive office (minimum age of twenty-five, a citizen of the United States and Louisiana for the preceding five years), the governor's term of office (four years), limitations on that term (two consecutive terms), and compensation. Section 5, titled "Governor; Powers and Duties," sketches out an expansive range of tasks and powers. As the titular head of state government, the governor has sole or shared responsibility for (nearly) every area of state government.[5] This proliferation of duties and responsibilities has led some to characterize governors as playing different "roles" in state government. For example, the governor acts as the state's chief executive; delivers the "state of the state" address providing guidance and recommendations to the legislature; appoints and supervises the fifteen members of the cabinet who lead state departments and agencies; supervises the creation and submission of the executive and capital outlay budgets; exercises veto power over all bills and budgetary items; grants pardons, commutations, reprieves, and remissions; makes an estimated fifteen hundred appointments while retaining removal power over most; calls special elections in times of need; and acts as the commander in chief of the state at all times, but particularly during states of emergency, which are, themselves, called by the governor.[6]

As figure 3.1 indicates, the governor interacts with nearly every political entity and enterprise, small or large, because of the varied powers of the office. Given the broad authority and control that the governor exerts over so many departments and agencies, the chief question is often "What does the governor think?" Projects and initiatives are uncertain without the governor's support, and with the governor's opposition they are usually sunk.

While impressive, this description of the governor's formal power is incomplete because it leaves out the many informal powers that governors rely on to gain their objectives. Power is not exercised in a vacuum, but rather in a complex and multifaceted political arena shaped by many factors, most of which are outside the governor's direct legal or constitutional control. For example, all governors advance a legislative package containing the bills they support for passage in each legislative session. This is a formal power of the governor, yet the real measure of a governor's legislative power depends on his or her ability to pass the most important bills and sign them into law. This achievement, in turn, depends on informal factors, such as whether the governor is popular or has a "mandate" from the last election, the number of seats the governor's party commands in each house, how tightly the governor is bound to the leaders in the House and Senate, the willingness of the governor to reward or punish legislators, how adept the governor and their staff are at engaging in the legislative process, and the pressure that powerful outside

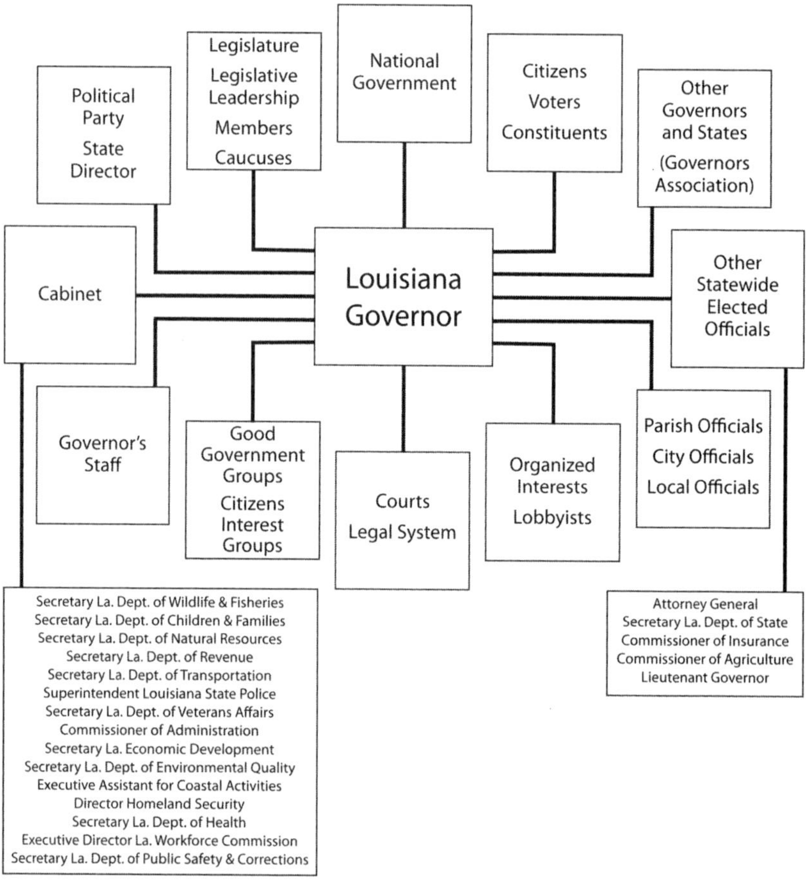

FIGURE 3.1. The Louisiana Governor's Connections to Political Offices and Organizations. Designed by Anna Kate Barnes.

groups can bring to aid the fight, to name just a few.[7] Article IV of the Louisiana constitution says nothing about these informal powers, yet they are arguably as important as the governor's formal powers—and may hold the key to success in office. In sum, governors combine, leverage, and wield their formal powers, informal powers, and native abilities to achieve their goals. All governors attempt to do this, but some are more successful than others. The passage of Governor Bobby Jindal's education legislation in 2012 is an example of how both formal and informal powers were crucial for a policy breakthrough.

PASSING EDUCATION REFORM IN LOUISIANA

Bobby Jindal began to plan his massive education initiative a year prior to being reelected to a second term. To pass the landmark legislation, he made remarkable use of both formal and informal powers and some powers unique to Louisiana governors. Campaigning as a reform candidate in 2007, Jindal was elected on the promise of accountability, competence, and bringing an end to corruption in Louisiana.[8] During his first term, Jindal passed ethics legislation and tightened state budgets, helped in part by the Great Recession. He supervised a mass evacuation during Hurricane Gustav and garnered public approval for his hands-on approach to the devastating British Petroleum oil spill in the Gulf of Mexico. Despite these and other successes, Jindal's first term initiatives were criticized by some for being too cautious, too unwilling to upset the status quo.

Easily reelected, Jindal set higher goals, focusing on remaking K–12 education in Louisiana. Jindal's reform plan reflected ideas popular among conservative education advocates: expanding vouchers, ending or limiting tenure for teachers, supporting private schools with public monies, and reducing the power of teacher unions. Passing sweeping education reform would require that Jindal use both his formal and informal powers.

THE EXERCISE OF POWER

In a democracy, representatives elected by a majority may justifiably claim to have the people's support. Governors who are elected (or reelected) by large margins often claim they've been given a mandate for change by the citizens. They enhance their power by helping to elect like-minded candidates for the legislature, typically those of their own party. Legislatures, in turn, defer to popular governors and are predisposed to support their initiatives. Already popular, Jindal raised an enormous amount of money for his 2011 campaign and swept to a staggering 48-point reelection victory (66–18 percent) over his nearest rival.[9] Concerned with building a Republican majority in the House and Senate, Jindal campaigned actively for those members most likely to be allies after the election. In this effort, he was aided by the Committee to Elect a Republican Majority, which, along with party switching by individual politicians, created a Republican Party majority in both the House and Senate, greatly enhancing Jindal's clout in the legislature.[10]

Jindal's influence in the House and Senate was enhanced by an unusual informal power exercised only by Louisiana governors: the selection of the president of the Senate and the speaker of the House and, usually, picking the persons leading important committees as well. In 2011, Jindal picked Chuck Kleckley as speaker of the House and Steve Carter as chair of the House Education Committee. In the Senate, Jindal tapped John Alario as president of the Senate and Conrad Appel, a long-time advocate for conservative education reform, as head of the Education Committee.

Although Jindal had the legislature well-in-hand, other parts of the puzzle were harder to achieve. For example, K–12 education in Louisiana is led by a state superintendent of education, who is appointed by the Board of Elementary and Secondary Education (BESE). BESE, which sets education policy, consists of eleven members: eight elected members and three who are appointed by the governor. Given Jindal's ambitions, control of this board was essential, but a majority opposed Jindal's plans for reform. To gain power over BESE, Jindal used his informal powers, reaching out to friendly lobbying and public interest groups, raising money, and campaigning against opposing board members.[11] The governor's intrusion was a shock in the normally quiet BESE races. With Jindal exerting his influence and with outside groups massing their power, ads, and fundraising ability, Jindal succeeded in replacing nearly all of the unfriendly board members.[12] BESE quickly rewarded Jindal for his efforts by selecting his preferred candidate, John White, for superintendent. Taking the campaign to the people, Jindal reached out to evangelical Christian churches and parochial schools with his plans to remake education. In so doing, Jindal made critical allies across Louisiana for education reform, parental choice, and funding for religious education. Their voices would provide crucial support for Jindal's legislative initiative in upcoming House and Senate committee meetings.

Jindal's use of informal powers to mobilize support for his legislative agenda paid off. With Senate and House leadership on board and Republican majorities in both houses, with the Board of Elementary and Secondary

Education led by a hand-picked ally, with organizations mobilized for a campaign and well-funded allies ready to exert pressure, Jindal introduced his landmark legislation package. The Senate and House education committees responded by passing the legislation in marathon sessions that sometimes extended late in the evening. Moving on to the entire House and Senate, the legislation—constituting the most sweeping education reform in Louisiana history—was passed in days. Jindal had interwoven the formal and informal powers at his disposal to create a tour de force. An exultant editorial in the *Wall Street Journal* heralded Jindal's reform legislation as a "Moon Shot" that "would create America's largest school voucher program, broadest parental choice system, and toughest teacher accountability regime" in one fell swoop, making Louisiana the first in the nation to "effectively dismantle a public education monopoly."[13]

Jindal's education reform legislation was a striking display of a governor's power to innovate and change entrenched policies. Yet, such examples may be rarer in the future, as governors have, on balance, been losing rather than gaining power, as illustrated by table 3.1. Even Jindal's stunning 2012 success did not carry over to 2013, when the centerpiece of his legislative package, an income tax proposal, was judged "dead-on-arrival" in the House, a fact that illustrates the ever-changing context of political power.[14] In fact, as the next section of this essay will illustrate, Louisiana governors are losing power in several areas, with individual, institutional, and societal factors all contributing to the diminishment of the governor's formidable power.

DECLINING GUBERNATORIAL POWER

The most noticeable element in the declining connection between individuals and the governor is the increasing scarcity of face-to-face contact. In Huey Long's day, governors met the people where they lived—on their farms, in their towns, and on the bayou. Governors gained support through countless face-to-face events, such as festivals, fairs, rallies, and speaking engagements. These personal contacts provided governors with direct connections with supporters. Patronage, the distribution of political and economic favors to supporters, strengthened this web of connections. Contractors doing busi-

TABLE 3.1. The Powers of the Louisiana Governor

Formal Powers	*Informal Powers*
Appointive	Election mandate
Budget/Capital Outlay (shared)	Legislative domination*
Veto/line-item	Popularity, charisma, leadership ability
Special Session (shared)	Media savvy
State of the State	Patronage, largesse*
Oversight of Departments (shared)	Slush funds, fundraising, endorsements*
Pardons, commutations, reprieves	Name speaker of House*
Commander in chief, national guard	Name president of Senate*
Emergency Declarations	Name chairs of committees in legislature*

*Denotes areas where power of the Louisiana governor has declined

Factors Limiting Governor's Power	*Examples*
Separately elected executive officials	attorney general, lieutenant governor, secretary of state, et al.
Low public expectations	Less ability for governor to redefine office aggressively
Lack of capacity in executive branch	Size of staff, independent analytical ability and advice
Strong structures in legislature	Legislative strength works against gubernatorial strength
Measures of legislative ideology	Ideological conflict leaves less room for compromise
Increasing outside money (PACS)	Campaigns increasingly run by out-of-state entities
Nationalization of politics	State politics/policy swamped by focus on national issues
Dedicated funds; budgetary inflexibility	Constrained budgets limit innovation; leadership initiatives

ness with the state funded much of this system. Despite weakening, vestiges of these practices extended into the 1990s.

However, with the rise of mass and social media, direct mail, television, and Internet ads, face-to-face connections are now largely a relic of the past. Eddie Rispone's 2019 gubernatorial campaign illustrates the new reality. Largely unknown prior to the election, Rispone gained 49 percent of the vote and nearly upset a popular incumbent while rarely leaving his living room.[15] Spending $10 million of his personal fortune, Rispone launched a barrage of ads on social media, television, and radio unmatched in Louisiana history. The individual connection, so much a part of Louisiana's past, was missing.[16]

Changes in the legislature, the electorate, and the rise of non-governmental organizations have also contributed to the decline of the governor's power. The recent independence of the Louisiana legislature has come largely at the governor's expense. As Republicans gained a majority in both houses and the institution began to operate more like other state legislatures, the governor lost many of his most important informal powers. While Governors Blanco and Jindal were still able to name House speakers and Senate presidents and punish members for imprudent votes, the 2015 legislature denied Democratic governor John Bel Edwards this privilege in a historic repudiation of the governor's traditional power.[17] No longer could a governor count on calling the shots in the legislature.

Another blow to the governor's ability to exert his or her will has been the rise of a more ideological legislature and electorate. As House and Senate members increasingly sorted themselves into ultra-conservative, conservative, liberal, and progressive camps, the ability of the governor to bridge differences between partisans has lessened. Historically, governors counted on support from both Republicans and Democrats in the legislature and made appeals bridging partisan and ideological divides. Increasingly, these divides are intractable, and governors concentrate on unity in their own party. The legislature both led and reflected this reality. For example, the Committee for a Republican Majority, initially formed to elect more Republicans to the legislature, was rechristened the Committee for a Conservative Majority (CCM), indicating that just being Republican was not enough.[18] The increasingly ideological tone of Louisiana politics militates against not only Democratic governors but also against Republican governors whose adherence to conservative ideology may be judged insufficient by the CCM.

Non-governmental organizations (NGOs), including business groups like the Louisiana Association of Business and Industry (LABI) and watchdog groups like the Public Affairs Research Council (PAR) and Council for a

Better Louisiana (CABL), have also challenged the governor's power. NGOs mobilize supporters for political action. Supporters testify in hearings, lobby the legislature, and work to shape public opinion. NGOs' political independence and ability to reach citizens directly insulates them from the governor's influence. Also challenging governors are the increasing number of PACS and super PACs that can spend as much (or more) money on a campaign as the candidates do. Previously the governor, covered by newspapers, television stations, and radio, was arguably the state's most important dispenser of information and political news. Today, with declining newspaper circulations and the penetration of states by national news coverage, there is very little independent state-based news coverage left, leaving the governor competing with powerful media campaigns often run by out-of-state organizations.[19]

Broad societal changes have undercut the informal power of Louisiana governors as well. The most damaging may be the public's lessening tolerance for corruption accompanied by a sharp reduction in the unregulated money that fueled it. By the late 1980s, Louisianans had tired of their state's well-deserved reputation for corruption. Edwin Edwards's departure for a federal prison marked a new era for Louisiana, one in which corruption was neither accepted nor ignored.[20] The governors elected after Edwin Edward's last term—Mike Foster, Kathleen Blanco, Bobby Jindal, and John Bel Edwards—all campaigned on ending corruption.[21] Jindal, in particular, focused on this issue. Making ethics the centerpiece of his first campaign, he called a special session of the legislature to pass ethics legislation, linking it with economic development and job creation. The publicity given this effort was perhaps as important as the laws passed.[22] Part of the anti-corruption agenda was the effort to prevent governors from raising and using money illegally. By the end of Jindal's term in 2014, the decline of political money and patronage, the emergence of a vibrant two-party system, and a robust campaign against corruption signaled the rise of a new "clean" era in Louisiana politics.

Yet not all changes in Louisiana politics have come at the expense of the governor's power. Governors today have large professional staffs, coordinate with national groups like governors' associations, have great fundraising ability, and are still uniquely able to speak to citizens and represent the state nationally. One area of gubernatorial power that remains important is crisis management. In other states, the governor's responsibility to manage crises might be rarely required, but in Louisiana crises of various types are a way of life. When a crisis threatens, the governor's power swells to meet the challenge. How a governor uses this power and responds during the crisis largely determines whether he or she can confidently seek reelection and enjoy a good reputation after leaving office.

Some crises are so massive or unprecedented that they overwhelm the ability of governors to address them, as Hurricane Katrina seems to have swamped Governor Kathleen Blanco in 2005. Learning from Blanco's misadventure, Bobby Jindal met the disasters of Hurricane Gustav and the BP oil spill with great care, determined not to be caught unprepared. However, a different kind of disaster, specifically the fiscal disaster that followed the Great Recession in 2008–2009, combined with Jindal's single-minded pursuit of higher office at the expense of the state, left his previously good reputation in tatters. After years of Jindal's budgetary chicanery, John Bel Edwards found it necessary to call seven special sessions before stabilizing the state's budget.[23] In so doing, he met the initial crisis of his administration admirably, although reviews of his handling of the second major crisis, the COVID-19 pandemic, vary across the partisan divide. While John Bel Edwards's power and visibility have grown, the threat this pandemic poses to his reputation and legacy has increased as well, a lasting paradox of gubernatorial power.

Finally, the question that matters most in terms of a governor's power: on whose behalf is this power used? Does the governor use his or her power to make things better for ordinary citizens, for children, for the environment, for the economy, for racial minorities, for women, for businesses, for entrepreneurs, or for the state as a whole? All governors come to office promising to make things better, yet none succeeds entirely. Looking back at the last four governors, all of whom had two terms except Blanco, there is a clear difference in energy, policy focus, and effect. Table 3.2 illustrates the different foci of the governors and their achievements. History will judge which governor has had the most lasting effect on Louisiana and which will serve as the best model for future Louisiana governors.

The Louisiana governor has transitioned from a circus master to a band director over the last thirty-five years. Although gubernatorial power ebbs

TABLE 3.2. The Policy Foci of Recent Louisiana Governors

Governor	*Achievements and Programs*
Murphy James "Mike" Foster Jr. 1996–2003	Created Louisiana Community and Technical College System Expanded Tuition Opportunity Program for Students (TOPS) Stelly Tax Reform Plan
Kathleen Babineaux Blanco 2004–2007	Rebuilt the Superdome following Hurricane Katrina Reorganized New Orleans schools under Recovery School District Teacher pay raised to southern regional average
Bobby Jindal 2008–2015	Ethics reform legislation K–12 education reform, enhanced charter schools Reorganization of Charity Health Care System
John Bel Edwards 2016–2023	Expanded Medicaid Ended perennial fiscal crises Led coronavirus response

and flows with the occupant of the office, several trends are clear: Governors of Louisiana have lost some of the unique informal powers that helped them achieve their goals. Governors have also been challenged by changes in partisan alignment, communication, and fundraising that make policy achievements more difficult. But in the area of crisis management, Louisiana governors remain extraordinarily important and powerful. Yet even this power may be subject to limitations in the future.[24] Regardless of the changes to come, the governor will always be at the center of Louisiana politics and remain the most powerful officeholder in Louisiana state government.

NOTES

1. Wayne Parent, *Inside the Carnival: Unmasking Louisiana Politics* (Baton Rouge: Louisiana State Univ. Press, 2004); John Maginnis, *The Last Hayride* (Baton Rouge, La.: Gris Gris Press, 1984).

2. The extraordinary latitude given governors during crises may be coming to an end, as the Louisiana legislature called itself into special session in 2020 to pass bills giving themselves a coequal role in facing crises. Governors since Edwards are Murphy "Mike" Foster (1996–2004); Kathleen Blanco (2004–2008); Bobby Jindal (2008–2016); and John Bel Edwards (no relation to Edwin Edwards) (2016–2024).

3. The article setting parameters for the current debate was Peter Bachrach and Morton S. Baratz, "Two Faces of Power," *American Political Science Review,* 56, no. 4 (1962), 947–952. See updates, arguments, and additions in Steven Lukes, *Power: A Radical View* (New York: Palgrave Macmillan, 2005). Thad Kousser and Justin H. Phillips take a deep dive into gubernatorial power in *The Power of American Governors: Winning on Budgets and Losing on Policy* (Cambridge: Cambridge Univ. Press, 2012), which contains a plethora of useful charts and graphs detailing gubernatorial power in many contexts.

4. Soon-to-be Governor Edwin Edwards led the effort behind the 1974 constitution that replaced the 1921 Louisiana constitution, which was routinely cited by critics as an example of how not to order a state government. For more discussion of the Louisiana constitution, please reference the essay by Haydel, Procopio, and Scott in this volume.

5. Responsibility for various governmental tasks is often shared with the legislature, as for example with crafting a budget.

6. Louisiana Constitution, Article IV, Section 5, subheadings A-K. The capital outlay budget is the list of road, dam, bridge, and other projects the state funds. The powers listed above merely scratch the surface of gubernatorial power. A good place to find out more about governors of other states is at the National Governors Association website, https://www.nga.org/.

7. Refer to Table 3.1. The Powers of the Louisiana Governor. A "mandate" is a term used to denote support for a victorious politician.

8. One example of corruption in the governor's office is illustrated by Edwin Edwards's selling casino licenses in exchange for cash. One such $400,000 payment, from 49ers owner Eddie DeBartolo to Edwards, resulted in DeBartolo's banishment from the NFL and culminated in Edwards's nearly ten-year stint in federal prison. See Tyler Bridges, *Bad Bet on the Bayou: The Rise of Gambling in Louisiana and the Fall of Governor Edwin Edwards* (New York: Farrar, Straus, and Giroux, 2002).

9. Jindal raised over $15 million for reelection and ended the campaign with $4.6 million in the bank. "Jindal Considers Third Term Bid After Historic Win," Associated Press, November 10, 2011; Jindal gained 673,239 votes out of a total of 1,023,163 cast, which bested Edwin Edwards's 62.31 percent victory over incumbent David Treen in 1983. "Ed Anderson, Bill Barrow, Governor Bobby Jindal Shows Strength Across Louisiana in Re-Election Landslide," *Times-Picayune,* October 23, 2011.

10. Louisiana politics has been reshaped by the increasing power of the Republican Party. The dramatic emergence of the Republican Party in Louisiana is well-covered in other essays in this volume. Bill Barrow, "Louisiana Republicans Take First House Majority with Latest Party Switch," *Times-Picayune,* December 18, 2010.

11. These groups included Council for a Better Louisiana (CABL), the Alliance for Better

Classrooms (ABC), the Louisiana Family Forum (LFF), and the most powerful business groups, led by the Louisiana Association of Business and Industry (LABI).

12. Lottie Beebe was the odd person out. Prior to Jindal's 2011 campaign, BESE was two votes short of electing Jindal's choice, John White. After the election, White was elected with nine of the eleven votes.

13. "Jindal's Education Moon Shot," editorial, *Wall Street Journal*, January 31, 2012.

14. Several factors are important in explaining why Jindal's bold victories in 2012 were not repeated in tax reform in 2013, but the most pertinent is the insularity of education as an issue as opposed to tax and revenue issues, which affect all state enterprises and engage an enormous number of powerful entities on both sides. See Bridges, "Once Called Governor's 'Lap Dog.'"

15. Blessed with a personal fortune that eliminated the need to raise money, Rispone launched an unprecedented media blitzkrieg aimed at winning the governor's race. Melinda Deslatte, "As He Runs for Governor, Eddie Rispone Gives Few Details," Associated Press, October 27, 2019. John Bel Edwards won 51 percent of the vote (774,498 votes) versus Eddie Rispone's 49 percent (734,286 votes). Louisiana Secretary of State, https://www.sos.la.gov.

16. The story of the 2019 election has yet to be told, although a riveting book has been written about John Bel Edwards's 2015 gubernatorial race by Tyler Bridges and Jeremy Alford: *Long Shot: A Soldier, a Senator, a Serious Sin, an Epic Louisiana Election* (Baton Rouge, La.: Lisburn Press, 2016).

17. Mark Ballard, "In a Rarely Seen Twist, Last-Minute Candidate Taylor Barras Selected Louisiana House Speaker," *The Advocate*, January 14, 2016.

18. Melinda Deslatte, "Louisiana PAC Trying to Elect More Conservative Lawmakers," Associated Press, August 29, 2019.

19. Robert Mann describes the declining arc of independent news in Louisiana in some detail in his essay in this book.

20. "Ten Years in Prison for Ex-Louisiana Governor," Associated Press, January 8, 2001.

21. Other important officials, such as Senator David Vitter, were strong supporters of ethics legislation and aided the movement, which was championed by the Republican Party in Louisiana.

22. Jindal's ethics reform was criticized for leaving the governor's office unreformed. Bob Barrow, "Jindal's Special Session Is Heavy on Ethics," *Times-Picayune*, February 2, 2008.

23. Only a significant hike in Louisiana's sales tax provided the revenue necessary to balance the budget and end the crisis.

24. Mark Ballard, "A Power Struggle Is at the Root of Louisiana's Latest Special Session, Starting Monday," *The Advocate*, September 26, 2020.

LOUISIANA'S LOCAL POLITICS

Institutional and Economic Tug-of-War

CHRISTIE L. MALOYED

Most outsiders recognize Louisiana by the distinct culture of its towns, cities, and localities. From the spectacle of Mardi Gras in New Orleans to the political lore of Baton Rouge to the rich Cajun and Creole music and food traditions of Acadiana, each locality in Louisiana celebrates its own rich style and flavor. While parishes and cities across the state are distinctly different culturally, they share many of the same political struggles. Two stand out: the resistance against state control and the struggle over the increasing national influence on local politics. This essay begins by explaining how parish and local governments are organized and subject to state oversight. We then investigate three areas of change and contention affecting local government. First, we explore how shared models of governance in East Baton Rouge and Lafayette Parishes have prompted debate over cities seeking independence from parish government. Second, we show how national partisan trends of ideological polarization and urban-rural political divides have trickled down to the local level and their effect on local politics. Third, the sharp peaks and drops in Louisiana's economy have strained the economic relationship between state and local governments. With a decentralized sales tax collection system and a controversial industrial tax exemption program, local governments face increasing economic uncertainty. These battles over control showcase the struggle for local autonomy amid an increasingly partisan backdrop.

THE STRUCTURE OF LOCAL GOVERNMENT IN LOUISIANA

In Louisiana, as in other states, municipal governments are primarily creatures of the state. As the Tenth Amendment to the US Constitution spells out, "The powers not delegated to the United States by the Constitution, nor prohibited by it to the States, are reserved to the States respectively, or to the people."[1] Hence, under the American system of federalism, local levels of government derive their authority from the state governments. This arrangement is accepted by states nationwide and is known as Dillon's Rule, allowing local governments only those powers specified in their governing charter.[2] This legal doctrine establishes that states have supremacy over the actions of local government. Thus, if a state and local government pass conflicting rules, the state's power holds and will invalidate the local rule. In Louisiana, the state regulates local economic activity by government entities. For instance, a city does not have the authority to control landlords' rent levels unless the local charter grants explicitly such power. Similarly, the state sets minimum wage levels. Local governments cannot require employers in their jurisdiction to pay a higher rate. Advocates of local control over wages in the state legislature have been unsuccessful, thus far, in contesting this rule.

As political scientist Wayne Parent has argued, in Louisiana "state politics invades almost every phase of local politics."[3] Though states have supremacy, local governments alleviate the burden of governing on states, providing the freedom to pass ordinances appropriate to each community. Louisiana's local government structure is divided into parish and municipal levels—the latter covers cities, towns, and villages (see figure 4.1). Parish government's responsibilities include services and offices that affect residents parish-wide, including road and drainage system maintenance, public health, and public safety. Parish governments are constitutionally required to have at least six offices: sheriff, coroner, tax assessor, clerk of the district court, registrar of voters, and district attorney.

Parish governments historically were organized as "police juries," and thirty-eight parishes continue to use this system. Unlike the American federal government, which separates the powers of making and enforcing laws between Congress and the president, a police jury serves both executive and legislative functions for the parish. Typically, there are five to fifteen elected members, and usually they select one of their members as chairperson to preside over meetings. Combining executive and legislative functions into a single governing body can make the process of governing more efficient and

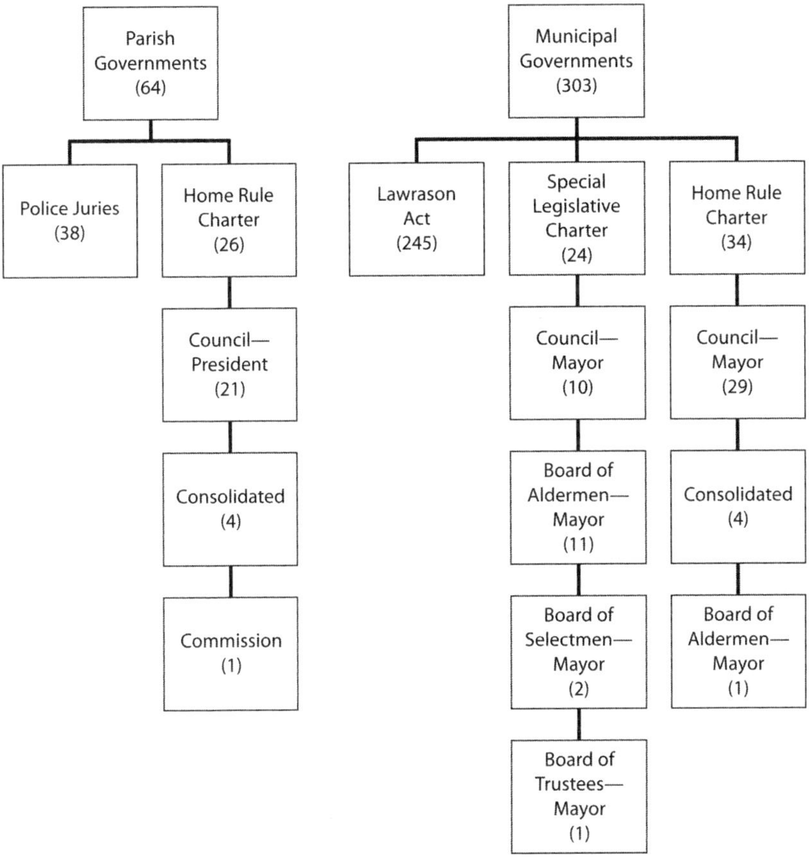

FIGURE 4.1. Forms and Numbers of Parish and Municipal Governments.

cheaper, especially since the states authorize a limited scope of power for parish governments.

A council-president system has been implemented by twenty-one other parishes, with the elected council performing the legislative function and the independently elected president serving as the executive. Caddo Parish uses a commission system, with twelve elected commissioners serving the legislative function, and one parish administrator, selected by the commissioners, acting as the executive. Four parishes have consolidated systems, discussed in greater detail below.[4]

Within Louisiana's parishes there are 303 independent municipal governments. Among those, the overwhelming majority, 245, were established under the Lawrason Act. This 1898 act standardized the process for creating a governing structure for an incorporated municipality. Municipalities established under the Lawrason Act tend to be small. The act provides only one option for the governing structure, a mayor–board of aldermen system, where elected board members hold legislative power and the mayor has executive power. Some cities have passed ordinances to call their legislative body a council rather than a board, though their powers remain the same. The board's size is proportional to the municipality's size, ranging from three to nine, with some elected from geographic districts while others may be elected at large.[5]

To provide increased efficiency for local decision-making, states have offered some local governments the option for home rule. Typically granted through a charter—a constitution for a local government—home rule spells out specific areas of autonomy and responsibility. In Louisiana, thirty-four cities have been established by home rule charters, primarily the larger cities, and twenty-four by legislative or special charters, typically mid-sized cities.[6] These charters provide the flexibility to adopt a governing structure different from the mayor-board of alderman structure offered in the Lawrason Act. Cities operating under home rule or a legislative charter often adopt a mayor-council system, or council-manager system, where the council appoints a professional city manager.

Local governments also have the power to create special districts, if needed. Special districts are governmental divisions created to oversee a particular sector, like a water district to ensure safety and cleanliness, or a fire district. Increasingly, localities are creating special districts to address economic issues, such as promoting economic development, and managing historical and cultural districts. Such districts have recently been established in Franklin, Lafayette, Orleans, St. Mary, and West Baton Rouge parishes. These give owners of registered historic homes tax credits to help make rehabilitation projects affordable. These districts also exempt artists' products from local sales tax. The goal is to invite investments into lower-income areas to make them cultural destinations.

Municipal governments are the closest to their citizens, and thus are typically responsible for establishing policies and ordinances that regulate everyday activities. These include building and land use, noise and animal control, and public safety. Both parish and municipal governments are staffed by civil service employees and range widely in size, from only a few to over five thousand employees in New Orleans. The offices staffed by municipal government also can vary widely. For villages and towns, municipal government services focus primarily on safety (police and fire), road and drainage maintenance, parks and recreation, and building and business permits. For larger cities, services extend to planning and zoning, economic development, community development, and housing. Many cities also utilize appointed boards and commissions. These boards oversee various special projects, such as arts programming, disability awareness, historical preservation, and regional planning. These boards allow residents to volunteer and be directly involved in local government.

REPRESENTATION AND CONSOLIDATED SYSTEMS OF GOVERNMENT

Four parishes have consolidated forms of government. Three of those have consolidated parish and municipal councils: Baton Rouge-East Baton Rouge Parish, Houma-Terrebonne Parish, and Lafayette-Lafayette Parish. This means that the parish government and city share a legislative council and executive officer, a mayor-president; however, other cities or towns within those parishes may have their own local governments. The City of New Orleans fully consolidated with Orleans Parish, making it one of only a few fully consolidated municipal-parish governments in America. There are no independent municipal governments within Orleans Parish, nor separate budgets for the parish city.

New Orleans experienced one of the earliest mergers in the country, a process that began at the inception of the city and was completed in 1870.[7] Though numerous consolidation proposals have been advanced across the country over the last decades, over 85 percent have been rejected because citizens are reluctant to give up local autonomy.[8] The movement toward consolidated governments picked up steam after the Second World War. The promise of economic savings, less red tape, and greater efficiencies made mergers appealing.[9] On the promise of just such savings, Baton Rouge consolidated with East Baton Rouge Parish (EBR) in 1949 and merged into a single metro council in 1982. Terrebonne Parish consolidated with Houma in 1981, passing by only a fifteen-vote margin, and Lafayette voters approved consolidation in 1992.

Business and financial interests often spurred the initial drive toward consolidation, but today, fractious debates about consolidated government often focus on concerns over equity in representation. In East Baton Rouge Parish, for example, leaders of Baton Rouge's chapter of the NAACP have argued that a split council is necessary to gain fair racial representation.[10] While the parish has a 45.9 percent Black population, the city of Baton Rouge is majority Black (55.0 percent).[11] The consolidated Metro Council currently has twelve members, seven white and five Black, which is reflective of parish but not city demographics. The Baton Rouge Area Chamber (BRAC) has opposed deconsolidation and argues that any split would create unnecessary layers of bureaucracy and create division.[12]

Meanwhile, St. George, a majority white community in the southeastern corner of EBR Parish, voted to incorporate into a separate city in October 2019. The BRAC adamantly opposed this movement, as has Mayor-President Sharon Weston Broome, whose administration filed a lawsuit in opposition, citing financial hardship to the consolidated government if they must forfeit taxes to St. George.[13] The impetus for St. George's break from Baton Rouge was the desire for control over their own school system. The more affluent and white community of St. George has decried the status of the lower performing, less economically secure, and racially diverse schools under Baton Rouge's control. These contemporary attempts to further racially segregate schools are happening nationwide through the "cityhood movement," where predominantly white suburbs seek incorporation to separate from their more racially diverse city centers and gain control over their school systems.[14]

Lafayette has also experienced bitter debates over its consolidated system since seating its first consolidated government in 1996. A mere fifteen years later, a charter commission was so dismayed by the problems facing the merged government that they proposed full deconsolidation, though it failed at the ballot box. Proposals for a complete restructuring of the merged council failed again in both 2013 and 2015, until finally, in 2018, Lafayette voters passed a proposal to split the city and parish councils. The mayor-president position, however, remains joined, and both councils must sign off on final budgets.

The division in Lafayette has focused more on the different priorities held by city and parish voters, though, as in Baton Rouge, race is a factor driving these debates. Voters in the municipalities and unincorporated areas have proven to be staunchly tax averse, while Lafayette City voters routinely vote in favor of tax proposals and renewals. For instance, parish opponents to a tax that funded the public library system recently voted down the renewal, outnumbering the city supporters. The economic downturn following COVID-19 spurred the administration to propose severe budget cuts to recreational centers located in the city's predominantly Black neighborhoods, showcasing the role of race and representation, or lack thereof, in Lafayette's consolidated government.[15] This rural-urban schism reflects national political trends. While the issues underpinning the consolidation debate in Lafayette and Baton Rouge are particular to each city, both instances reflect the growing influence of national partisan politics and ideological polarization as driving forces in local government.

NATIONALIZATION OF LOCAL POLITICS

While the state government has formal control over local government, national trends are taking greater hold at the local level in terms of politics. Historically, the issues that drove local politics, like fixing potholes, were not partisan. However, the changing nature of political media coverage, campaign spending, and hyperpartisanship has shifted the balance toward national influence.

One of the largest drivers of this shift is the nationalization of media. Local media has dedicated more time to national issues, covering fewer local ones.[16] With less information about local candidates, voters are less likely to know much about the candidates and thus depend more on partisan labels to make election day decisions.[17] As local newspapers and television news stations have closed, there has also been a reduced number of people running for local offices.[18]

In local races, Louisiana has also seen a greater national influence from increased campaign contributions. Even school board races, the most local of local races, have been targeted for out-of-state donations. Charter school proponents associated with businesses that own, manage, or supply these quasi-private schools typically make these contributions. For instance, in the 2012 New Orleans school board elections, Sarah Newell Usdin ran for the District 3 seat and accepted more than $110,000 in campaign contributions, including out-of-state donations.[19]

The *Citizens United v. FEC* (2010) court decision allows campaign donations from "dark money" groups. These are nonprofits permitted to engage in some political activity without disclosing the names of donors, making it impossible to know who funds the organization. In 2018, the dark money group Education Reform Now Advocacy—affiliated with the New York-based pro-charter school group Democrats for Education Reform—spent over $100,000 on media advertising to influence local school board elections in Baton Rouge.[20] In Lafayette, the dark money group Citizens for a New Louisiana—a conservative, anti-tax organization—made contributions in Lafayette local tax campaigns, including successfully opposing tax proposals that would support building new school infrastructure and support the public library.[21]

In addition to the influence of outside money in campaigns, candidates for local offices are increasingly expected to take a position on national issues. Campaign materials, including push cards and websites, routinely mention the candidate's position on hot-button national issues like Second Amendment gun rights, abortion rights, and support or opposition to the president. Candidates still address typical local issues, like local taxes and maintenance of roads. However, local races that used to be primarily shielded from national politics have shifted to stress political ideology and connections to national political parties and issues.

Louisiana has experienced a profound shift in its partisan alignment in the past two decades, one that has been felt both in state and local elections. The state has experienced an increase in hyperpartisanship. Those who identify with a political party do so strongly and are more likely to have an unfavorable view of members of other political parties.[22]

Though Louisiana had remained the last Democratic stronghold in the

South, party registration has followed the trend of neighboring states, with increased Republican Party membership. From 2000 to 2020, the Democratic Party has dropped in statewide registered members by 17.9 percent, with Republican registration gaining by 9.5 percent, and other parties, including No Party and Independents, gaining by 8.3 percent. This transition has not been felt equally across the state. Following a nationwide trend, partisan shifts have broken along the lines between urban and rural communities. In both New Orleans and Baton Rouge, the majority of voters are registered Democratic Party members and have Democratic mayors and majority control of their councils. By contrast, more rural cities and parishes have increasingly supported Republican candidates for both local and state offices. However, party registration does not always reflect this shift, as some voters have remained registered Democrats but consistently vote for Republican candidates. And while partisan conflicts have increasingly shaped some local policy debates, many issues, especially economic ones, fall more along the familiar battle lines of local governments seeking to wrest power from the state.

THE BATTLE FOR ECONOMIC CONTROL

Across the nation, local governments have faced increasing financial burdens. Especially in the wake of the economic downturn following the COVID-19 pandemic, local governments have increased spending for public health measures while collecting fewer tax revenues, leading to impending and widespread budget shortfalls. As compared to most states, Louisiana's local governments rely disproportionately on sales taxes over property taxes to fund government operations. Some, like Cameron Parish and the city of Broussard, rely exclusively on sales tax revenues. Sales tax collections can lead to sharp peaks and drops in tax revenues depending on local economic cycles. In contrast, property values fluctuate less dramatically and thus provide more stable sources of revenues.

While the state maintains a 4.45 percent sales tax (as of spring 2021), local taxing authorities—such as municipal and parish governments, school boards, and sheriffs—can levy sales taxes with voter support. Local taxes vary widely, averaging 5 percent but as high as 7.95 percent in LaSalle Parish for a

TABLE 4.1. Parishwide Millage Rates Ranked Highest to Lowest, 2019

Rank	*Parish*	*Millage Rate*	*Rank*	*Parish*	*Millage Rate*
1	Grant	161.1	33	Webster	105.7
2	LaSalle	154.8	34	Jackson	105.3
3	Allen	150.5	35	Assumption	104.9
4	St. Helena	149.9	36	Iberville	104.1
5	Cameron	146.9	37	Jefferson Davis	103.6
6	St. Tammany	145.6	38	St. Martin	103.4
7	Orleans	145.4	39	St. Mary	98.5
8	St. Bernard	143.2	40	Terrebonne	96.2
9	Caddo	136.1	41	Ouachita	94.1
10	Caldwell	133.7	42	Natchitoches	92.2
11	East Carroll	129.1	43	Madison	92.0
12	St. John	125.7	44	Morehouse	91.2
13	Tensas	125.4	45	Vermilion	90.6
14	Lafourche	123.7	46	Winn	90.4
15	Vernon	123.0	47	Catahoula	89.6
16	Beauregard	120.5	48	Tangipahoa	89.1
17	East Baton Rouge	119.2	49	Sabine	86.7
18	St. Charles	118.4	50	Claiborne	83.6
19	Bossier	116.1	51	Lafayette	82.9
20	Bienville	113.7	52	Union	82.2
21	Jefferson	113.0	53	Richland	80.4
22	West Baton Rouge	112.8	54	West Feliciana	79.8
23	DeSoto	111.9	55	Lincoln	79.3
24	Rapides	111.2	56	West Carroll	76.2
25	Washington	110.3	57	Avoyelles	75.9
26	Calcasieu	109.9	58	Acadia	75.7
27	Ascension	109.4	59	Evangeline	72.5
28	Livingston	108.8	60	Iberia	72.0
29	St. James	107.6	61	Plaquemines	68.7
30	Concordia	106.1	62	St. Landry	56.6
31	Franklin	106.0	63	Pointe Coupee	53.5
32	Red River	105.7	64	East Feliciana	49.5

Source: Data from the Louisiana Tax Commission Annual Report, 2019.

combined state and local rate of 12.45 percent (see table 4.1). Sales taxes often go into a general fund to be used at the local government's discretion, but they also support specific projects. For instance, voters have approved designated local sales taxes to fund the construction of a new airport terminal (Lafayette Parish), build a new sport and recreational complex (Youngsville), and pay for public school employee salary raises (Lincoln Parish).

The sales tax collection process in Louisiana exemplifies the complicated relationship between local governments and the state. With over four hundred local taxing authorities in the state, Louisiana has one of the country's most byzantine sales tax systems. It is one of only two states in the United States that does not utilize a state-level, centralized collection process, and is a rare example of local autonomy and one that local governments are fighting to retain.[23] Lobbying organizations representing local taxing authorities' interests have opposed the state's efforts to centralize tax collections. This includes the Louisiana Municipal Association, the Police Jury Association, and the Louisiana School Board Association. Recent proposals for centralized collection in the state legislature have called for a portion of local tax revenues to be diverted to the state to cover administrative costs. Local governments also fear their state authorities will be less vigilant with collections, further reducing their revenues.

Internet sales have forced Louisiana's sales tax collections into the limelight. The US Supreme Court decision *South Dakota v. Wayfair, Inc.* (2018) affirmed states' right to collect sales taxes on remote purchases. Before this case, Louisiana only collected taxes on sales from businesses physically located within the state, which meant they missed out on substantial revenue collections. Given the complicated patchwork of local tax rates, since 2018, remote sellers have been allowed to collect and remit taxes at an average 8.45 percent rate. As of July 2020, the Louisiana Sales and Use Tax Commission for Remote Sellers may require the collection of local taxes based on the purchaser's zip code going forward. If successful, this may be a pilot program for Louisiana to become the forty-ninth state to centralize sales tax collections from all businesses against local governments' wishes.

Another contentious issue surrounding local tax collection revolves around the state's Industrial Tax Exemption Program (ITEP). As in many other states, Louisiana offers industrial and manufacturer corporations economic incentives to expand operations by providing exemptions from local property taxes. Applications for the program must propose a specific expansion project that will create jobs. For decades, the state-level Commerce and Industry Board handled all ITEP applications without input from local governments. In 2016, newly elected Governor Jon Bel Edwards issued an executive order that routed all ITEP requests to local taxing authorities. Following his order, if a corporation wanted to apply for local tax exemptions, they had to appeal to each local authority, including the school board, sheriff, and municipal and parish governments.

Whereas the state board had approved virtually all applications that met the ITEP program criteria, some local governments rejected proposals under the new rules. For example, in December 2018, the Lafayette Consolidated Council rejected a request from Stuller Inc., a jewelry equipment supplier, because the parish budget was facing shortfalls. In February 2020, St. James Parish attempted to negotiate an amended tax rate exemption for a new hydrogen plant, agreeing to an 80 percent exemption for the first five years but collecting 50 percent for the next five, a move that the Louisiana Economic Development office says violates ITEP rules.[24]

The financial stakes over tax exemptions are high, especially for fiscally strapped local governments. For instance, in January 2019 the East Baton Rouge School Board and Baton Rouge Metro Council rejected a retroactive $2.9 million exemption request from ExxonMobil because they completed the project two years prior. ITEP proponents argued that Exxon would use the money to grow the company and job opportunities further. The school board, facing a $30 million deficit, argued that those tax dollars would prevent jobs from being eliminated in the school district. Together Baton Rouge, a community organization, has led the opposition to such exemptions, arguing that Baton Rouge taxing authorities received an additional $10.5 million since gaining local control over approvals.[25]

The influential lobbying group Louisiana Association of Business and Industry (LABI) led the opposition against Edwards's ITEP reforms. They argued that the changes created a confusing scenario for corporations. Some local tax authorities might approve the request and others reject it, making an already complicated tax system even more challenging to navigate. Governor Edwards relented somewhat, and as of February 2020 corporations can appeal to the state board if local authorities reject their proposals. Despite some prominent application denials, many local governments have approved ITEP proposals and have sought additional tax breaks to lure businesses.

The ITEP program showcases the tension in Louisiana governance. The issue at hand is not an outright rejection of incentivizing economic development; instead, it is over who should have a say in whether corporations pay local taxes: the local government or the state? Though the state has exercised considerable control over local governments for decades, these struggles demonstrate how local governments seek autonomy, especially over their economic affairs. Though national partisan trends increasingly influence state and local politics, the local struggle for greater power over their affairs is not a Democratic or Republican issue. Despite strong oversight from the statehouse in Baton Rouge, local governments continually seek opportunities to experiment and innovate.

NOTES

1. US Constitution, Tenth Amendment.

2. This rule was named for Iowa Supreme Court Justice John Dillon, presiding judge in the case that established this precedent.

3. Wayne Parent, *Inside the Carnival: Unmasking Louisiana Politics* (Baton Rouge: Louisiana State Univ. Press, 2004), 91.

4. Louisiana House of Representatives, House Legislative Services, *State and Local Government in Louisiana: An Overview,* October 2011, https://house.louisiana.gov/SLG/index.htm.

5. Jerry J. Guillot, "The Lawrason Act," *Louisiana Municipal Association,* August 2016.

6. Louisiana Municipal Association, *2019 Handbook for Louisiana Municipal Officials,* 2019, https://www.lma.org/LMA/Publications/Municipal_Handbook/LMA/Publications/Handbook_old.aspx?hkey=303c6109-1261-4cca-9b6f-596107734f8a.

7. S. S. Sheppard and L. L. Moak, "New Orleans Leads in Consolidation," *National Municipal Review* 29 (1940): 724–727.

8. Suzanne Leland and Kurt Thurmaier, *Case Studies of City-County Consolidation: The Changing Local Landscape* (Armonk, N.Y.: M. E. Sharpe, 2004).

9. The evidence on whether or not consolidated government leads to economic savings is mixed. Some preliminary research suggests Lafayette may have gained some financial savings

since consolidating: Joshua Hall, Matti, Josh, and Zhou, Yang, "The Economic Impact of City-County Consolidations: A Synthetic Control Approach," *Economics Faculty Working Papers Series* 35 (2017), https://researchrepository.wvu.edu/econ_working-papers/35. Other scholars have found consolidation in general may not produce savings: Charles D. Taylor, Dagney Faulk, and Pamela Schaal, "Where Are the Cost Savings in City-County Consolidation?," *Journal of Urban Affairs* 39, no. 2 (February 2017): 185–204.

10. Terry Jones, "St. George Vote Revives Chatter of Dismantling Consolidated Government in East Baton Rouge," *The Advocate,* October 19, 2019, https://www.theadvocate.com/baton_rouge/news/article_e3f2dff0-f031-11e9-bd90-5fcc670feb01.html.

11. US Census Bureau, 2018 American Community Survey 5-Year Estimates.

12. Andrea Gallo, "Making St. George Comparison, Mayor Broome, BRAC Oppose Effort to Create Separate City Council," *The Advocate,* September 5, 2018, https://www.theadvocate.com/baton_rouge/news/article_c6f61b92-b13f-11e8-a71d-1b65272bb95f.html.

13. "Baton Rouge Area Chamber Voices Opposition to St. George Incorporation," Baton Rouge Area Chamber, May 15, 2018, https://brac.org/baton-rouge-area-chamber-voices-opposition-st-george-incorporation/; Terry Jones and Blake Paterson, "St. George Incorporation in Limbo after Mayor, Others Sue to Stop Creation of New City," *The Advocate,* November 4, 2019, https://www.theadvocate.com/baton_rouge/news/article_1a07709a-fb65-11e9-81e7-9fcc950f12f5.html.

14. Sam Rosen, "Atlanta's Controversial 'Cityhood' Movement," *The Atlantic,* April 26, 2017, https://www.theatlantic.com/business/archive/2017/04/the-border-battles-of-atlanta/523884/.

15. Claire Taylor, "White Lafayette Parish Councilmen Kill Attempt to Keep Rec Centers Open in Black Neighborhoods," *The Advocate,* July 28, 2020, https://www.theadvocate.com/acadiana/news/article_619e7a50-d0eb-11ea-b886-e7e975424cbb.html.

16. See Robert Mann's essay on Louisiana's media coverage of politics for more information.

17. Joshua P. Darr, Matthew P. Hitt, and Johanna L. Dunaway, "Newspaper Closures Polarize Voting Behavior," *Journal of Communication* 68, no. 6 (November 5, 2018): 1007–1028.

18. Meghan E. Rubado and Jay T. Jennings, "Political Consequences of the Endangered Local Watchdog: Newspaper Decline and Mayoral Elections in the United States," *Urban Affairs Review* 56, no. 5 (April 2019): 1327–1356.

19. Andrew Vanacore, "Orleans Parish School Board Candidate Sarah Usdin Laps the Field in Fund-Raising," *Times-Picayune,* October 10, 2012.

20. Charles Lussier, "Charter-School Friendly Group Launches Ad Campaign Ahead of East Baton Rouge School Board Election," *The Advocate,* May 29, 2018, https://www.theadvocate.com/baton_rouge/news/education/article_3cb35870-5f76-11e8-a40a-9bab8c3981a5.html.

21. Christie L. Maloyed, "Dark Money in Local Politics," *The Current,* October 18, 2018, https://thecurrentla.com/2018/dark-money-in-local-politics/.

22. See Michael Henderson's essay of partisanship and polarization in Louisiana for additional information.

23. Public Affairs Research Council, "Having It Both Ways on Sales Taxes," June 26, 2018, http://revenue.louisiana.gov/Miscellaneous/PAR%20Policy%20Brief%20-%20Sales%20taxes%206-26-18.pdf.

24. Sam Karlin, "Change to State's Largest Tax Break Would Give Companies Ability to Appeal Rejections by Locals," *The Advocate,* February 20, 2020, https://www.theadvocate.com/baton_rouge/news/politics/legislature/article_ddddb63c-5420-11ea-92a1-dbf8f92bd50f.html.

25. Terry Jones, "Changes to ITEP Tax Break Netted East Baton Rouge about $10 Million, Advocacy Group Says," *The Advocate,* https://www.theadvocate.com/baton_rouge/news/article_030a640e-62fa-11ea-ab62-5b798889642e.html.

PART II

POLITICS

THE LATEST LAST HAYRIDE

Louisiana's Political Journalism in Transition

ROBERT MANN

When the late political journalist John Maginnis published his book chronicling the raucous 1983 Louisiana governor's race between incumbent governor Dave Treen and former governor Edwin Edwards, he called it *The Last Hayride.* Harnett T. Kane's 1941 book about Huey Long's era, *Louisiana Hayride,* had inspired the title of the newer book. In his chronicle, Maginnis argued that the 1983 campaign was the last gasp of the corrupt politics that had dominated Louisiana since the Long era. Maginnis wrote, "Louisiana is running out of time," adding, "Our free and easy, banana republic, oil sheikdom days are numbered."[1]

While Maginnis's book was an indictment of Louisiana government, implicit was the suggestion that the 1983 race was the last to feature the flamboyant campaigning style that long characterized Louisiana politics. This had included caravans of candidates roaming the state, delivering stump speeches in dozens of small towns. From Huey Long to Earl Long to Jimmie Davis to John McKeithen, a Louisiana governor's campaign resembled a traveling circus, a tent revival, a patent medicine show, or some parts of all three: high on entertainment and low on useful information. For example, at his rallies Earl Long handed out hams and watermelons. Davis and Long both used country and western bands to warm up crowds. A renowned singer, Davis not only spoke about politics, he also sang hit songs like "You Are My Sunshine" to adoring crowds.[2] "Candidates for major statewide offices spent several months stumping the state," political scientist Joseph B. Parker wrote in 1988 for the book *Readings in Louisiana Politics.* "They made several stops each day, frequently in the oppressive heat of summer."

Parker argued that the crowded 1963–1964 governor's race was the first contest of a new era that "established professional campaigning statewide." Each candidate ran thirty- and sixty-second television spots, conducted polls, and hired media strategists. "This was also the last campaign in which stumping was used extensively," Parker observed, adding, "Stumping virtually died and newspaper advertising was little used as campaigns were increasingly conducted via television and radio."[3]

While noting the waning use of retail campaigning in statewide races, Parker's most important contribution to understanding the evolution of Louisiana campaigns may have been his recognition that the media and advertising strategies candidates began using in the early 1960s had shattered the state's traditional Long vs. anti-Long bifactionalism. "Media-oriented campaigning has, to a large extent, negated the need for organized politics," Parker asserted. "Television and radio allow a candidate to communicate directly with the electorate without the need for grassroot organization."

This essay will examine the dramatic evolution in Louisiana political news coverage, particularly by the state's daily newspapers, during the period between the governor's election of 1983 and that of 2019. This thirty-six-year period featured not only an evolution in campaign strategies and practices, it also heralded the Internet's rise, a phenomenon that wrought severe economic damage to the state's newspapers and resulted in less state and local political news.

LOUISIANA'S EVOLVING POLITICAL LANDSCAPE

By the late 1980s, big changes were occurring in Louisiana politics. Partisan alignments and alliances shifted. In 1983, 85.5 percent of voters were Democrats, and 90 percent of state legislators elected that year were Democrats. Every statewide elected official in January 1984 was a Democrat. By the 2019 elections, the picture was radically different. As in every other southern state, Republicans controlled the state's legislature. Republicans held every statewide office except for the governorship. By 2019, 42 percent of the state's voters were Democrats (half of what it was in 1983), while GOP registrations increased to 31 percent. Twenty-seven percent belonged to neither party.[4] During this period, the state's legislative politics also shifted. From the 1960s through the early 2000s, the partisan lines in both houses had evolved into a loosely organized anti-governor/pro-governor division. Legislators often cooperated with and supported governors of the opposite party.

Despite recognizing the changes affecting Louisiana politics beginning in the 1960s, it is unlikely most political scientists and other observers understood how Louisiana's media landscape would evolve, and why and how these changes would influence the state's politics. Some, like Joseph Parker, already recognized that television advertising would render rallies irrelevant to informing and persuading voters. But, like most observers, Parker could not have envisioned the Internet and the havoc it would wreak in the newspaper business throughout Louisiana and in every other state. He and others could not have known about the coming decline in newspaper readership and the media fragmentation that would make it difficult for voters to make informed choices. And they might not have anticipated that voters would learn as much or more about campaigns from television commercials and partisan national news sources than from local political news.

In the almost four decades from the "the last hayride" of 1983 to the 2019 governor's race between Governor John Bel Edwards and business executive Eddie Rispone, the state's politics and media environment evolved dramatically. The period 1983–2019 saw a profound drop in newspaper readership, a decline in newspaper stories about politics and campaigns, and a simultaneous reduction in the airtime television stations devoted to political news.[5]

By the early 2000s, partly to fill this vacuum of statewide political news, partisan news organizations—on the local and national levels—blossomed. While some readers found these sites welcome additions to the political news ecosystem, they contributed to the partisan fragmentation of political news. The decline of local political news and the simultaneous rise of partisan national outlets ensured that Louisiana voters would view local and state politics through an increasingly partisan lens.

THE DECLINE OF LOUISIANA NEWSPAPERS

In 1983, the state's largest newspaper, the *New Orleans Times-Picayune,* enjoyed an average daily circulation of 278,000 and Sunday circulation of 332,000. The same year, *The Advocate* of Baton Rouge reported 77,000 daily circulation. In 2019, business executive John Georges, owner of *The Advocate* of Baton Rouge, purchased the *Times-Picayune.* Now rebranded the *Times-Picayune/New Orleans Advocate,* along with its Baton Rouge sister publication, *The Advocate,* the two papers reported a combined daily circulation of about 98,000 in 2021. The market disruption and declining circulation played out across Louisiana, where other daily newspapers experienced significant declines and ownership changes. For example, the *Alexandra Daily Town Talk* reported a daily circulation of 38,500 in 1983, which plunged to less than 16,000 by 2017 (the last year for which we have reliable statistics). The *Lafayette Daily Advertiser* reported daily circulation of 31,000 in 1983; in 2017 it was 22,400. In North Louisiana, the decline in newspaper circulation was the same. The *Shreveport Times* reported daily circulation of 84,000 in 1983, but only 33,800 in 2017. (The city's afternoon paper, the *Shreveport Journal,* closed in 1991.) Many daily newspapers in the state suffered steep declines in paid circulation during this period (see table 5.1).[6]

Newspaper circulation plunged across the country. According to the Pew Research Center, total national weekday daily newspaper circulation fell from 62.6 million in 1983 to an estimated 28.5 million in 2018.[7] Declining revenues meant fewer news stories. For example, in January 1983 the *Baton Rouge Advocate*'s Sunday edition had an average of 275 pages of news and advertisements. By January 2019, the paper's average Sunday edition had 92 pages. The same occurred with other Louisiana papers. The average Sunday edition of the *Shreveport Times* in January 1983 offered readers 219 pages of news and advertisements. In January 2019, the average Sunday *Times* comprised 44 pages. In Alexandria, the *Town Talk*'s average Sunday edition in January 1983 was 147 pages; in January 2019, only 26. In Lafayette, the *Daily Advertiser*'s average Sunday edition in January 1983 was 129 pages; in January 2019, 59 (see table 5.2).[8]

Declining circulation resulted in fewer reporters and editors at most, if not all, daily papers. Nationwide, newsroom employment fell from 71,000 in 2004 to 38,000 in 2018, a 46 percent decline.[9] While statistics about Louisiana newspaper employment are not available for this same period, they were probably similar. Even the relatively healthy *Baton Rouge Advocate/New Orleans Times-Picayune/New Orleans Advocate* (for which this writer was once

TABLE 5.1. Louisiana Daily Newspaper Circulation, 1983–2017

	1983	*2000*	*2017*
Alexandria Daily Town Talk	38,551	36,951	15,983
Baton Rouge Advocate	77,181	109,230	93,148
Hammond Daily Star	9,622	12,199	9,595
Houma Daily Courier	21,152	19,753	11,044
Lafayette Daily Advertiser	31,198	44,283	22,460
Lake Charles American-Press	41,483	37,942	25,433
Monroe News-Star	40,516	36,711	22,974
New Orleans Times-Picayune	278,284	273,076	83,860
Shreveport Times	84,204	73,023	33,843

TABLE 5.2. Average Pages of Selected Louisiana Dailies, 1983 vs. 2019 (Sunday Editions)

	1983	*2019*
Alexandria Daily Town Talk	147	26
Baton Rouge Advocate	275	92
Lafayette Daily Advertiser	129	59
Shreveport Times	219	44

Source: Newspapers.com, data from January 2019.

a columnist) was not immune from the financial pressures. In March 2020, during the coronavirus pandemic, the newspaper furloughed 10 percent of its workforce, cut pay for many employees, and asked readers for charitable contributions.[10]

Among other consequences, shrinking Louisiana newsrooms meant fewer reporters covered local and state politics. Here, again, comparing 1983 to 2019 is useful to show the difference in campaign coverage in the two eras. The 1983 race between Edwin Edwards and Dave Treen attracted widespread media attention, in and out of state. In October 1983, for example, Edwards embarked on a three thousand-mile, ten-day series of campaign events in each of the state's sixty-four parishes. More than a dozen Louisiana-based journalists reported on the caravan. Several national news organizations—including ABC News, NBC News, *Time*, and the *Philadelphia Inquirer*—covered the first day's events. On that day, Edwards had so many journalists along (at least thirty, including this writer, then a *Shreveport Journal* reporter) that the campaign provided a bus to transport them. In 1983, there were at least fifteen full-time newspaper reporters from a half-dozen Louisiana newspapers covering the race. Several smaller dailies, like the *Shreveport Journal* and the *Alexandria Town Talk*, assigned two reporters to the campaign. Even the smaller *Opelousas Daily World*, circulation 14,600, had a full-time reporter covering the race. The campaign also attracted sustained coverage from at least a half-dozen Louisiana television stations.

As late as 2003, at least twelve Louisiana newspaper reporters covered that year's governor's race between Kathleen Blanco and Bobby Jindal. By contrast, the 2019 race had no more than six full-time newspaper reporters covering the candidates. There were no television reporters covering the governor's race full time in 2019. There were not only fewer reporters covering 2019 compared to 1983, there also was much less news about that race, including fewer detailed examinations of the candidates' records and policy proposals.[11] A word search of the twenty-eight daily and weekly Louisiana newspapers archived on Newspapers.com for 1983 yielded 499 stories that mentioned "governor's race" and the names of the candidates. A similar search for the 2019 governor's race (of the nineteen then-active Louisiana papers archived on the site) yielded 229 stories. An examination of other daily newspapers' coverage also suggests that Louisiana newspapers produced fewer political stories. The *Alexandria Town Talk* published eighty-four stories in 1983 about that year's governor's race; in 2019, it published thirty-seven. The *Lafayette Daily Advertiser* published sixty-two stories about the 1983 race and fifty-two stories about the 2019 contest. The *Opelousas Daily World* published forty-four stories about the 1983 governor's election and thirty-five stories in 2019.

One notable exception to the apparent statewide decline in coverage about the two races was in *The Advocate* of Baton Rouge, which, while smaller than in 1983, maintains a sizeable news staff compared to other Louisiana papers, including its sister publication, the *Times-Picayune/New Orleans Ad-*

vocate. In 1983, the *Baton Rouge Advocate* published 120 stories about the governor's race; in 2019, that rose to 160. But even *The Advocate*'s increased coverage could not make up for diminished circulation. No matter how many stories it published, there were far fewer people reading them in 2019 than thirty-six years earlier.

THE DECLINE OF LOCAL TELEVISION POLITICAL COVERAGE

Quantifying the diminished political coverage by newspapers, however, is only one part of the story of Louisiana's transformed media landscape. Television newsrooms have shrunk, to be sure, but not as much as newspapers. However, television news—which is less in-depth and more personality driven than newspapers—often echoes newspaper coverage, especially political news.

Most Americans rate local television news as the most desirable and credible source of information about their communities. According to a 2018 survey of thirty-five thousand Americans by the Pew Research Center, "The 41% of Americans who say they prefer getting their local news via TV and the 37% who prefer it online far outpace those who prefer a printed newspaper or the radio (13% and 8%, respectively)." Pew reported that despite the rapid rise in digital news delivery, "local television stations retain a strong hold in the local news ecosystem. They top the list of nine types of local news providers, with 38% of US adults saying they often get news from a local television station. That is followed by 20% who often turn to local radio stations and 17% who rely on local daily newspapers."

One problem for those interested in political coverage in Louisiana, as previously noted, is that beyond carrying live candidate debates and election night coverage, local television stations have quit covering all but the most superficial political news events. It is likely that most Louisiana voters in 2019 got as much information about the candidates running for governor from the candidates' television spots as they did from television news coverage of the race. As the 2018 Pew report stated, "There is some mismatch between the information news consumers want and the level of ease they have in finding it." While 87 percent of those surveyed said they watched local television for news about government and politics, only 30 percent of respondents found it "very easy" to stay informed about it. This suggests that television is not providing the news content viewers desire.[12]

The massive Pew survey contained sample sizes large enough to report findings on the Baton Rouge and New Orleans markets. These numbers suggest the problem of Louisiana's political coverage is worse than in many other media markets. For example, of those respondents in Baton Rouge who said news about local politics and government is important or interesting to them, only 24 percent said it was easy to stay informed about those subjects.[13] This number was better in New Orleans, where 31 percent of respondents found it easy to stay informed about local politics.[14] While Pew provided no statistics for other Louisiana markets, it is doubtful viewers elsewhere would report receiving all the political and governmental news they desire from local television stations.

DOES DECLINING POLITICAL NEWS DEPRESS VOTER TURNOUT?

During the 1983–2019 period, voter turnout in Louisiana tracked the decline in newspaper circulation and political reporting. In the 1983 governor's race, 75.6 percent of those registered voted. In every governor's election for the next thirty-six years, turnout declined or remained relatively low: 73.1 percent in 1987; 67 percent in 1995; 58.4 percent in 2003; 46.62 percent in 2007; 37.4 percent in 2011; 40.1 percent in 2015; and, 51 percent in 2019 (see figure 5.1).

In 1983, 2.13 million Louisiana residents were registered. By 2019, 2.97 million people were on the state's voter rolls, but the number of citizens voting in that election—1.5 million—was less than the 1.6 million people who voted in the 1983 governor's election. While it would be hard to prove that the steep and chronic decline in voting participation in Louisiana is the result of reduced news coverage about elections, such strong correlation indicates the need for further research on this topic.

PARTISAN, NATIONAL POLITICAL COVERAGE IS ASCENDANT

While news about campaigns and candidates has declined, information about the candidates has not. It may be that only the source of this information has

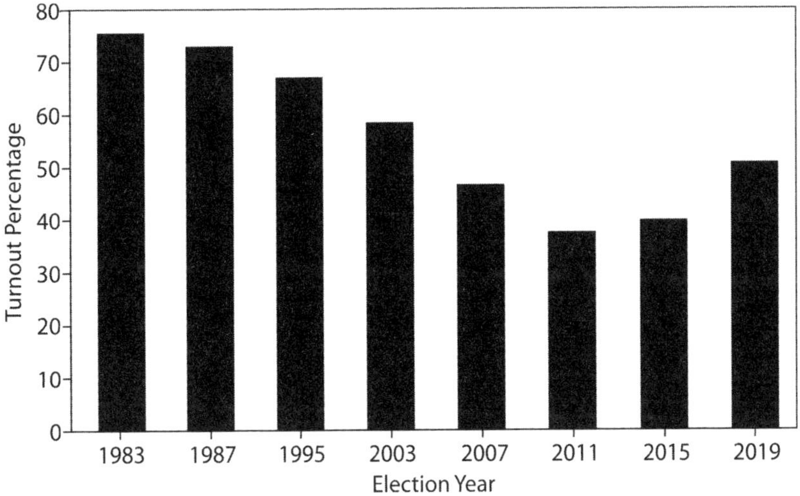

FIGURE 5.1. Turnout in Contested Louisiana Governor's Elections, 1983–2019.

changed. In the past, voters learned about the candidates from the news media, campaign advertisements, or by attending a campaign event. Today, Louisiana voters still have three major sources of information for evaluating local and state candidates: local coverage, national coverage, and campaign advertisements (on television, radio, online, and by mail). But, given the steep decline in local political coverage, candidate advertising and national news may now play an outsized role in voters' decisions. Put another way, as statewide and local political coverage fades, Louisiana voters are left to rely on partisan sources for political information.

Partisan news sourcing, however, is more pronounced among conservatives. A 2020 survey of more than twelve thousand adults conducted by the Pew Research Center revealed, "Overall, only one source, Fox News, was used by at least one-third of Republicans for political and election news in the past week. There are five different sources from which at least one-third of Democrats received political or election news in the last week (CNN, NBC News, ABC News, CBS News and MSNBC)."[15] This trend may have profound implications for voter behavior in places like Louisiana, where conservatives constitute a significant percentage of voters.[16]

Partisan affiliation, combined with declining local news influence, may be partly to blame for increased voter apathy and partisanship. In 2005, political scientist James Druckman found "strong support for the hypothesis that increased newspaper reading leads to significantly more information" than people learn from television.[17] A 2014 study examining the impact of the closure of daily newspapers in Denver and Seattle concluded, "There is a positive relationship between newspaper readership and civic engagement."[18] Studies suggest that exposure to political news can stimulate voter participation.[19] In their 2015 study of hundreds of US House races, political scientists Danny Hayes and Jennifer L. Lawless found that "citizens exposed to a lower volume of coverage are less able to evaluate their member of Congress, less likely to express opinions about House candidates in these districts, and less likely to vote." The researchers concluded, "this is true for people regardless of levels of political awareness, indicating that the deleterious consequences of a decline in local coverage are widespread, not restricted to just the least attentive citizens." Furthermore, they observed, "When local news outlets like daily newspapers devote less coverage, and less substantial coverage, to politics—whether it be about a House race, state legislative contest, or municipal election—there are few alternative sources to which citizens can turn." As Hayes and Lawless noted, most communities have no local *Politico* providing political news. "As a result," they concluded, "the quality of information to which all citizens have access—not just the least attentive—is reduced. That, in turn, lowers the prospect for political knowledge and participation for everyone."[20]

Other studies have found that local television news is a poor substitute for the lack of political coverage by local newspapers. As noted, local television stations often ignore politics, and when they do pay attention, coverage is often shallow or focuses on simplistic aspects of the race (that is, who leads the polls or sensationalistic statements by candidates).[21] A study in 2019 by three media researchers may provide the most telling conclusions about the drastic changes in Louisiana and national politics over the past four decades. The researchers focused on political polarization in the 110 communities that lost a newspaper from 2009 to 2012. The findings may have implications for Louisiana, where several newspapers have closed or downsized drastically in recent years. The loss of any newspaper resulted in "a decline in split-ticket voting across votes for the presidency and the Senate." In other words, voters became more partisan after a local newspaper closed. The researchers concluded that this is because "as newspapers close, Americans rely more heavily on available national news or partisan heuristics to make political decisions." In other words, without useful news about a local or state candidate, voters take their cues from partisan national sources.[22]

THE FUTURE OF LOUISIANA NEWS AND CAMPAIGNS

In Louisiana and elsewhere, the futures of media organizations are in doubt. In ten years, Louisiana will almost certainly have fewer newspapers than today. This could spark a cascading effect that will mean even fewer reporters. Fewer reporters will mean less in-depth political coverage. Many voters, however, will continue consuming information about politics. They will find it, and their voting cues, from other sources—and many of those will be partisan news outlets. That could harden the partisan divide at the local level, where until recently a candidate's party was not as important as other qualifications.

Despite the economic challenges of the recession, innovations in campaigning will continue. Nothing is more consistent than the ability of political professionals to adapt to societal and technological change. Just as Huey Long was among the first politicians to use radio, some Louisiana politicians will probably be at the forefront of change in the post-pandemic era.

While it is impossible to predict how profound the effects of the pandemic will be, we can envision a future in which candidates, cognizant of the need for sensible social distancing, conduct town hall meetings online. While some candidates in 2020 adapted to the new reality by broadcasting from living rooms and home offices, it might become standard practice for candidates to equip their homes with sophisticated broadcast equipment that allows for high-quality broadcasts and easier interaction with voters. Campaigns and elected officials will improve their technical capabilities to communicate more effectively. As these skills and methods become standardized, voters may see changes in political advertising, which were already becoming more personalized. As political advertising turns toward the Internet and away from television, television station revenue may suffer. Targeted spots might also make it harder for journalists to report what the candidates are saying, since these messages may not be viewed as easily as those aired previously on television.

Political journalism may rise to the occasion and improve and expand its reporting. Voters may find good journalism more valuable, even vital, to a well-functioning society. Readers and viewers may pay a fair price for this information. Local newspapers might monetize content and survive, even expand. If so, voters will enjoy a media environment less controlled by politicians. If not—that is, if the trend of the last three-plus decades continues—historians may one day consider the 2019 election not just "the last hayride" in Louisiana politics, but among the last gasps of a campaign ably covered by a healthy news media.

NOTES

1. Harnett T. Kane, *Louisiana Hayride: The American Rehearsal for Dictatorship, 1928–1940* (Gretna, La.: Pelican Publishing, 1941); John Maginnis, *The Last Hayride* (Baton Rouge, La.: Darkhorse Press, 1984), 353.

2. Terry L. Jones, *The Louisiana Journey* (Layton, Utah: Gibbs-Smith Press, 2007), 297; Glen Jeansonne, "Jimmie Davis: The Sunshine Governor," *64 Parishes*, https://64parishes.org/jimmie-davis.

3. Joseph B. Parker, "Professional Political Campaigning in Louisiana," in *Readings in Louisiana Politics*, 2nd ed., ed. Mark T. Carleton, Perry H. Howard, and Joseph B. Parker (Baton Rouge, La.: Claitor's Publishing, 1988), 555. Parker noted, however, that stumping made a brief revival in the 1983 Edwards-Treen race. See Maginnis's "*Last Hayride*." Parker observed: "The [1983] campaign disappointed no one looking for a show. It was a circus of media campaigning, fundraising, and spending."

4. "Voter Registration Reaches All Time High in Louisiana," *Caldwell Watchman*, October 19, 1983; Louisiana Secretary of State, Elections Division, https://www.sos.la.gov.

5. Jessica Mahone et al., "Who's Producing Local Journalism? Assessing Journalistic Output across Different Outlet Types," *DeWitt Wallace Center for Media and Democracy*, August 2019, https://dewitt.sanford.duke.edu/whos-producing-local-journalism-nmrp-report/.

6. *Editor & Publisher International 1983 YearBook* (New York: Editor & Publisher Co., 1983), I-133-138; *Editor and Publisher 96th Annual Newspaper DataBook, 2017* (Fountain Valley, Calif.: Duncan McIntosh Co., 2017), I-125-30.

7. "Newspaper Fact Sheet," Pew Research Center, July 9, 2019, https://www.journalism.org/fact-sheet/newspapers/.

8. This is based on a review of editions of these papers on Newspapers.com.

9. "U.S. Newsroom Employment Has Dropped by a Quarter since 2008, with Greatest Decline at Newspapers," Pew Research Center, April 20, 2020, https://www.pewresearch.org/fact-tank/2020/04/20/u-s-newsroom-employment-has-dropped-by-a-quarter-since-2008/.

10. "A Challenging Time for the *Times-Picayune,* and for Louisiana," *New Orleans Advocate,* March 23, 2020.

11. Taken from the author's analysis of newspaper coverage, using the newspaper's websites and newspaper databases, including NewsBank and Newspapers.com.

12. "For Local News, Americans Embrace Digital but Still Want Strong Community Connection," Pew Research Center, March 26 2019, https://www.journalism.org/2019/03/26/for-local-news-americans-embrace-digital-but-still-want-strong-community-connection/.

13. "What Are the Local News Dynamics in Your City?" Pew Research Center, March 29, 2019, https://www.journalism.org/interactives/local-news-habits/12940/.

14. Ibid.

15. "U.S. Media Polarization and the 2020 Election: A Nation Divided," Pew Research Center, January 24, 2020, https://www.journalism.org/2020/01/24/u-s-media-polarization-and-the-2020-election-a-nation-divided/.

16. "Conservatives Greatly Outnumber Liberals in 19 U.S. States," Gallup, February 22, 2019, https://news.gallup.com/poll/247016/conservatives-greatly-outnumber-liberals-states.aspx.

17. James N. Druckman, "Media Matters: How Newspapers and Television News Cover Campaigns and Influence Voters," *Political Communication* 22, no. 4 (2005): 474.

18. Lee Shaker, "Dead Newspapers and Citizens' Civil Engagement," *Political Communication* 31, no. 1 (2014): 139.

19. William P. Eveland Jr. and Dietram A. Scheufele, "Connecting News Media Use with Gaps in Knowledge and Participation," *Political Communication* 17, no. 3 (2000): 215–237.

20. Danny Hayes and Jennifer L. Lawless, "As Local News Goes, So Goes Citizen Engagement: Media, Knowledge, and Participation in US House Elections," *Journal of Politics* 77, no. 2 (2015): 460.

21. R. D. Arnold, *Congress, the Press, and Political Accountability* (Princeton, N.J.: Princeton Univ. Press, 2004); Joshua P. Darr, Matthew P. Hitt, and Johanna L. Dunaway, "Newspaper Closures Polarize Voting Behavior," *Journal of Communication* 68, no. 6 (2018): 1007.

22. Darr, Hitt, and Dunaway, "Newspaper Closures," 1007, 1021.

THE NEW POLITICS OF LOUISIANA'S ELECTIONS

JOSHUA STOCKLEY

The shared traumatic history of the eleven former states of the Confederacy resulted in a unique political bond, an overwhelming partisan identification with the Democratic Party that would last a century. The Democratic Party maintained authority primarily by manipulating electoral rules and stoking racial, social, and economic resentments. As V. O. Key observed, "In its grand outlines the politics of the South revolves around the position of the Negro."[1] As long as Democrats could effectively deal with the issue of race and maintain racial barriers, they were able to preserve their electoral monopoly; however, the Civil Rights Act of 1964 and the Voting Rights Act of 1965 shattered the racial mechanisms keeping the Democratic Party in power. Sensing an opportunity, the Republican Party adopted racial, social, and economic positions more amenable to southerners and, in turn, the South gave way to two-party competition. Yet, the partisan arc of the South did not stop; rather, it bent back toward one-party dominance—this time with the Republican Party in control. While the degree of Republican dominance varies by state, the story of the South writ large lies within the story of Louisiana. This essay explores the rise of the Republican Party, the demise of the Democratic Party, and whether there is a future for two-party competitiveness in Louisiana.

Scholars have traditionally divided the South into two subregions—the Deep South and the Peripheral South. The Deep South includes Louisiana, Mississippi, Alabama, Georgia, and South Carolina, while the Peripheral South includes Texas, Arkansas, Tennessee, Virginia, North Carolina, and Florida. V. O. Key wrote in 1949, "The character of the politics of individual states will vary roughly with the Negro proportion of the population."[2] He found that southern states with a higher percentage of African Americans had a different partisan environment than states with a lower percentage of African Americans. This explained why one-party Democratic rule was more firmly entrenched in the Deep South. These racial differences persist today. The proportion of African Americans in the Deep South (30 percent) remains higher than in the Peripheral South (16 percent). In Louisiana, African Americans make up 32.7 percent of the population and 31.3 percent of registered voters.[3] Seth McKee, in *The Dynamics of Southern Politics,* finds that sectional and locational differences, which are historically and culturally rooted in race, remain a significant factor shaping southern political behavior, explaining why the Republican Party today performs better in the Deep South.[4]

The story of Republican Deep South domination starts with race and realignment. Following the passage of the Voting Rights Act in 1965, African Americans joined the Democratic Party, which led the party to accommodate more liberal issue positions. White officeholders and white voters began to exit the Democratic Party, finding the Republican Party more receptive to conservative positions.[5] This racial realignment featured two groups. First, lower-class, rural whites attuned to socially conservative issues found their concerns marginalized or ignored by Democrats and co-opted by Republicans—issues like busing, school prayer, and abortion. Second, middle-class, suburban whites found their economic positions supported by a pro-business Republican Party. Republican candidates who fused social and economic conservatism were rewarded with electoral success. White conservatives and white moderates voted or registered with the Republican Party, while the Democratic Party became increasingly Black and liberal.

Today, Blacks disproportionately identify with the Democratic Party, while whites disproportionately identify with the Republican Party. Racial polarization has brought ideological polarization. A higher percentage of white voters in the Deep South identify as conservative than do those in the Peripheral South. According to Gallup, four of the ten most conservative states are the Deep South states of Alabama (1st), Mississippi (2nd), Louisiana (3rd), and South Carolina (10th). In Louisiana, 43 percent of residents identify as conservative, versus 35 percent as moderate and 15 percent as liberal.[6] Racial polarization and ideological polarization, together with the lack of in-migration and less urbanization, have contributed to the growth of the Republican Party in the Deep South. Prior to the 2020 elections, Republicans held 97 percent of all statewide offices (37/38), 66 percent of all state Senate seats (151/228), 64 percent of all state House seats (407/636), 74 percent of all US House seats (28/38), and 90 percent of all US Senate seats (9/10) in the Deep South.

Like the rest of the Deep South, Louisiana has exchanged one-party Democratic rule for one-party Republican rule. In 2020, Louisiana Republicans controlled all but one statewide office, held large majorities in both state legislative chambers, and occupied all but one federal office. Republican voter registration is increasing while Democratic voter registration is decreasing. Democratic office holding is largely confined to majority-minority or urban districts. Nevertheless, there are some critical differences. Louisiana was the last southern state to enter the Republican fold because of the state's heterogeneity stemming from a large African American population, a large Catholic population, and the nonpartisan blanket primary. In the 1990s, while Republicans made major gains throughout the South, Democrats in Louisiana still controlled the governorship, a majority of statewide offices, both houses of the state legislature, a majority of the congressional delegation, and both US Senate seats.[7] Today, the governor of Louisiana, John Bel Edwards, is the only Democrat elected to a statewide executive office in the Deep South. While his victories were fortuitous, on the one hand, as discussed below, they offer some insight into how a Democrat can still win state-wide office in Louisiana.

NONPARTISAN BLANKET PRIMARY

The most distinctive electoral feature in Louisiana is the nonpartisan blanket primary, commonly referred to as an open primary or jungle primary. In a nonpartisan blanket primary, all candidates running for an office, regardless of political party, are placed on a single ballot. If a candidate obtains a simple majority in the primary, then they are elected outright. Otherwise, the top two vote-getters compete in a general election a month later. The absence of partisan restrictions allows two candidates of the same party or opposite parties to compete in the general election. For federal elections, Louisiana's primary election occurs in November on the same day as the general election for the rest of the nation, and the general election occurs in December. For state elections, the primary election occurs in October, and for any races where no candidate obtained a majority in the primary, a general election occurs in November between the top two candidates.

The concept of a nonpartisan primary was initially proposed by former governor Edwin Edwards in 1975, who envisioned it as a mechanism to impede growing popularity for the Republican Party. As the minority, the Republican Party benefited from being homogenous and unified; decades of one-party dominance left Democrats faction-ridden and organizationally weak. Traditionally, victories in competitive Democratic primaries were tantamount to election victories, but this assurance was receding with the increasing perception of competitiveness and Edwards's own election in 1972. A less competitive closed primary allowed the Republican Party organization to handpick a lone nominee and reserve its resources for the general election, where they could appeal to disaffected Democratic supporters. Edwards was hoping the nonpartisan blanket primary would force Republicans to expend their resources on intra-party struggles. With Democrats holding a substantial advantage in party registration at the time, the nonpartisan blanket primary could produce a Democrat versus Democrat general election or a Democrat versus Republican general election, albeit with a damaged Republican.

However, Edwards's scheme went awry as the Republican Party of Louisiana accommodated themselves to this reform, enacting party rules authorizing pre-primary endorsements and exercised heavy-handed discipline discouraging competing candidacies. Democrats were slow to respond. Meanwhile, the diminution of party symbols in the nonpartisan primary worked to the advantage of Republican candidates. It encouraged a conservative though nominally Democratic electorate to consider moderate or conservative candidates without regard to party affiliation, enabling Republican candidates to appeal to a conservative electorate.[8] The effectiveness of the nonpartisan primary in assisting Republicans can be seen in 1995 (Mike Foster) and 2004 (David Vitter). In each contest, a lone Republican emerged victorious over a crowded Democratic field because the Democrats reserved their ferocity for fellow Democrats while Republicans remained above the fray. Democrats split the votes of other Democrats and of Democratic-leaning independents, allowing Republicans to siphon the support of white Democrats. While the nonpartisan blanket primary aided the growth of the Republican Party, it has also worked for Democrats. For example, John Bel Edwards benefitted from competing and divisive Republican candidacies to win an upset election in 2015 and reelection in 2019. Today, the nonpartisan blanket primary is a mechanism that keeps Democrats competitive in Louisiana.

PARTISANSHIP AND ELECTIONS

The nonpartisan primary helps explain why party registration lags electoral behavior. All voters receive the same ballot regardless of partisan affiliation, so there is no incentive for voters to align party registration with actual voting behavior. For example, in 1995, Democrats comprised 68.4 percent of the state's population, while Republicans were only 20.0 percent.[9] Despite a three-to-one registration advantage, this was the year that Louisiana's Republican advance began in earnest, as Mike Foster became only the second Republican governor since Reconstruction. Foster defeated US Representative Cleo Fields (D-4th District) in a highly divisive and racially charged election. Democrat state treasurer and rival gubernatorial candidate Mary Landrieu was accused of arguing that Fields could not win because an African American could not win statewide in Louisiana—that African Americans would be wasting their vote in voting for Fields. To date, since Reconstruction, Louisiana has yet to elect an African American statewide. Fields blistered Landrieu for the allegation and, in the process, mobilized a higher than average number of Black voters to turnout. Fields finished second, ahead of Landrieu. In response, Landrieu refused to support Fields and endorsed Foster. Foster won in a lopsided contest—64 percent to 36 percent. It was an embarrassing loss for a Democrat. It was also a warning to Democrats that racial divides in the party jeopardized electoral success; they needed a biracial voting coalition to win. Nevertheless, Louisiana's white voters are not a monolithic voting bloc.

South Louisiana is predominantly Catholic, the product of French and Acadian heritage. North Louisiana is predominantly Protestant, home to Duck Dynasty and culturally like Mississippi or Arkansas. The two regions are similar on the issue of fiscal conservatism and abortion but have split over issues such as gambling, alcohol, and prayer in schools. Endorsements by evangelical groups, such as the Christian Coalition, Family Research Council, and Louisiana Family Forum, resonate powerfully in the north but have at times alienated more tolerant and less socially conservative Catholics in southern Louisiana. Therefore, moderate-to-conservative Catholic Democrats—like Mary Landrieu, and later Kathleen Blanco and John Bel Edwards—were attractive because of their ability to appeal to both Blacks and southern whites. Socially conservative Republicans, like Woody Jenkins and Tony Perkins, were often too conservative for southern Catholics.

The story of Republican advancement in Louisiana includes party switching. In 1995, two Democrats in the US House of Representatives—Billy Tauzin (3rd District) and Jimmy Hayes (7th District)—defected to the Republican Party, creating a 4–3 Republican congressional advantage and the first post-Reconstruction Republican congressional delegation (see table 6.1). Tauzin and Hayes were actively recruited by House Speaker Newt Gingrich, who promised chairmanships and coveted committee assignments in the Republican-controlled US House of Representatives. Partisan switches signaled that officeholders and candidates found the Republican Party a better option for future electoral success. Other notable party switchers included Secretary of State Fox McKeithen (1989), State Senator Mike Foster (1995), US Representative Rodney Alexander (2005), State Treasurer John Kennedy (2007), Lieutenant Governor Scott Angelle (2010), and Attorney General Buddy Caldwell (2011).[10]

The election of Foster and the defections of Tauzin and Hayes were offset by the Democrats' ability to maintain control of a majority of statewide offices, both houses of the state legislature, and both US Senate seats. Louisiana was also one of only three southern states carried by Bill Clinton in both 1992 and 1996, and Democrats won US Senate races in 1996, 1998, and 2002. In 2003, behind Kathleen Blanco, Democrats regained the governor's mansion, won all but one statewide office, and held a decisive 67–37 majority in the state House and a 24–15 majority in the state Senate.

Yet, cracks were emerging in the Democratic foundation. In 1996, US Senator J. Bennett Johnston (D) announced his retirement. Democrats restored party and racial unity, with Fields endorsing Landrieu for the Senate after intervention from fellow southerners President Clinton and Vice President Gore. Landrieu finished second to Republican Woody Jenkins in the primary. The problem with Jenkins for southern Catholics was that he was perceived to be too conservative. Specifically, white Catholics bristled at many of Jenkins's socially conservative positions, including his advocacy of school prayer (there had been a history of Catholic and French cultural suppression in Louisiana public schools). Landrieu won by less than six thousand votes out of 1.6 million cast. Her numbers were buttressed by a one-hundred-thousand-vote margin in Orleans Parish and an above average performance among white Catholics in southern parishes. Landrieu's narrow victory demonstrated that Democratic success required a biracial coalition comprised of Blacks, white moderates, and white Catholics. Jenkins's defeat taught Republicans that electoral success could only come by unifying northern white Protestants and southern white Catholics.

When George W. Bush carried Louisiana with 53 percent of the vote in 2000, Republicans made Landrieu a national political target in 2002. Landrieu won reelection with a little luck. The presumed Republican frontrunner, US Representative John Cooksey, was caught saying after 9/11, "If I see someone's coming in and he's got a diaper on his head and a fan belt around that diaper on his head, that guy needs to be pulled over and checked." Cooksey refused to drop out despite national criticism. Suzanne Haik Terrell was recruited to run at the last minute. She was a natural alternative because she had recently defeated Jenkins in a statewide race for commissioner of elections (the first female Republican to win a statewide race in Louisiana). It was too little, too late. Senator Landrieu won by forty-two thousand votes, relying on a lopsided performance in Orleans Parish and another strong showing among Catholics in southern Louisiana.

Landrieu's win defied voter registration trends. Democratic voter registration was steadily decreasing (see table 6.2). In 1995, 68.4 percent of the state's population was Democrat; however, a mere five years later, the percentage of registered Democrats dropped to 61.1 percent. In 2011, Democrats lost their majority for the first time since Reconstruction, becoming 49.8 percent of registered voters. In 2020, Democrats comprise only 42.0 percent of the state's registered voters. The Democratic Party was also losing white voters. In 2000,

TABLE 6.1. Partisan Makeup of Louisiana's Legislative Chambers and Statewide Offices

	State House		*State Senate*		*Statewide*		*US Congress*		*US Senate*	
	D	R	D	R	D	R	D	R	D	R
1962	101	2	39	0	7	0	8	0	2	0
1964	103	2	39	0	7	0	8	0	2	0
1966	103	2	39	0	7	0	8	0	2	0
1968	105	0	39	0	7	0	8	0	2	0
1970	104	1	38	1	7	0	8	0	2	0
1972	101	4	38	1	7	0	7	1	2	0
1974	101	4	38	1	7	0	6	2	2	0
1976	101	4	38	1	7	0	6	2	2	0
1978	96	9	38	1	7	0	5	3	2	0
1980	95	10	39	0	6	1	6	2	2	0
1982	93	11	38	1	6	1	6	2	2	0
1984	91	14	38	1	7	0	6	2	2	0
1986	87	15	34	5	7	0	5	3	2	0
1988	86	17	34	5	6	1	5	3	2	0
1990	89	16	34	5	5	2	4	4	2	0
1992	88	16	34	5	6	1	4	3	2	0
1994	89	16	33	6	6	1	4	3	2	0
1996	77	27	25	14	5	2	**2**	**5**	2	0
1998	77	27	25	14	5	2	2	5	2	0
2000	70	33	26	13	5	2	2	5	2	0
2002	71	34	26	13	5	2	2	5	2	0
2004	69	36	26	13	6	1	3	4	1	1
2006	64	41	24	15	5	2	1	6	1	1
2008	55	50	24	15	**2**	**5**	2	5	1	1
2010	52	50	23	16	1	6	1	6	1	1
2012	**45**	**58**	**14**	**24**	0	7	1	5	1	1
2014	44	59	13	26	0	7	1	5	**0**	**2**
2016	42	61	14	25	1	6	1	5	0	2
2018	41	61	14	25	1	6	1	5	0	2
2020	35	68	13	26	1	6	1	5	0	2

*Numbers in bold indicate the switch to a Republican majority.

Source: Wayne Parent and Huey Perry, "Louisiana: African Americans, Republicans, and Party Competition," in *The New Politics of the Old South,* 4th ed., ed. Charles S. Bullock III and Mark J. Rozell (Lanham: Rowman & Littlefield, 2010), 115.

Note: Updated data through 2020 from Louisiana Secretary of State, https://www.sos.la.gov/ElectionsAndVoting/Pages/default.aspx.

Blacks comprised 39.9 percent of all registered Democrats; however, in 2013, they became the majority of registered Democrats (51.4 percent). In 2020, Blacks made up 57.4 percent of all registered Democrats. In contrast, 93.9 percent of registered Republicans were white. There has been a racial realignment in Louisiana. Making matters worse for Democrats, a critical electoral base had shrunk. Orleans Parish, for decades an electoral bedrock for Democrats, was decimated by Hurricane Katrina in 2005. Today, the parish contains only 391,000 people, down from 485,000 pre-Katrina, forcing Democrats to make up votes in other areas of the state.

In 2004, Republicans broke the Democratic monopoly on the US Senate when US Senator John Breaux (D) announced his retirement and US Representative David Vitter (R-1st District) was elected Louisiana's first Republican senator since Reconstruction. Vitter ran against three Democrats—Black State Representative Arthur Morrell, State Treasurer John Kennedy, and US Representative Chris Johns (7th District). The Democratic candidates attacked each other mercilessly under the pretense that the leading vote-getter among them would face Vitter in the general election and win—as Landrieu had done in 1996 and 2002. Vitter stunned everyone by winning outright. Representative Alexander's defection (5th District) increased the Republican's congressional majority from a 4–3 to a 5–2 margin. Exit polls revealed that 41 percent of the state's voters, a plurality, identified as Republicans, voter registration notwithstanding. In 2006, Republicans held their 5–2 congressional advantage even though the party lost thirty-three seats nationwide.

In 2007, US Representative Bobby Jindal (R-1st District) became the first nonincumbent candidate for governor to be elected outright during the primary. Jindal had narrowly lost four years earlier to Blanco, who had announced her retirement after taking a political beating for her response to Hurricane Katrina. Jindal, a self-described "evangelical Catholic," united southern Catholics and northern Protestants like Vitter in 2004. Riding Jindal's coattails, Republicans won five out of seven statewide contests, giving them the majority of statewide offices in Louisiana for the first time since Reconstruction. Thanks to term limits and party defections, Republicans narrowed a 67–37 Democratic advantage in the state House to a razor-thin 51–49 margin, though the state Senate remain unchanged. The solitary bright spot

TABLE 6.2. Registered Democratic Voters in Louisiana, 2000–2020

	Total Voters	*Total Democrats*	*Percentage*	*Black Democrats*	*Percentage*
2000	2,725,473	1,665,901	61.1%	665,144	39.9%
2001	2,763,121	1,626,084	58.8%	655,601	40.3%
2002	2,719,540	1,617,581	59.5%	663,344	41.0%
2003	2,786,940	1,580,178	56.7%	665,188	42.1%
2004	2,924,895	1,565,865	53.5%	677,815	43.3%
2005	2,842,443	1,553,095	54.6%	678,790	43.7%
2006	2,893,674	1,553,009	53.7%	678,789	43.7%
2007	2,831,831	1,512,630	53.4%	667,370	44.1%
2008	2,940,985	1,498,015	50.9%	670,481	44.8%
2009	2,912,682	1,523,428	52.3%	721,186	47.3%
2010	2,939,372	1,506,736	51.3%	720,850	47.8%
2011	2,854,515	1,420,585	49.8%	686,754	48.3%
2012	2,969,729	1,407,885	47.4%	693,745	49.3%
2013	2,915,672	1,405,131	48.2%	722,027	51.4%
2014	2,917,833	1,383,437	47.4%	719,021	52.0%
2015	2,879,068	1,342,640	46.6%	709,706	52.9%
2016	2,910,086	1,331,636	45.8%	711,711	53.4%
2017	2,976,695	1,321,549	44.4%	725,331	54.9%
2018	2,976,945	1,303,300	43.8%	723,533	55.5%
2019	3,001,240	1,287,153	42.9%	726,513	56.4%
2020	2,991,206	1,256,701	42.0%	720,917	57.4%

Source: Wayne Parent and Huey Perry, "Louisiana: African Americans, Republicans, and Party Competition," in *The New Politics of the Old South*, 4th ed., ed. Charles S. Bullock III and Mark J. Rozell (Lanham: Rowman & Littlefield, 2010), 127.

Note: Updated data through 2020 from Louisiana Secretary of State, https://www.sos.la.gov/ElectionsAndVoting/Pages/default.aspx.

for Democrats occurred in 2008 when Senator Landrieu retained her seat by defeating Democrat-turned-Republican state treasurer John Kennedy by a 52 percent to 48 percent margin.

A new decade confirmed Louisiana's status as a solid, one-party Republican state. In 2010, Senator Vitter easily won reelection by a 57 percent to 38 percent margin over US Representative Charlie Melancon (D-3rd District). Republicans increased their congressional majority to a 6–1 margin, leaving only a Black Democrat, US Representative Cedric Richmond, in the state's majority-minority 2nd Congressional District. In 2010, two state representatives switched parties to create the first post-Reconstruction Republican majority in the Louisiana House of Representatives. In February of 2011, Republicans won a special election to obtain their first post-Reconstruction majority in the Louisiana Senate. In 2011, Democrats failed to elect a single major candidate to any statewide office as Republicans swept all seven statewide offices for the first time in state history. Republicans increased their margins in the state House (58–45) and the state Senate (24–15). The final blow for Democrats came in 2014 when US Representative Bill Cassidy (R-6th District) defeated Senator Mary Landrieu, a three-term incumbent. Cassidy hit Landrieu on two issues—her vote for the Affordable Care Act and her voting record during the Obama presidency. In this election, Landrieu carried only 18 percent of the white vote, down from 33 percent in 2008, and became the first sitting Louisiana senator to lose reelection since 1932. For the first time since Reconstruction, the state of Louisiana lacked a single statewide elected Democrat. Landrieu's loss signaled the completion of the Republican takeover of Louisiana.

THE NEW POLITICS OF LOUISIANA

With Landrieu's defeat, Republicans had every reason to be optimistic heading into the 2015 gubernatorial election. The Republican field featured a political heavyweight—incumbent US senator Vitter—and two other formidable Republicans—Lieutenant Governor Jay Dardenne and Public Service Commissioner Scott Angelle, while the Democrats countered with State Representative John Bel Edwards (no relation to former governor Edwin Edwards), a relatively unknown two-term representative from the small town of Amite. Edwards was a pro-life, pro-gun, Army Ranger veteran. Except for the issue of Medicaid expansion, little appeared to separate Edwards from Vitter and, in fact, Republicans.

Vitter was polarizing and uncompromisingly conservative. He had attacked the Republican Party establishment loyal to former governor Dave Treen, grown openly critical of Governor Jindal, financed Republican challengers to run against Republican incumbents, and held a reputation of being difficult to work with—even among Republicans. Having alienated Republicans, Vitter felt his best chance of winning was to concentrate his vitriol on Dardenne and Angelle to ensure a general election matchup against the Democrat, Edwards. Given Landrieu's catastrophic defeat, chaos within Democratic Party ranks, Edwards's poor name recognition, and paltry fundraising, a Republican-Republican runoff was possible. This did not happen, though, as Vitter's negative campaign was hugely successful in suppressing support for Dardenne and Angelle. Vitter finished second in the primary and moved into a general election against Edwards.

Vitter's strategy was undone as his attacks on Republicans created a backlash; his competitors refused to endorse him in the general election. Republican and Democratic opponents hammered at the scandal surrounding Vitter, which involved him soliciting prostitutes while working as a US Senator. Vitter was not well-liked—with a 38 percent favorable versus 41 percent unfavorable rating. Edwards held only an 11 percent unfavorable rating. Edwards's conservatism, combined with Vitter's unfavorable rating, negative campaign tactics, and well-publicized prostitution scandal, allowed Edwards to defeat Vitter by a 56 percent to 44 percent margin, the exact opposite result of the Cassidy-Landrieu election eleven months prior. Vitter's 44 percent was the worst showing for a Republican candidate in a competitive race since 1991, when Edwin Edwards defeated David Duke 61 percent to 39 percent.

Edwards's coalition included white voters, Black voters, and Republican voters. Approximately eighty thousand Republican voters crossed over to support Edwards (he received the same number of votes as the winning Republicans for lieutenant governor and attorney general). He also received an estimated 35 percent of the white vote. Edwards also benefitted from an election in an odd-numbered year, which insulated his campaign from national partisan trends.

Edwards's victory was historic and significant. A white southern Democrat won in the Deep South. Louisiana still is more likely to elect conservative Republican candidates than Democrats, but if a Democratic candidate checks the correct conservative boxes, then he or she can still win, albeit with a little help. The help in 2015 came in the form of the blanket primary, an off-year election, and a flawed Republican candidate.

The 2015 gubernatorial election appeared to be a deviant event. Down ticket, Republicans won every other statewide office and retained decisive majorities in the state House and state Senate. Republicans retained their 5–1 congressional majority in 2016, while Trump carried Louisiana by a 58 percent to 38 percent margin.

In 2019, Edwards was opposed by political novice and businessman Eddie Rispone, who narrowly bested US Representative Ralph Abraham (R-5th District) in the primary by running negative advertisements against him. Rispone attempted to nationalize the election by emphasizing his alignment with Trump and having the president visit Monroe and Shreveport to rally northern conservatives and former Abraham supporters. Ultimately, Edwards defeated Rispone by a narrow 51 percent–49 percent margin; only forty thousand votes separated them out of 1.5 million cast. Edwards's victory was partly a product of an impressive voter turnout operation: first, he increased turnout in Orleans parish to create a one hundred thousand-vote difference over Rispone; and second, he increased his voter turnout in the 4th and 5th Congressional Districts by approximately twenty-five thousand and fifty thousand votes, respectively. In these two districts, sixty thousand Republican voters crossed over to vote for Edwards. Unfortunately for Louisiana Democrats, the reelection of Governor Edwards had more to do with Edwards than with the party. Republicans won the other six statewide races and increased their share of seats in the House (68–35) and Senate (27–12) to their largest margins since Reconstruction.

CONCLUSION

Democrats once dominated the southern landscape. However, the rise of the nation's first Black president accelerated an ongoing migration of southern whites from the Democratic to the Republican Party. Today, Democratic registration in Louisiana is declining while Republican registration is increasing. Demographic trends favoring Democratic growth elsewhere in the South—Hispanic population growth, in-migration, and urbanization—are not present in Louisiana. The election of Governor John Bel Edwards in 2015 provided one electoral blueprint for how Democrats might win in Louisiana, but relying on splits in the Republican Party and flawed candidates is not a solid long-term electoral strategy. Unfortunately for Democrats, there do not appear to be many, if any, politicians with Edwards's conservative resume seeking office in Louisiana. The election results of 2020 bear this out, as Democrats fielded a weak slate of candidates and Republicans strengthened their hold on the Pelican State. Trump carried Louisiana by a 58–40 margin; however, US Senator Bill Cassidy won reelection by a more impressive 59–19 margin over token opposition. Likewise, Democrats were not competitive in any congressional district outside Louisiana's majority-minority 2nd Congressional District. The Democratic Party must find a way to attract white voters in the absence of demographic changes propelling party competitiveness in other states. Until then, Louisiana will remain a Republican stronghold.

NOTES

1. V. O. Key, *Southern Politics in State and Nation* (1949; reprint, Knoxville: Univ. of Tennessee Press, 2014), 5.

2. Ibid., 5.

3. Registration data results obtained from the Louisiana Secretary of State, https://www.sos.la.gov; census data from the US Census Bureau.

4. Seth McKee, *The Dynamics of Southern Politics: Causes and Consequences* (Thousand Oaks, Calif.: CQ Press, 2019).

5. M. V. Hood III, Quentin Kidd, and Irwin L. Morris, *The Rational Southerner: Black Mobilization, Republican Growth, and the Partisan Transformation of the American South* (Oxford: Oxford Univ. Press 2014).

6. Jeffrey M. Jones, "Conservatives Greatly Outnumber Liberals in 19 U.S. States," Gallup.com, February 22, 2019, https://news.gallup.com/poll/247016/conservatives-greatly-outnumber-liberals-states.aspx.

7. Wayne Parent and Huey Perry, "Louisiana: African Americans, Republicans, and Party Competition," in *The New Politics of the Old South*, 3rd ed., ed. Charles S. Bullock III and Mark J. Rozell (Lanham, Md.: Rowman and Littlefield, 2007).

8. Harold F. Bass, Albert C. Ringelstein, Henry B. Sirgo, and Joshua Stockley, "Melancon Defeats Romero in a Louisiana House Race," in *The Roads to Congress, 2006*, ed. Sunil Ahuja and Robert Dewhirst (New York: Nova Science Publishers, 2007).

9. Registration data and election results obtained from the Louisiana Secretary of State, https://www.sos.la.gov/ElectionsAndVoting.

10. For a list of Louisiana's elected representatives who have switched parties, see table I.3.

PUBLIC OPINION IN LOUISIANA

More Change, More of the Same

MICHAEL HENDERSON

Pundits and other political observers often paint contemporary politics in America—and Louisiana—as an intensely bitter conflict between deeply polarized parties. A key feature of this commentary is a vast ideological gulf between liberal Democrats and conservative Republicans fervently opposed to each other with little middle ground between them. Yet, while *polarization* has become a frequent topic of political commentary, it remains one of the most misunderstood features of contemporary American politics. The confusion arises from the conflation of two concepts. The first is *ideological disagreement,* that is, the extent to which partisans cluster at opposite ends of the ideological spectrum or hold contradictory positions on political issues. The second is *hyperpartisanship,* that is, the intensity with which people identify with their side and dislike or distrust the other side. Failure to distinguish between these two concepts misconstrues the nature of partisan divisions in public opinion—whether looking at the United States as a whole or Louisiana specifically.

A political ideology is a general worldview about political issues. In the United States, it is often thought of as how liberal or conservative a person is. Today, elected officials in the federal and state governments are more ideologically divided than at any point since, perhaps, the Civil War. In state legislatures, Republicans are more conservative and Democrats are more liberal than just two decades ago, leaving the parties further apart and with less room for agreement.[1] The ideological gap between Democrats and Republicans in the Louisiana legislature, for example, approximately doubled from

1996 to 2017, as moderate and conservative Democrats either switched parties or were replaced by Republicans.[2] This growing divide in state legislatures dampens the potential for compromise and sparks increasingly bitter policy fights.[3] Since Louisiana's elections of 2015 yielded a Democratic governor and a majority Republican legislature, political observers in the state—and even the politicians themselves—routinely decry "Washington-style politics," by which they mean the gamesmanship and gridlock between the branches of state government.[4]

In other words, the history of the Louisiana legislature in recent decades is one of both growing ideological disagreement and rising hyperpartisanship. But what about Louisiana voters? This essay examines whether Democratic and Republican voters in Louisiana are growing more ideological polarized and whether they are becoming more partisan in their approach to political questions. Though it is true that ideological differences and disagreements over certain issues are somewhat larger among Americans today than they were three decades ago, that expansion has been modest.[5] Significant overlap remains between rank-and-file Democrats and Republicans on ideology and issues—much more so than among their elected representatives.[6] At the same time, however, partisanship—and its effects on political choices—has increased far more significantly among the population.[7]

The trends in Louisiana are illustrative. Democrats and Republicans in Louisiana are modestly more divided over ideology and issues than they were even a decade ago. Nevertheless, Louisianans remain less divided over ideology and issues than Americans as a whole, and considerable overlap remains between the two groups. If political divisions centered on ideological disagreement, then party competition would be less fervent in Louisiana than elsewhere in the country. That is decidedly not the case. Louisianans are just as divided by partisanship as their fellow Americans—whether measured as commitment to their partisan groups, their (un)willingness to seek compromise, or the consistency of their support for their party's candidates across a variety of elected offices. Thus, there is fervent partisan dislike without (much) ideological disagreement.

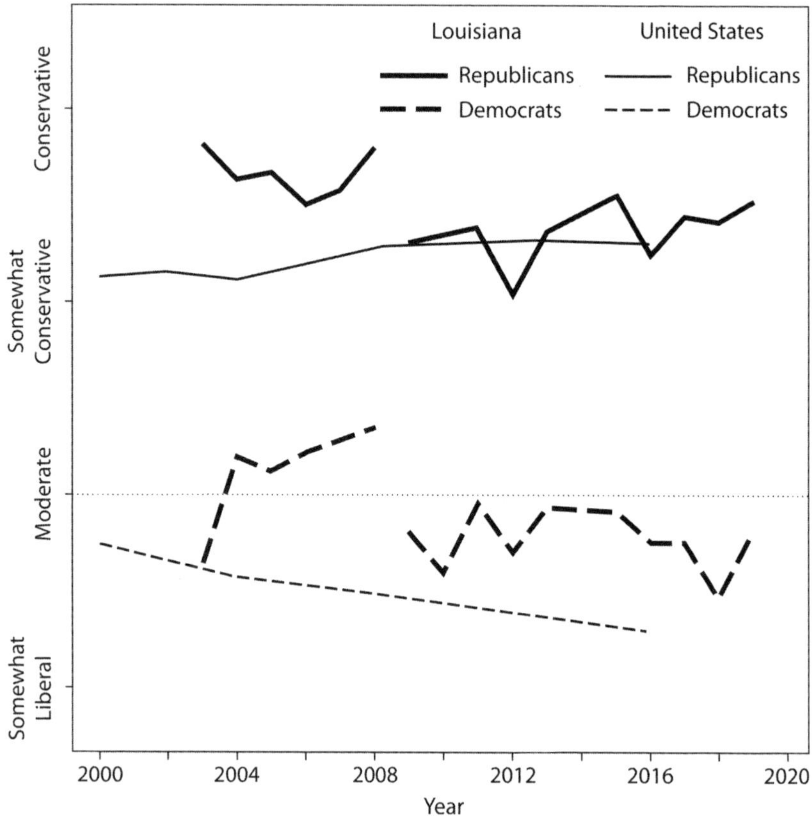

FIGURE 7.1. Trends in Ideology by Partisanship in Louisiana and the United States, 2000–2019. Lines show average responses to ideology question by party identification. Louisiana data are from the annual *Louisiana Survey*, a project of Louisiana State University's Reilly Center for Media and Public Affairs, with the exceptions of the 2014 and 2015 surveys that did not include ideology questions. State ideology responses for 2015 are taken from another Reilly Center survey administered that year. No state ideology data are available for 2014. National data are from the *American National Election Study* (ANES), which is administered every four years during presidential elections. Averages are based on a seven-point response scale for the ANES and the *Louisiana Survey* (2009–2019). Prior to 2009 the *Louisiana Survey* used a three-point response scale.

THE IDEOLOGICAL GAP BETWEEN DEMOCRATS AND REPUBLICANS IS GROWING . . .

Figure 7.1 displays the trends in the ideological tilt of Republicans and Democrats in Louisiana over nearly the past two decades. The data are from the annual *Louisiana Survey,* which regularly asks adult residents of the state what party they identify with and how they think about themselves ideologically. The solid lines show the average response to the ideology questions for Democrats and Republicans since 2003, when the survey began. Positive values indicate a group leans more conservative, while negative values indicate a more liberal lean. Until 2008, the survey asked respondents if they thought of themselves as liberal, moderate, or conservative. Since 2009, the survey has used a more nuanced response scale allowing for "very liberal," "liberal," "somewhat liberal," "moderate," "somewhat conservative," "conservative," and "very conservative." This change in wording makes it problematic to compare responses across these two periods. Differences between 2008 and 2009 may be due to actual changes in political context, such as the election of Barack Obama to the presidency, but they may just as well stem from the difference in wording. However, it remains possible to examine the trends within each period.

Partisans do indeed think of themselves differently in ideological terms. On average, Louisiana Republicans place themselves near the "somewhat conservative" response, while Louisiana Democrats fall somewhere between "moderate" and "somewhat liberal." The gap between them has widened slightly in recent decades. Democrats remain at about the same point in 2019 as they were in 2009. Republicans are just a bit more conservative on average than ten years before.

The same pattern appears when looking at how Democrats and Republicans think about specific issues. Figure 7.2 shows the party trends in attitudes toward a perennial topic in Louisiana's politics—taxes. For seventeen years, the *Louisiana Survey* has asked Louisiana residents whether they favor cutting state income taxes, raising them, or keeping them the same. The figure shows average responses for each party, with positive values indicating more support for cutting taxes and negative values indicating more support for raising taxes. There is clear evidence that the gap between parties widened since about 2012.

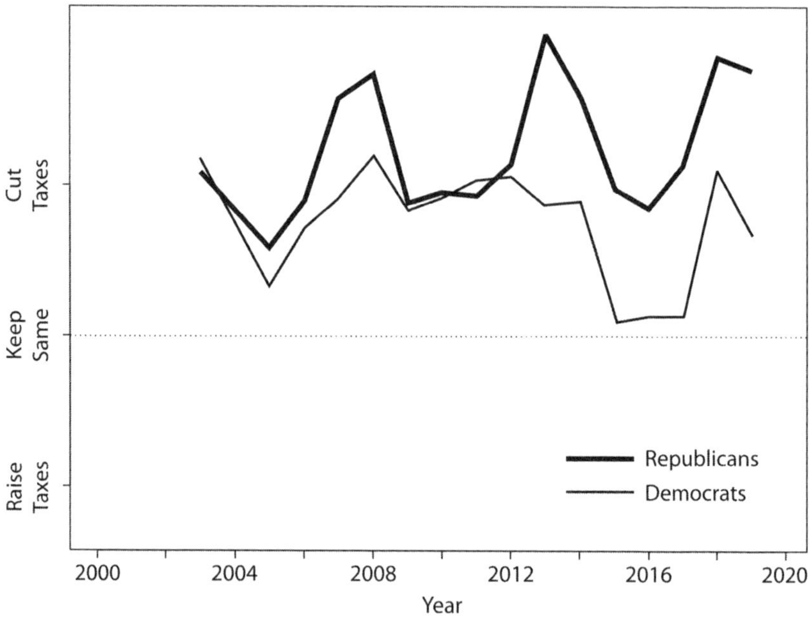

FIGURE 7.2. Trends in Attitudes toward State Income Tax Policy in Louisiana, 2003–2019. Lines show average responses to the tax question by party identification from the annual *Louisiana Survey.* Averages are based on a three-point response scale (cut taxes, keep the same, or raise taxes).

. . . BUT SIGNIFICANT OVERLAP REMAINS

Does growing disagreement mean that Louisianans are ideologically polarized? The most obvious definition of polarization is one in which Democrats and Republicans cluster at opposite poles of the ideological spectrum.[8] This is not the case in Louisiana. The left panel of figure 7.3 shows the overall distribution of ideology among the adult population of the state in 2019. Only about one in eight Louisianans are on the extremes, either very liberal or very conservative. Most state residents (60 percent) cluster in the center—that is, they are moderate, somewhat liberal, somewhat conservative, or unable to identify with an ideology at all.

The next two panels display the distributions for each major party. Generally, Republicans do cluster to the right. Most (78 percent) place themselves on the conservative side of the scale, and only 5 percent think of themselves as liberal. Yet, nearly one-fifth of Republicans describe themselves as moderate. Democrats are less concentrated on one side. Only 41 percent describe themselves as liberal. Nearly a third describe themselves as some shade of conservative and a similar amount describe themselves as moderate.

The sizable share of conservatives among Democrats, as well as the moderates within both parties, yields a significant amount of overlap between the parties in Louisiana. Furthermore, most partisans avoid the extremes. Just 10 percent of Louisiana Democrats describe themselves as "very liberal." The share of Republicans at the farthest right end of the response scale is more than twice as high (24 percent) but remains only a minority of the party. This is hardly a vast ideological gulf separating Democratic and Republican voters.

The same pattern holds for political issues. For example, Republicans are more favorable to state income tax cuts than Democrats are, but pluralities in both parties favor cuts over the status quo or tax hikes (47 percent among Re-

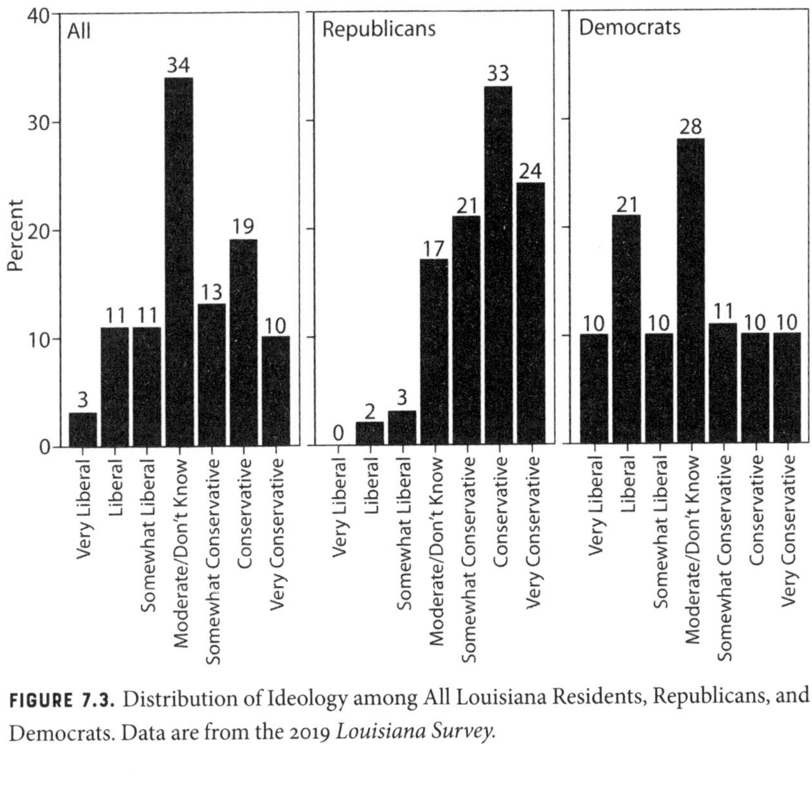

FIGURE 7.3. Distribution of Ideology among All Louisiana Residents, Republicans, and Democrats. Data are from the 2019 *Louisiana Survey.*

publicans and 38 percent among Democrats). In fact, an examination of forty policy issues polled in the past five years shows more consensus than polarization across a range of social, economic, and other issues. Table 7.1 shows the distribution of responses for Democrats and Republicans to these questions. While there is nearly always some difference between the parties, these gaps rarely put the majority of Democrats and the majority of Republicans on opposing sides. For example, more Democrats (79 percent) than Republicans (60 percent) favor criminal justice reform, but majorities of both nevertheless favor these reforms. In all, majorities of both Democrats and Republicans are *on the same side* for half of these issues (twenty out of forty), ranging from cutting state sales taxes to protecting members of the LGBT community from workplace discrimination.

There is clear evidence for disagreement between the majority of Democrats and the majority of Republicans for less than a third of these issues (twelve of forty). These disagreements include a mix of economic issues (for example: regulations on business, a $15 minimum wage, raising taxes on corporations and the wealthy), social issues (for example: abortion, concealed carry rights, and requiring individuals to use public restrooms designated for their gender at birth), and other issues (for example: expanding policies for racial equality, school vouchers).

It is possible to identify this sort of disagreement for four additional issues related to government spending by designating those who favor maintaining current spending levels as opposed to increases or cuts. Viewed in this way, a majority of Democrats favor increased spending for K–12 education, higher education, and health care while a majority of Republicans oppose these increases (although they do not favor spending cuts to these areas). Likewise, a majority of Republicans favor cuts to welfare spending while a majority of Democrats oppose these cuts (although they do not necessarily support increased spending for welfare). Even with this more lenient approach to classifying disagreements, Democrats and Republicans stand on opposite sides on fewer than half (sixteen) of these forty policy issues.

Finally, looking back at figure 7.1, the gap between the parties is noticeably smaller in Louisiana than in the United States as a whole. The graph shows the polarization trend for the nation. The mix of ideology within the

LE 7.1. Issue Positions of Democrats and Republicans in Louisiana

	Democrats			Republicans		
	Increase	*Decrease*	*Keep same*	*Increase*	*Decrease*	*Keep same*
ome tax (2019)	22	38	36	4	47	46
es tax (2019)	5	53	41	3	50	45
12 ed spending (2018)	73	1	26	47	4	47
gher ed spending (2018)	75	5	19	47	14	38
althcare spending (2018)	65	5	29	30	21	43
rastructure spending (2018)	63	6	29	60	5	33
son spending (2018)	13	47	37	8	42	45
lfare spending (2018)	34	15	47	3	64	29
	Approve	*Disapprove*		*Approve*	*Disapprove*	
iminal justice reform (2019)	79	16		60	28	
dicaid expansion (2019)	99	0		53	39	
	Support	*Oppose*		*Support*	*Oppose*	
ise gas tax 5 cents/gal. (2019)	83	17		52	46	
ise teacher pay (2019)	93	7		80	18	
ise min. wage to $8.50 (2019)	94	6		72	28	
ise min. wage to $15.00 (2019)	85	15		44	56	
pand alternative to prison (2019)	91	8		82	17	
ndatory minimum sentences (2019)	35	61		29	68	
otect coverage of pre-existing conditions (2019)	83	13		66	26	
low sports gambling (2019)	53	40		57	37	
galize recreational marijuana (2019)	55	42		47	50	
n assault weapons (2019)	59	41		26	71	
n high capacity magazines (2019)	44	54		33	64	
pand concealed carry (2019)	31	68		84	14	
n sale of firearms to mentally ill 2019)	62	37		75	22	
ath penalty (2018)	42	53		73	19	
ual pay (2017)	93	7		90	8	
n workplace discrimination for exual orientation (2017)	85	12		66	30	
n workplace discrimination for gender identity (2017)	83	14		59	34	

(continued on next page)

TABLE 7.1. Issue Positions of Democrats and Republicans in Louisiana *(continued)*

	Democrats		*Republicans*	
	Support	*Oppose*	*Support*	*Oppose*
Same sex marriage (2016)	44	50	32	61
Remove Confederate monuments (2016)	34	56	6	92
Allow refugees from Syria (2016)	39	50	11	84
Charter schools (2016)	67	30	73	25
School vouchers (2016)	52	40	39	55
More spending to help needy (2018)	75	22	26	70
Regulations on businesses (2018)	56	41	39	57
Allow refusal of services to same sex couple (2017)	23	73	70	27
More spending to help needy (2018)	75	22	26	70
Transgender use public restroom of gender identity (2017)	51	39	20	74
	Necessary	*Harmful*	*Necessary*	*Harmful*
Regulations on businesses (2018)	56	41	39	57
	Do more	*Done enough*	*Do more*	*Done enough*
To achieve gender equality in workplace (2018)	92	6	57	41
	More programs	*Lower taxes*	*More programs*	*Lower taxes*
To reduce poverty (2016)	67	18	23	61
	Illegal	*Legal*	*Illegal*	*Legal*
Abortion (2016)	39	53	69	27
	Do more	*Done enough*	*Do more*	*Done enough*
To achieve equal rights between races (2016)	79	18	26	67

Note: Response frequencies are from the *Louisiana Survey* with specific year in parentheses. In instances where a question repeats across multiple years, the most recent responses are included. Majority shaded where appropriate. Cells displaying "50" are shaded if unrounded value exceeds 50 percent. Shares of respondents who volunteered they "don't know" are not displayed.

parties in Louisiana (particularly among Democrats) keeps them closer together than in the rest of the country. This raises two questions. First, why is there less ideological disagreement between the parties in Louisiana than in the United States as a whole? Second, does the ideological overlap between the parties mean Louisianans are more open to bipartisanship and compromise?

LOUISIANA PARTISANS ARE INCREASINGLY POLARIZED BY RACE

Louisianans have followed a pattern of racial sorting that has mitigated the growing ideological distance between Democrats and Republicans. Continuing a pattern that began as far back as the 1960s, whites have increasingly abandoned the Democratic Party in Louisiana through recent decades. The left side of figure 7.4 shows the share of whites who identify as Republicans and Democrats in the *Louisiana Survey* since 2003. For comparison, the national pattern (from the *American National Election Study*) appears on the right side. The solid lines show the percent of whites identifying as Democrats and Republicans when initially asked. The dashed lines show results when including so-called "leaners"—that is, people who initially do not say they identify as either a Democrat or Republican but say they lean toward one party or the other when answering a follow-up question.

The figures show the declining Democratic fortunes among white Louisianans. Today, nearly 60 percent of whites consider themselves Republicans or lean toward the Republican Party. In contrast, only about one in five lean or identify as Democrats. Put another way, political parties sort along racial lines in Louisiana more than they do in the United States as a whole. Yet, because Black voters and white voters do not divide as clearly along ideological lines, the racial polarization of parties in Louisiana mitigates their ideological polarization.

Most whites in Louisiana identify as conservative (59 percent), but a significant number identify as moderate (19 percent) or liberal (17 percent). Except for white liberals (who tend to identify as Democrats), the gravitational pull of whites toward the Republican Party in Louisiana has drawn both conservatives and moderates. The tendency of moderate whites in Louisiana to

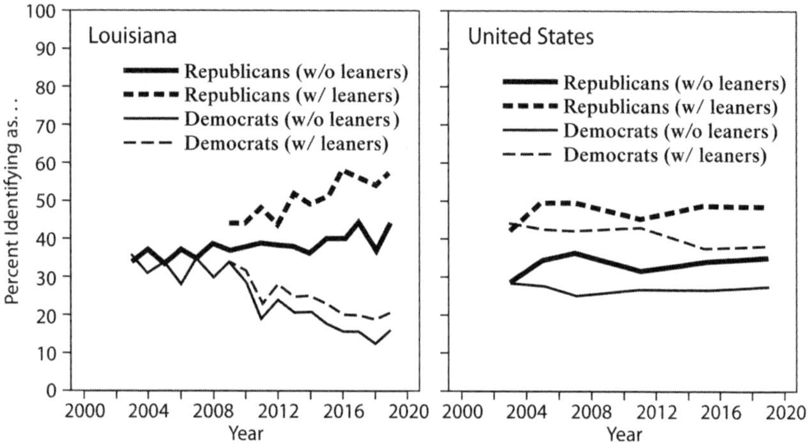

FIGURE 7.4. Trends in Party Identification among Whites in Louisiana and the United States, 2000–2019. Lines show percentage of white respondents to the *Louisiana Survey* or the ANES who identify as Republicans or Democrats.

identify as Republicans rather than Democrats is what sets Louisiana apart from the United States as a whole. Across the country, moderate whites split almost evenly between the Democratic Party (40 percent) and the Republican Party (37 percent). In Louisiana, the Republican Party has more than a two-to-one advantage over the Democratic Party among white moderates (46 percent of whom identify as the former, while only 19 percent identify as the later).

Thus, the Republican Party in Louisiana is mostly a mix of conservative and moderate whites. Liberal whites identify as Democrats. Black Louisianans make up the majority of Democrats in the state and split almost evenly in their identification as liberals (33 percent), moderate or unsure (34 percent), and conservative (33 percent). To put it another way, Black voters who identify as conservative also tend to identify as Democrats. The relative scarcity of liberal whites in Louisiana and ideological diversity among Black Democrats in the state means the party is less liberal than it is nationally. At the same time, the increasing movement of moderate whites into the Republican Party helps offset the increasing conservatism among Republicans. The political parties in Louisiana are less *ideologically polarized* than in the rest of the country, but it is because they are more *racially polarized.*

PARTISAN DISLIKE WITHOUT (MUCH) IDEOLOGICAL DISAGREEMENT

If rank-and-file Democrats and Republicans in Louisiana have only modest disagreements over ideology or political issues, is the state less divided and more open to bipartisan cooperation? No. In fact, disagreements over political polarization largely miss the forest for the trees. Hyperpartisanship neither depends on ideological disagreement nor necessarily produces it. Partisanship itself is a powerful political force shaping how we think, feel, and behave.

Party identification is a psychological attachment to a particular group, and it filters how we acquire and process political messages.[9] To be clear, party identification is not the same as party registration. The former is an ongoing feature of how we think about ourselves politically, while the latter is simply an administrative record describing a behavior that many engage in just once (when they first register to vote) and do not update as their thinking changes.[10]

Part of the reason party identification exerts such a strong influence on how we engage politics is because it is a group identity. This group identity gives rise to a sort of tribalism in which partisans are biased toward their own group and against others outside of the group.[11] This group-based mentality increasingly divides Americans and stokes antagonism toward the opposite party.[12] It has little, if anything, to do with ideological differences of opinion.[13] This mentality is akin, in some ways, to being a fan of a sports team. Fans of NFL rivals the New Orleans Saints and the Atlanta Falcons might agree about issues such as the importance of balancing a running and passing offense, but they consistently root against the opposing team (even in games that do not involve their own team), mock fans of the opposing team, and interpret officials' calls in wildly different ways. Americans increasingly approach politics in much the same way. They are increasingly faithful to their own party's candidates in elections.[14] And they increasingly dislike partisans on the other side.[15] Republicans distrust Democratic voters without necessarily disagreeing with them over taxes or trade policy, for example, while Democratic voters doubt their Republican neighbors without being far apart from them over gun access or abortion. Democrats and Republicans do not simply see the other side as people who *disagree* with them, but rather as people who are *different* from them.

TABLE 7.2. Partisan Dislike in Louisiana and the United States

	Among Louisiana Democrats			*Among Louisiana Republicans*		
	Favorable	*Unfavorable*	*Net*	*Favorable*	*Unfavorable*	*Net*
Attitude toward Democrats	79	20	+59	14	84	−70
Attitude toward Republicans	18	80	−62	73	24	+49
	Among US Democrats			*Among US Republicans*		
	Favorable	*Unfavorable*	*Net*	*Favorable*	*Unfavorable*	*Net*
Attitude toward Democrats	79	18	+61	14	82	−68
Attitude toward Republicans	16	79	−63	68	28	+40

Note: Data from 2016 *Louisiana Survey*. Percent favorable includes share of respondents answering "favorable" and "very favorable." Percent unfavorable includes share of respondents answering "unfavorable" and "very unfavorable."

Unsurprisingly, then, party identification remains strong in Louisiana despite small declines in the share of voters registering with the major parties. Since 2009, the *Louisiana Survey* has asked individuals who do not initially identify themselves as Republicans or Democrats whether they lean toward one of these parties or not. In 2019, 77 percent of state residents either identified with or leaned toward one of the two major parties; that is, most Louisianans expressed a group attachment to one of these parties. This share had not shifted in any noticeable way over the previous decade despite a drop in the share of voters registered as Democrats or Republicans from 77 percent to 73 percent. The strength of these partisan attachments remained robust. In 2019, nearly half of Louisiana residents (46 percent) said they think of themselves as a "strong" Democrat or Republican—the highest share on record in the state since the *Louisiana Survey* began asking about the strength of partisan attachments in 2009. In other words, regardless of how they register, partisan identities persist in the minds of Louisiana voters.

At the same time, Louisiana voters express deep disaffection for the opposing side. In this respect, Louisiana partisans are very much like American partisans as a whole despite having fewer ideological disagreements. Table 7.2 shows the favorability ratings of Democrats and Republicans among partisans from each side both in the United States and in Louisiana. In 2016, 79 percent of Democrats held a favorable view of the Democratic Party while only 20 percent held an unfavorable view of their party, for a net favorability rating of +59. At the same time, only 18 percent of Democrats had a favorable view of the Republican Party and 80 percent had an unfavorable view, for a net favorability rating of −62. Republicans were similar. Just 14 percent held a favorable view of the Democratic Party, and 84 percent held an unfavorable view, for a net favorability of −70. Their net favorability toward their own party was +49. The magnitude of these gaps in attitudes toward opposing partisans outstrips most differences in issue opinions shown in table 7.1. In other words, Democrats and Republicans are more divided in how they view one another than they are over political issues.

This dislike of the opposite party has consequences for what voters want from their own side in political debates. The 2016 *Louisiana Survey* included a question asking respondents about their support for political compromise. The survey asked respondents whether elected officials in state government who share their positions on the most important issues facing Louisiana should work with elected officials they disagree with, even if it results in some policies the respondent does not like, or whether they should stand up for their positions, even if that means little gets done in state government. As shown in figure 7.5, voters who have a favorable view of the opposite party (in other words, Democrats who think well of Republicans and vice versa) prefer compromise, even if they end up with some policies they dislike. However, partisans who have a very unfavorable view of the opposite party would rather see the government get little done than have their leaders compromise with the other side.

Finally, as has occurred across the country, partisanship is strongly associated with how Louisiana voters choose among candidates. In the 2012 presidential election, 91 percent of Louisiana Democrats voted for the Democratic candidate, Barack Obama, and 95 percent of Republicans voted for the Republican candidate, Mitt Romney. Four years later, 89 percent of Democrats voted for the Democratic candidate, Hillary Clinton, while 95 percent of Republicans voted for the Republican candidate, Donald Trump. No policy issue in table 7.1 comes close to pitting 90 percent of Republicans against 90

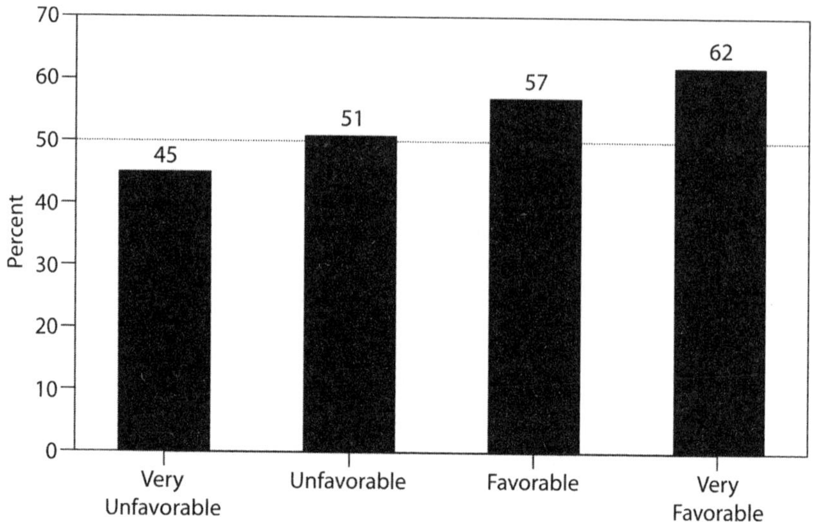

FIGURE 7.5. Support for Compromise by Favorability toward the Opposing Party. Data are from the 2016 *Louisiana Survey.*

percent of Democrats. Hyperpartisan voting extends well beyond presidential elections. Across the United States, voters increasingly approach state and national elections in the same way.[16]

In Louisiana, the election of Democratic governor John Bel Edwards is an exception to the general tendency of the majority of voters in the state to back Republicans. Including Edwards's two gubernatorial victories, Democratic candidates have won just four of thirty-one statewide elections (13 percent) for an office in state government since 2007. Over the same period, Democratic candidates for national office (US Senate or president) have carried the state in just once out of seven contests (14 percent)—and not since former US senator Mary Landrieu last won in 2008. Louisiana statewide elections are also remarkably consistent in party vote shares across state and federal offices. Voters average 59 percent support for Republican candidates and 39 percent support for Democratic candidates across all statewide elections from 2007 to 2019 (including all first-round and runoff contests that include at least one candidate from each major party).[17] There is also strong consistency between presidential election returns and state legislative returns in Louisiana even though these elections do not occur in the same year. In the

2019 state legislative elections, for example, candidates from the same party of the presidential nominee who carried the district three years earlier won 94 percent of districts. Republican candidates won ninety-four of the 101 House and Senate districts that Trump won in 2016, while Democrats won forty-one of the forty-three Clinton districts. The degree of consistency in voting patterns across offices and over time strongly suggests that most voters consistently support the same party, and few voters swing from one side to the other.

This strong and consistent commitment to one's own team—and deep distaste for the other side—sustains a system in which voters who are only mildly split over issues continue to elect candidates to government who are far more divided ideologically. This likely means that Louisiana will continue to tilt Republican in statewide elections and legislative control for the near future—until generational change or a national realignment of party constituencies shift partisan attachments.[18]

NOTES

1. Boris Shor and Nolan McCarty, "State Polarization, 1996–2016," *Measuring American Legislatures,* July 20, 2017, https://americanlegislatures.com/2017/07/20/state-polarization-1996-2016/; Boris Shor, "How U.S. State Legislatures Are Polarized and Getting More Polarized (in 2 graphs)," *Washington Post,* January 14, 2014, https://www.washingtonpost.com/news/monkey-cage/wp/2014/01/14/how-u-s-state-legislatures-are-polarized-and-getting-more-polarized-in-2-graphs/.

2. Boris Shor and Nolan McCarty, "Polarization in the South, 1996–2017," *Measuring American Legislatures,* July 20, 2017, https://americanlegislatures.com/2017/05/03/polarization-in-the-south-1996-2017/.

3. National Conference of State Legislatures, "State Legislative Policymaking in an Age of Political Polarization," February 2018, https://www.ncsl.org/Portals/1/Documents/About_State_Legislatures/Partisanship_030818.pdf.

4. Julia O'Donoghue, "Louisiana House Republicans Chafe at John Bel Edwards' Comments about 'Washington-Style Politics,'" *Times-Picayune,* April 11, 2017, https://www.nola.com/news/politics/article_2867f452-c4f6-53ee-9e67-11352d5b99e4.html; Julia O'Donoghue, "Louisiana Senate to Consider 'Obamacare' Replacement," *Times-Picayune,* May 2, 2019, https://www.nola.com/news/article_5efaf95e-36a5-56b5-a5da-6357a14e1dbe.html.

5. Alan I. Abramowitz and Kyle L. Saunders, "Is Polarization a Myth?," *Journal of Politics* 70, no. 2 (2008): 542–555; Pew Research Center, "The Partisan Divide on Political Values Grows Even Wider," October 5, 2017, https://www.people-press.org/2017/10/05/the-partisan-divide-on-political-values-grows-even-wider/; Pew Research Center, "Political Polarization in the Ameri-

can Public," June 12, 2014, https://www.people-press.org/2014/06/12/political-polarization-in-the-american-public/.

6. Morris P. Fiorina, Samuel J. Abrams, and Jeremy C. Pope, *Culture War? The Myth of a Polarized America* (New York: Pearson, 2005); Karen M. Kaufmann, John R. Petrocik, and Daron R. Shaw, *Unconventional Wisdom: Facts and Myths about American Voters* (Oxford: Oxford Univ. Press, 2008); Morris P. Fiorina, Samuel J. Abrams, and Jeremy C. Pope, "Polarization in the American Public: Misconceptions and Misreadings," *Journal of Politics* 70, no. 2 (2008): 556–560; Morris P. Fiorina and Samuel J. Abrams, "Where's the Polarization?," in *Controversies in Voting Behavior,* 5th ed., ed. Richard G. Niemi, Herbert F. Weisberg, and David C. Kimball (Washington, D.C.: CQ Press, 2011), 309–318; Marc Heatherington, "Partisanship and Polarization," in *New Directions in Public Opinion,* ed. Adam J. Berinsky, (New York: Routledge, 2012), 101–118.

7. Kaufmann, Petrocik, and Shaw, *Unconventional Wisdom;* Marc Heatherington, "Resurgent Mass Partisanship: The Role of Elite Polarization (Updated)," in *Controversies in Voting Behavior,* 5th ed., ed. Richard G. Niemi, Herbert F. Weisberg, and David C. Kimball (Washington, D.C.: CQ Press, 2011), 242–265; Heatherington, "Partisanship and Polarization."

8. Paul DiMaggio, John Evans, and Bethany Bryson, "Have Americans' Social Attitudes Become More Polarized?" *American Journal of Sociology* 102, no. 3 (November 1996): 690–755.

9. Angus Campbell, Phillip E. Converse, Warren E. Miller, and Donald E. Stokes, *The American Voter* (Chicago: Univ. of Chicago Press, 1960); Heatherington, "Partisanship and Polarization"; Christopher H. Achen and Larry M. Bartels, *Democracy for Realists: Why Elections Do Not Produce Responsive Government* (Princeton, N.J.: Princeton Univ. Press, 2016).

10. In Louisiana, for example, party registration reflects current party identification for just two-thirds of registered voters. Indeed, 10 percent of registered Democrats in the state actually think of themselves as Republicans. There is no definitive evidence for why party registration lags party identification, but it may result in part from the fact that Louisiana does not use closed party primaries except for presidential elections. In states with closed primaries, voters must register in a party to vote in its primary elections. Therefore, Louisiana voters who registered as Democrats when they first registered to vote decades ago during a time when most southerners thought of themselves as Democrats now have little incentive to change their registration even if they no longer identify as Democrats. The fact that older, white registered Democrats are the most likely to have a mismatch between their party identification and registration suggests this may be the case. In fact, only slightly more than half of white registered Democrats over the age of sixty-four actually think of themselves as Democrats. Michael Henderson, "What Does Party Registration Tell Us? Less Than You May Think," *Louisiana by the Numbers,* November 14, 2019, http://louisiananumbers.com/blog/2019/11/14.

11. Donald Green, Bradley Palmquist, and Eric Schickler, *Partisan Hearts and Minds: Political Parties and the Social Identities of Voters* (New Haven, Conn.: Yale Univ. Press, 2002).

12. Lillliana Mason, *Uncivil Agreement: How Politics Became Our Identity* (Chicago: Univ. of Chicago Press, 2018).

13. Donald R. Kinder and Nathan P. Kalmoe, *Neither Liberal nor Conservative: Ideological Innocence in the American Public* (Chicago: Univ. of Chicago Press, 2017).

14. Heatherington, “Resurgent Mass Partisanship”; Heatherington, “Partisanship and Polarization.”

15. Kaufmann, Petrocik, and Shaw, *Unconventional Wisdom;* Shanto Iyengar, Gaurav Sood, and Yphtach Lelkes, “Affect, Not Ideology: A Social Identity Perspective on Polarization,” *Public Opinion Quarterly* 76, no. 3 (fall 2012): 405–431; Shanto Iyengar, Yphtach Lelkes, Matthew Levendusky, Neil Malhotra, and Sean J. Westwood, “The Origins and Consequences of Affective Polarization in the United States,” *Annual Review of Political Science* 22 (2019): 129–146.

16. Daniel J. Hopkins, *The Increasingly United States: How and Why American Political Behavior Nationalized* (Chicago: Univ. Chicago Press, 2018).

17. The shares do not total 100 percent because of the small share of votes that go to first-round candidates who are neither Democrats nor Republicans.

18. There is some evidence that traditionally Republican-leaning suburbs in Louisiana shifted slightly toward Democrats in 2016, 2018, and 2019, following a national pattern. However, like the national pattern, it is not clear whether this is the first sign of a long-run trend or a short-term reaction to the candidacy and presidency of Donald Trump.

GONE WITH THE WIND (AND WATER)

Hurricane Katrina, the Great Recession, and the Death of Populism

ALBERT L. SAMUELS

On August 29, 2005, Hurricane Katrina slammed into South Louisiana as a monster Category 3 storm. While the metropolitan New Orleans area experienced minimal wind damage from Katrina, the storm surge from this mammoth storm breached the levee system built to protect the below-sea level city. The ensuing floodwaters precipitated a major catastrophe that forced tens of thousands of New Orleanians to flee for their lives. At the height of the flood, 80 percent of New Orleans was underwater. Television viewers nationwide were overwhelmed with images of poor African Americans in desperate need of rescue, left behind because they had no means to evacuate on their own. The storm's impact displaced thousands of Louisianans in the parishes most directly affected (Orleans, Jefferson, St. Bernard, Plaquemines, and St. Tammany). Notably, the drastic reduction in the large African American population in the New Orleans area portended profound ramifications for politics all over the state of Louisiana. Three years later, the state was rocked again by disaster—this time an economic meltdown on Wall Street that brought down the entire national economy. The "double-whammy" effect of these two disasters set in motion a chain of events that would dramatically shift the center of gravity of Louisiana politics to the right.

This essay focuses on how the twin impacts of these two disasters—Hurricane Katrina and the Great Recession—laid the groundwork for Bobby Jindal and a more conservative legislature to dramatically alter the trajectory of Louisiana politics to the right. For most of the twentieth century, Louisiana politics was dominated by a populist tradition, a type of politics predicated on severance taxes on the petrochemical industries and the wealthy to finance a robust social safety net. Bobby Jindal benefited from the wreckage that Hurricane Katrina and the Great Recession left in their wake to chart a decidedly more conservative course for Louisiana than would have been politically possible otherwise.

HUEY LONG AND LOUISIANA'S POPULIST LEGACY

Louisiana's populist legacy can be traced back to the administration of Governor Huey Long, whose "common man" populist appeals turned the Louisiana political establishment on its ear. After easily vanquishing his opponents in the 1928 election, Long transformed state government from an elitist club run primarily for the benefit of the well-to-do to a generous provider of economic and social programs for the common man. His agenda was financed primarily by taxing the rich (and especially the oil and gas industry). Populist politics formed the basis for a bi-factional political system pitting Longites versus anti-Long Democrats, an ideological divide that approximated a two-party system for decades after Huey Long's death in 1935. During the 1970s, Governor Edwin Edwards, the political heir to the Long coalition, built on the traditional alignment of rural whites, Catholics, Cajuns, and labor unions by adding the newly enfranchised African American population to forge a new majority.

Populist politics worked so long as Louisiana's budget coffers were overflowing. Relying disproportionately on severance taxes levied on oil and gas reserves enabled Louisiana to finance a significantly more robust public sector than would have been possible otherwise, given its low income and property taxes. This luxury, however, ended when the decline in world oil prices during the 1980s devastated Louisiana's oil-dependent economy and state government. With severance tax revenues in decline, Louisiana resorted to greater reliance on sales tax revenues and legalizing several forms of gambling in order to finance state operations. By 2002, revenues derived from gambling exceeded oil and gas taxes as the largest source of the state's revenues, but it never fully replaced the vast resources available to populist governors during the heyday of the "Louisiana hayride."

Politically, the weakening of the economic basis for Louisiana's populist style of governance and a more conservative national political landscape opened the door for Republicans to gradually make inroads in the state's politics. By the Blanco years, Republican legislators (while still a minority) had become an increasingly important and cohesive voting bloc, occupying forty-three seats in the Louisiana House of Representatives (where all revenue bills originate). They had demonstrated their political muscle during the 2005 legislative session when they scuttled Governor Kathleen Blanco's central legislative priority: a pay raise for the state's teachers. In doing so, they delivered an embarrassing political setback to the governor. Then came Hurricane Katrina. The "political storm" that Katrina unleashed would radically reshuffle the deck of Louisiana politics.

KATRINA PUSHES LOUISIANA TO THE RIGHT

Hurricane Katrina took the lives of 1,833 Louisianans and led to hundreds of billions of dollars in property damage and other economic losses, making it easily the costliest hurricane in American history.[1] The storm was almost immediately followed by a political blame game erupting between national, state, and federal officials with respect to which level of government was responsible for the inept response to the hurricane's aftermath. Governor Kathleen Blanco's reputation was the biggest political casualty of Hurricane Katrina. The governor's recovery agenda, despite some achievements, was overshadowed by the administrative and political debacle of the "Road Home" program—a state-sponsored initiative designed to help displaced Louisianans settle their mortgages with their lenders and return home. Homeowners languished for months with excruciating bureaucratic delays, only to be bitterly disappointed by settlements that were significantly less than what they expected. The failures of the "Road Home" program clung to Governor Blanco's shoulders like a political albatross, dooming any possibility that she might be able to engineer a political resurrection. In March 2007, six months before the October gubernatorial primary, Blanco announced that she would not seek reelection. After former US senator John Breaux passed on the race, Democrats were left without a strong candidate for governor. Only Public Service Commissioner Foster Campbell, a North Louisiana populist and longtime state senator, Walter Boasso, a state senator from Arabi (who had changed parties from the Republican Party to the Democrats in May 2007), and John Georges, who entered the race as an independent, were left to challenge presumptive favorite Bobby Jindal, who had won election to Congress in District 1 in the fall election.

In the aftermath of the storm, Jindal's rapid speaking style and encyclopedic grasp of complex information stood in strong contrast to Blanco's less polished presentations. The political fallout resulting from the storm's impact represented a political windfall for Jindal, enabling him to present himself as the candidate of change. He campaigned on a platform that made ethics reform one of its central tenets. Jindal argued that the state's poor national image discouraged out-of-state businesses from investing in Louisiana. The national press produced critical stories about the state's legacy of cronyism and corruption as the key explanation for the state's dismal rankings in national measures of state well-being. The reluctance of the federal government to support key aspects of Louisiana's recovery wish list seemed to amplify Jindal's point.

In addition, the "2007 Fact Book" by the Council for a Better Louisiana (CABL), a nonpartisan public policy group, seemed to buttress the case for change. It cited statistics ranking Louisiana forty-first in the nation in per capita income, with the nation's second highest poverty rate. *Forbes* magazine rated Louisiana dead last among the states in which to do business in the country. Moreover, the report cited recent census figures indicating that Louisiana had lost nearly 250,000 of its 4.5 million people in the year after Hurricane Katrina. In the five years prior to Katrina, 70,000 people departed Louisiana, even as the population of neighboring southern states expanded. The population under the age of eighteen had declined nearly 11 percent since 2000; additionally, the number of women of childbearing age fell by nearly 10 percent.[2]

Certainly, the Blanco administration was not responsible for all of Louisiana's problems. However, in the period when CABL was compiling these statistics, it was led predominantly by Democratic governors and Democratic-controlled legislatures. This situation enabled Louisiana Republicans in the 2007 election to genuinely campaign as the party of change. They also bene-

TABLE 8.1. Referendum on Legislative Term Limits, 1995

Term Limits	*Vote Total*	*Percentage*
Yes	842,659	76%
No	271,153	24%

Source: Louisiana Secretary of State, October 21, 1995, election, https://voterportal.sos.la.gov/graphical.

fited from another "perfect storm" in that the 2007 election represented the first time that legislative term limits, enacted overwhelmingly in 1995 by a statewide referendum, would take effect (see table 8.1). Thus, many rural districts where voters had been trending Republican for years but were represented by Democrats would be "ripe pickings" for GOP gains.

The 2007 primary election results are displayed in table 8.2. Jindal won an unusual first-round victory in the October primary, triumphing with 54 percent of the vote statewide over his three outmatched opponents. He carried sixty of the state's sixty-four parishes. A mere ninety thousand votes were cast in Orleans Parish—a figure smaller than the Democratic *margin of victory* in recent statewide elections in New Orleans. Republicans ran their total to near parity with Democrats in both houses of the Louisiana legislature: winning fifty of 105 seats in the House of Representatives and fifteen of thirty-nine seats in the Senate. Shortly following the election, Senator Robert Adley of Bossier City switched from Democrat to Republican, setting off a wave of defections that, by early 2011, would put both legislative chambers in Republican hands.

TABLE 8.2. Louisiana Gubernatorial Primary Election Results, 2007

Candidate	*Vote Total*	*Percentage*
Bobby Jindal—Republican	699,275	54%
Walter Boasso —Democrat	226,476	17%
Foster Campbell—Democrat	161,615	14%
John Georges—Independent	185,682	12%

Source: Louisiana Secretary of State, October 20, 2007, https://voterportal.sos.la.gov/graphical.

In his inaugural address, Governor Jindal promised the dawning of a new day in Louisiana:

> We will come to this Capitol to make a clean break from the past. To give Louisiana the highest standards for accountability anywhere in the nation. To take our government 180 degrees from the darkest chapters of our past. . . . We cannot settle for cosmetic change. And we must recognize the stakes. When we succeed, the world will take note. They will take note in Silicon Valley. They will take note in the board rooms of Wall Street. And they will take note in the living rooms across Houston and Atlanta and Dallas, where former Louisianians now live—many of them our best and brightest—in exile from an uncertain future at home. We must bring them home.[3]

When the new governor took office, he inherited a hefty budget surplus. With the infusion of federal recovery dollars, higher sales tax revenues associated with Hurricanes Katrina and Rita (also in 2005), and record oil prices, Louisiana's financial posture was rosier than it had been in decades. The budget surplus stood at approximately $2 billion, including $1.1 billion in unanticipated revenues left over from the 2006–2007 fiscal year. The governor and the legislature, in short order during a special session, divided up the revenues. Lawmakers, at the governor's urging, swiftly approved a slew of business tax breaks totaling $367 million and $20 million in private school tuition and home schooling tax credits. They also spent the $1.1 billion surplus on a host of infrastructure projects, including roads and bridges, hurricane protection, coastal protection, coastal restoration, deferred maintenance at state universities, and improvements to Pennington Biomedical Center. During the regular session, the legislature voted to repeal the voter approved "Stelly Tax Plan" of 2002, which had rolled back state sales taxes in favor of higher income taxes on individuals. Despite warnings that in the event of an economic downturn the state would not have enough money to pay for recurring expenses, legislators repealed the Stelly Tax Plan unanimously.[4]

Jindal and the legislature had enacted a far more sweeping tax cut agenda than would have been possible prior to Katrina. However, as fortune would have it, Louisiana's leaders would not have to wait long to see the fears of those who warned against repealing the Stelly Tax Plan borne out.

LOUISIANA TURNS EVEN MORE TO THE RIGHT

The abrupt collapse of Wall Street stalwart Lehman Brothers in September 2008 triggered a panic that threatened not just the American economy, but economies all over the globe. Oil prices, previously at historical highs, plummeted as demand collapsed virtually overnight. Louisiana's budget surplus rapidly evaporated in the face of the national catastrophe. By Christmas, "the Grinch" greeted the Jindal administration with the news of an estimated $341 million midyear deficit. Even worse, forecasters warned of a possible $2 billion deficit for the 2009–2010 fiscal year beginning July 1.

Jindal, the governor who had prided himself on being a fiscal conservative, had somehow managed to turn the largest surplus in Louisiana history into a deficit in the space of less than a year. One might have thought that this would have prompted Jindal to reconsider his ideological preference for tax cuts in light of the new fiscal realities of the state. No longer could Jindal act like a congressman, a member of a legislative body not constitutionally mandated to produce a balanced budget. Rather, as governor of Louisiana, he was constitutionally bound to end each year with the state's books in balance. However, rather than bending his conservative principles in order to meet this exigency, Governor Jindal "doubled down" on conservative orthodoxy. As one of hundreds of Republican politicians who had signed national anti-tax advocate Grover Norquist's pledge to oppose any and all tax increases, Governor Jindal refused to reconsider any of the tax cuts enacted in 2008—including the Stelly Tax Plan repeal. Instead, he promised to veto any new proposals to raise taxes, regardless of the situation or rationale. Instead of compromising his principles to confront a circumstance that he did not anticipate, Jindal saw the new fiscal reality as an opportunity to pursue a more aggressively conservative agenda than what might have been politically possible in the absence of the economic downturn.

Accordingly, the governor "held the line" against every tax proposal emanating from the legislature, regardless of who proposed it or what public priorities it might advance. Defeated proposals ranged from a 2009 bill to index the state's gasoline tax to inflation in order to address the state's backlog of highway projects to taxes to offset steep budget cuts to higher education. No matter their provenance or purpose, they were all shot down by Jindal and his allies within the legislature. Even though the Stelly Tax Plan had been credited with helping to stabilize the state's finances and raising its bond rating, no serious consideration was given to the 2008 decision to repeal it. Not only were tax increases "off the table," but the Jindal administration dramatically expanded—with the legislature's acquiescence—new tax exemptions ostensibly to foster economic development, further exacerbating the state government's revenue losses.[5]

Universities, public health, and hospitals were the hardest hit because their funds were not constitutionally protected from budget cuts, making them easier targets for reductions during times of scarcity. Scrambling to make up for the lost state appropriations, universities raised tuition and fees, shifting a greater share of the burden of financing higher education to students and their parents (especially those not covered by the state's TOPS scholarship program). Moreover, without the infusion of federal funds during the 2010 and 2011 fiscal years, the cuts that would have been required to balance Louisiana's budget would have been far more draconian than they turned out to be given the governor's adamant refusal to consider tax increases.[6]

But Jindal's reform agenda was not limited to tax cuts and cuts to state agencies; rather, the administration used the fiscal crisis to make the case for "streamlining government." Streamlining, in practice, privatizes many of the functions formerly performed by state employees and state agencies. In 2009, the legislature passed a Jindal-backed bill authorizing the creation of the Commission on Streamlining Government (CSG). In December 2009, the commission issued its initial report, outlining 238 recommendations estimated to save $1 billion through privatization, streamlining, consolidation, and the elimination of government activities. These initiatives covered a wide range of state agencies. In November 2011 a progress report submitted to the CSG estimated that sixty-two of the CSG's 238 recommendations had been implemented, another sixty-two had yet to be acted upon, and the rest were underway. The report declared that, to date, the savings accrued to the state from implementing the CSG recommendations had exceeded $750 million.[7]

The two most significant policy fields where Jindal pressed his privatization agenda were in health care and education. In the former, the Jindal administration privatized the delivery of Medicaid services, the state's health care program for the poor. In July 2011, the state announced the selection of five health care insurers that would provide state-subsidized policies to over eight hundred thousand Medicaid recipients statewide. In 2012, the administration privatized the Office of Group Benefits (OGB), the state agency responsible for managing the health care plans for state employees, and awarded the contract to Blue Cross/Blue Shield of Louisiana. In 2013, the Jindal administration scored its biggest privatization victory: it secured legislative approval to turn over management of the state's charity hospital system to a network of private health contractors. In doing so, Bobby Jindal dismantled one of the last vestiges of the Long legacy in Louisiana. What made this transition particularly galling for health care advocates was the Jindal administration's simultaneous refusal to accept Medicaid expansion (as part of the Affordable Care Act), which would have extended health insurance coverage to nearly four hundred thousand Louisiana residents.[8]

In education, Jindal used the political capital he had accumulated in 2012 after his easy reelection victory to champion a sweeping education reform package. One part of the education reform instituted a statewide voucher program providing taxpayer subsidies for parents to send their children to private or parochial schools. The plan also made it significantly easier to establish and operate charter schools by authorizing the Board of Elementary and Secondary Education (BESE) to establish charters and do "end-runs" around resistant local school boards. It also imposed a new accountability system for public schools and a new evaluation system for teachers. The administration pushed these measures swiftly through the legislative process over the bitter objections of teachers' unions and other advocates of public education, who resented the diversion of tax dollars from already cash-strapped schools to private institutions and charter schools.[9]

In pushing privatization at virtually every turn, the Jindal administration was mirroring Republican governors all over the country who were pursuing similar policies. The Republican privatization agenda became particularly emboldened in the wake of the 2010 elections, which brought twenty-nine Republican governors to power. Governors from a diverse array of states, including Jan Brewer (Arizona), Rick Scott (Florida), Scott Walker (Wisconsin),

John Kasich (Ohio), and Chris Christie (New Jersey), pushed to privatize prisons, state parks, welfare eligibility programs, and state lottery management, and to strip public employee unions of their collective bargaining rights. In each state, the rationale for these policy agendas was the same: "big government" was to blame for the fiscal morass that the states found themselves in. Ending "big government" meant slashing the public sector and privatizing as many of the functions of state government as possible. State workers were, in turn, scapegoated by GOP governors and conservative lawmakers for their supposedly lavish retirement and health care benefits that were deemed to be fiscally unsustainable in the long term. Louisiana politics during the Jindal era certainly fit easily within this larger national pattern.

CONCLUSION

Bobby Jindal seized the political opportunity given him by the twin disasters of Hurricane Katrina and the Great Recession to push the political center of gravity in Louisiana decidedly to the right. He was aided in this effort by the most conservative legislature since Bourbon Democrats dominated the state's politics. The impact of federal stimulus dollars obscured the immediate economic impacts of Bobby Jindal's fiscal policies, which would not become apparent to most Louisiana voters until late in his second term. Jindal's popularity declined as the state's budget woes mounted. His frequent out-of-state visits deepened popular dissatisfaction. Yet, despite these facts, Jindal's legacy of tax cuts and downsizing government narrowed the range of what was politically possible for his successors. As Republicans increased their majorities in the state legislature, the political prospects for old-style populist economic policies were dimmed. Therefore, no matter who succeeded him after the 2015 election, Bobby Jindal's eight years in the governor's mansion ensured that there would be no going back to Huey Long-style populist politics anytime soon.

NOTES

1. David L. Johnson, "Service Assessment, Hurricane Katrina, August 23–31, 2005," National Oceanic and Aeronautic Administration, https://www.weather.gov/media/publications/assessments/Katrina.pdf.

2. Council for a Better Louisiana, "Louisiana Fact Book for the 2007 Election: How Do We Measure Up? How Far Do We Have to Go?" http://cabl.org/wp-content/uploads/2016/06/2007_FactBook-2.pdf.

3. Bobby Jindal, "Inaugural Address," January 14, 2008, https://www.americanrhetoric.com/speeches/bobbyjindalinauguraladdress.htm.

4. Public Affairs Research Council, "PAR Says Proposed Tax Cut Is Shortsighted Fiscal Policy," May 30, 2008, http://parlouisiana.org/par-says-proposed-tax-cut-is-shortsighted-fiscal-policy/.

5. Public Affairs Research Council, "PAR Guide to the State Budget Crisis: How We Got Here—The Jindal Record—The Real Priorities," April 10, 2015, http://parlouisiana.org/wp-content/uploads/2016/02/PAR_Guide_to_State.pdf.

6. During the 2010 and 2011 fiscal years, federal dollars from the American Recovery and Reinvestment Act, more popularly known as "the stimulus," softened (but did not totally eliminate) the blow to higher education and other state services from Jindal's budget cuts. These dollars were part of the rescue package enacted by Congress during the first month of the Obama administration in 2009 in response to the Great Recession.

7. Leonard Gilroy, "Jindal Continued Louisiana Privatization Push in 2011: Initiatives Advanced in Medicaid, Public Employees Health Care, and More," www.reason.org, May 15, 2012 (accessed June 5, 2021).

8. For more information on the privatization of Louisiana's health care system, see Jan Moller's essay in this volume.

9. More information on this initiative may be found in Pearson Cross's essay on the governor in this volume.

WOMEN IN LOUISIANA POLITICS

Barriers and Opportunities

MIRYA R. HOLMAN AND
ANNA MITCHELL MAHONEY

Women are underrepresented in political office in Louisiana. The state routinely ranks in the bottom five in the nation for women's representation in the state legislature. As figure 9.1 shows, the level of women's representation in Louisiana today is not a new pattern but is instead the continuation of a long trend. The dotted line represents the share of the state legislative seats that are held by women and reveals three main takeaways: women have never held even one-in-five of the seats in the legislature;[1] the share of women in office increased fairly steadily from 1975 to 2007 and then dipped during the late 2000s and early 2010s;[2] and women hold more seats in 2020 than in any previous session. The gray shaded area is the state's ranking versus other states, in terms of the share of women in political office.[3] In 2005, Louisiana reached the best ranking in the state's history, with the state's share of women holding office placing it thirty-fourth in the country. Women of color are particularly underrepresented: while Black women make up more than 16 percent of the state's population, they hold only 8 percent of state legislative seats.[4]

Women's underrepresentation is not just limited to the state legislature. In 2020, no women held statewide office in Louisiana. Only one woman (Kathleen Blanco) has ever served as Louisiana's governor, and only five women have ever served in Congress.[5] Of the state's three US Senators (Rose McConnell Long, who served in 1936; Elaine S. Edwards, 1972; and Mary L. Landrieu, 1997–2014) and two Representatives (Corinne "Lindy" Claiborne Boggs, 1973–1990; Catherine S. Long, 1985–1986), all came from politically important families, and three of the five either entered office following the

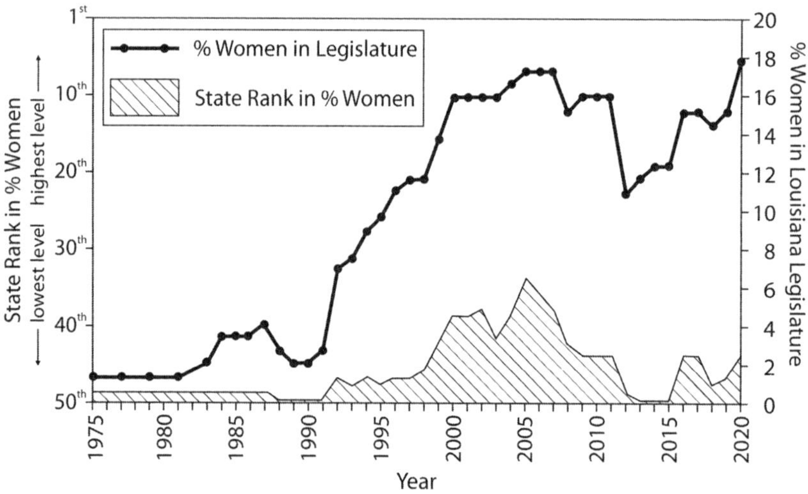

FIGURE 9.1. Representation of Women in Louisiana's Legislature. Data are from the Center for American Women in Politics.

death of their office-holding husband or were appointed to office by their husband.[6] All five representatives in Congress and eight of the nine women to hold statewide office have been members of the Democratic Party. A woman of color has never held statewide office in Louisiana, nor have any women of color represented the state in Congress.

But recent elections have revealed shifting patterns in women seeking and holding political office in Louisiana. The mayors of the state's three largest cities are Black women: LaToya Cantrell in New Orleans, Sharon Weston Broome in Baton Rouge, and Ollie Tyler in Shreveport. Women hold the majority of seats on many city councils and parish boards. For example, in New Orleans women have held half or more of city council seats since 2005,[7] and more women ran for state legislative office in 2019 than at any other point in the state's history.[8] Seventy-seven women qualified as candidates, besting the previous record of sixty-three in 2007.[9] Are patterns changing in the Pelican State?

To further explore these data, we ask: how well does the underrepresentation of women in Louisiana fit with dominant theories of women in politics in the United States? We consider two potential sets of explanations: that the *supply* of women is low in Louisiana, as there simply are not the structures in place to encourage women to run for office; or that the *demand* for women in office is low in Louisiana, as party leaders and voters are uninterested in supporting women running for office. In doing so, we argue that the patterns of women in Louisiana politics today look more like the patterns in other states than they have in the past. As a result, there may be more opportunities for increasing the share of women in office in Louisiana in the future than there have been in the past.

SUPPLY AND DEMAND THEORIES OF WOMEN'S REPRESENTATION

Women are descriptively underrepresented in almost every political body in the United States. When Nevada elected its legislature in 2018, for the first time women held more than half of the seats in any state or federal elected body.[10] Scholars of representation, gender and politics, and elections argue that the descriptive underrepresentation of women in political office stems from multiple sources.[11] Findings suggest that women's low numbers in public office are in part a consequence of fewer women candidates running and argue that to reach parity, interventions in electoral rules and campaigns will be necessary, such as the implementation of gender quotas.

THE SUPPLY OF WOMEN INTERESTED IN POLITICAL OFFICE

The *supply* idea of representation argues that women do not run for office because they do not have high levels of interest in running, which might stem from excess demands on their time, from seeing politics as incompatible with their more general career and life goals, or because they lack resources.[12] Women often lack the time necessary to run for political office. For example, because women disproportionately perform childcare and household maintenance, those women have less time to dedicate to political participation, including engaging in the work that is important for political candidates, such as attending meetings, raising funds, and meeting voters.[13] Women also may be less interested in running for office because they see political office as incompatible with their other career goals.[14] Finally, running for office in the United States is expensive and is largely limited to economic elites who have the resources necessary to run for office.[15] These factors shape who considers themselves potential political candidates, or who hold nascent political ambition.

Looking at the demographics of women in Louisiana suggests a small potential supply of women candidates. Women in Louisiana routinely fall at the bottom of state-level rankings of women's economic power, education levels, and socioeconomic status. For example, 56 percent of women participate in the labor force, and 38 percent of women hold managerial or professional occupations; these rates place Louisiana in fortieth and thirty-eighth place in the nation, respectively.[16] Yet, the status of women in the state has improved over the last decade: more women own businesses (36.5 percent, up from 23.9 percent in 2004), have health insurance (86.8 percent, up from 74.2 percent in 2004), and have bachelor's degrees (24.6 percent, up from 18.2 percent in 2004). Women's increased education, business ownership, and benefits would suggest that a greater share of women would be economically positioned to run for office if they should choose to do so.

DEMAND FOR WOMEN TO RUN FOR OFFICE

A second set of explanations focus on whether there is *demand*—from political parties, elites, and voters—for women to run for and hold political office.[17] In essence, women do not run because parties will not recruit them, because donors do not give them money, and because voters discriminate against them.[18] The dominance of political parties in shaping voter choices in the United States[19] is particularly important here: women are much more likely to be candidates in the Democratic Party, and research suggests that Democratic voters are more interested in supporting women in their party.[20] In this context, national patterns show an increase in the total number of women (and women of color) who run under the Democratic ticket and decreasing numbers of women running in the Republican Party.[21] In 2020, State Senator Karen Carter Peterson stepped down as the chair of the Louisiana Democratic Party, the first woman to hold this post, after serving eight years. She was succeeded by Katie Bernhardt in September 2020. Research indicates that having women serve as party chairs is critical to increasing the number of women in office.[22]

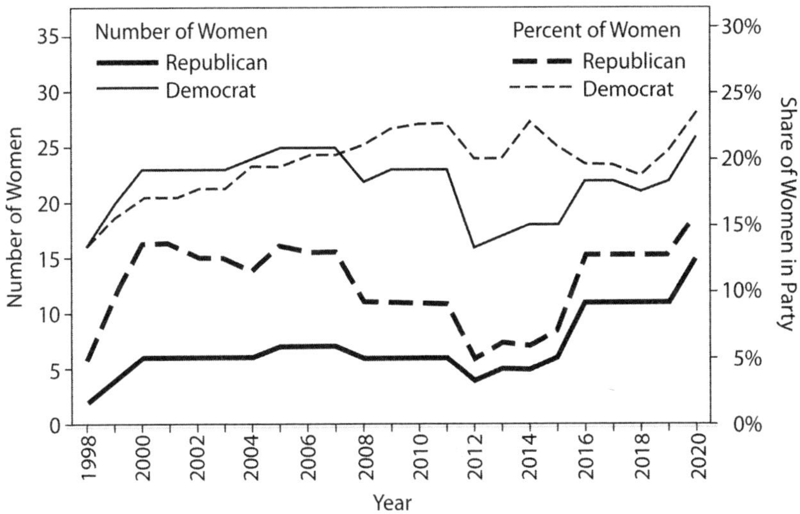

FIGURE 9.2. Women in the Democratic and Republican Parties in Louisiana.

How, then, does Louisiana do on recruitment and support of women candidates? To evaluate this question, we look at two factors: the political party representation of women in Louisiana politics and the role of organizations specifically aimed at increasing the number of women in politics.

Like in national trends, women who are active in Louisiana state politics, both running for and winning office in the state legislature, are much more likely to be members of the Democratic Party, a trend that has been consistent since 2000. Figure 9.2 provides the raw number of women in the Democratic Party (thin line) and the Republican Party (thick line) and the percent of women legislative representatives in the Democratic Party (thin dashed line) and the Republican Party (thick dashed line). While women legislative representatives are consistently more likely to be members of the Democratic Party (by a 2:1 ratio in most years), women's representation is increasing in both parties in recent elections, particularly as seen in the 2019 election.[23]

The state has undergone a major change in the last decade that has the potential to dramatically shift the number of women candidates: the institutionalization of a variety of programs specifically aimed at training women to run for office. Women's candidate training programs exist across the United

States (and around the world!), take many different forms, and represent an avenue for convincing women to run for office, supporting them in their attempts, and networking politically ambitious women with each other.[24] For example, in March of 2015, the Louisiana Legislative Women's Caucus sponsored Ready to Run, a bipartisan candidate training program.[25] The training includes helping women who are already ambitious and have identified the race they plan to enter[26] as well as those who are generally interested in politics but have not yet decided if they are going to run for office. Emerge Louisiana, a Democratic campaign training program launched in 2017 recruits cohorts who train together for a year in public speaking, voter outreach, fundraising, and more. These programs, the first in Louisiana's history, may provide an avenue to increasing women's political representation in the state.

CHILDCARE AND WOMEN RUNNING

A 2019 decision by the Louisiana Ethics Board to allow campaign funds to be used for childcare expenses associated with the candidate's campaign activities illustrates the challenges that women face running for office in the state and the changes that could help more women to run for office and win.[27] Changes like these are hard-fought. Initially, when Morgan Lamandre, a Baton Rouge state legislative candidate and Emerge Louisiana alumna, asked for permission from the Louisiana Ethics Board to use campaign funds for campaign-related childcare expenses, the board ruled that "The use of campaign funds to pay for child care expenses [a candidate] would incur as a result of your participation in campaign events and activities is not an allowable expenditure" (despite having allowed it for male candidates in the past).[28] In doing so, Peppi Bruneau, a male member of the board (and prior member of the Louisiana House of Representatives), told Lamandre, "You have children. It's your responsibility. It's your decision to make as to how to balance your priorities."[29] Advocacy by Lamandre and other concerned members of the community led to a successful appeal of the ruling.

The Louisiana Ethics Board ruling demonstrates that cultural issues in the state still stand as barriers to women running *and* that possible changes are underway. Antiquated gender role expectations still hold women back,[30] but this episode in Louisiana political history demonstrates that change is possible when people draw attention to disparities and demand redress. Further, candidate training programs may have effects far into the future, as alumna can network together to push for changes in the structures of campaigns and elections in Louisiana.

THE FUTURE FOR LOUISIANA WOMEN IN POLITICS

While women have not achieved parity in Louisiana politics, some structural shifts, including training programs and campaign rule reform, may lead to more women running for office and winning. Likewise, political contexts are rarely static, and changes are sometimes favorable to women candidates. A 2019 public opinion poll noted: "A majority of Louisiana residents wants to see their elected officials compromise, but few expect to actually see it."[31] Evidence suggests that women in office are more likely to compromise and work across political divides.[32] Particularly in an environment where the governor is a Democrat and Republicans control the state legislature, electing more women to office may help the state overcome its increasing partisanship and accomplish more for its citizens.

Race as well as gender shapes Louisiana politics, with sometimes confounding results. For example, Senator Katrina Jackson, from the Monroe area, has long been an outspoken opponent of abortion despite belonging to the Democratic Party. Other Black women Democrats, including Mayor-President Sharon Weston Broome and Senator Regina Barrow, share Jackson's anti-abortion stance. Their positions reflect the conservative state culture around women's autonomy. Despite this conservatism, these same women supported the expansion of Medicaid, criminal justice reform, and other traditionally liberal policy positions. Their careers remind us to question monolithic political identity categories.[33]

The issues that are most important to Louisiana voters (education, transportation infrastructure, and economy) are among those where women have important contributions to make.[34] The lived experience they bring to governing is vital for representation for all Louisiana residents. Research suggests that diverse bodies come to better decisions, so a more diverse legislature may come up with more creative solutions to the many pressing problems the state faces.[35] In fact, a majority of state residents lack confidence in state government.[36] Women in office are more successful in achieving their policy goals, meaning more women in office could increase the public's satisfaction and confidence in its governing institutions.[37]

Despite the small number of women in Louisiana's political history, they have made a significant impact on citizens' lives. Women with credit cards and bank loans have Representative Lindy Boggs to thank for the Equal Credit Opportunity Act of 1974. Following Hurricane Katrina, Senator Mary Landrieu worked to secure a $250 billion aid package for the state. More recently, Helena Moreno worked tirelessly in the state legislature for equal pay measures, and when thwarted in that venue she brought the fight to the New Orleans City Council, where she has been successful in implementing a salary history ban for public employees. Women like Representative Julie Stokes and Senator Karen Carter Peterson have spoken out against gender bias within the state legislature, fighting for a better work environment for the women who will serve in years to come.[38]

Despite a long history of women's exclusion from public office in Louisiana, women have contributed to the state economically, socially, and politically since its inception. In this essay we have identified the many structural challenges women face in achieving public office. These challenges include gender expectations for household responsibilities and disparities in economic power and social capital. To overcome these institutional barriers, women have worked together to challenge antiquated gender norms and change electoral rules. Organizations have stepped up to recruit and train women candidates, leading to record numbers in 2019. In particular, women have been successful at the local level serving on city councils and as mayors throughout the state. Black women's political history in Louisiana is important, complicated, and a potential source of future statewide or federal candidates. The road to parity in elective office will require interventions in the status quo, and Louisiana women are poised to meet that challenge.

NOTES

1. Louisiana, like many southern states, commonly appears among the bottom ten states for women's presence in state legislatures. Other states, like Alabama and Mississippi, also have not broken the 20 percent barrier.

2. The dip in women's representation may be due to the introduction of term limits, the economic recession, or part of national trends of stagnation in women's representation. Susan J. Carroll and Krista Jenkins, "Unrealized Opportunity? Term Limits and the Representation of Women in State Legislatures," *Women and Politics* 23, no. 4 (September 1, 2001): 1–30.

3. Center for American Women and Politics (CAWP), "State Fact Sheet—Louisiana," CAWP, 2020, https://www.cawp.rutgers.edu/state_fact_sheets/la.

4. Ibid.

5. Ibid.

6. Thomas H. Ferrell and Judith Haydel, "Hale and Lindy Boggs: Louisiana's National Democrats," *Louisiana History: The Journal of the Louisiana Historical Association* 35, no. 4 (1994): 389–402.

7. Ashley Cusick, "As New Orleans Mayor Is Sworn in Monday, La. Has Three Black Women Leading Its Largest Cities," *Washington Post,* May 8, 2020, https://www.washingtonpost.com/national/as-new-orleans-mayor-is-sworn-in-monday-la-has-three-black-women-leading-its-largest-cities/2018/05/06/6a80bcbe-4fd8-11e8-84a0-458a1aa9ac0a_story.html.

8. Mark Ballard, "Record Number of Women Running for the Louisiana Legislature," *The Advocate,* August 9, 2019, https://www.theadvocate.com/baton_rouge/news/politics/elections/article_5f3be6dc-bb05-11e9-b1bb-ff98f7476156.html.

9. More than half of those candidates were Democrats, which speaks to the infrastructure within that party of more training programs and recruitment efforts specifically targeted to women.

10. Jennie Sweet-Cushman and Rebecca Gill, "Nevada Bets on Women's Political Leadership: An Examination of the First-Ever Majority Women State Legislature" (working paper, 2020).

11. Melody Crowder-Meyer, "Gendered Recruitment without Trying: How Local Party Recruiters Affect Women's Representation," *Politics & Gender* 9, no. 4 (2013): 390–413; Mirya R. Holman and Monica C. Schneider, "Gender, Race, and Political Ambition," *Politics, Groups, and Identities* 6, no. 2 (April 3, 2018): 264–280; Andrea Silva and Carrie Skulley, "Always Running: Candidate Emergence among Women of Color over Time," *Political Research Quarterly* 72, no. 2 (2019): 342–359; Mia Costa, "He Said, She Said: The Gender Double Bind in Legislator-Constituent Communication," *Politics & Gender* OnlineFirst (2020): 1–24; Elizabeth N. Simas, "But Can She Make America Great Again? Threat, Stability, and Support for Female Candidates in the United States," *Political Behavior,* April 3, 2020.

12. Shauna L. Shames, *Out of the Running: Why Millennials Reject Political Careers and Why It Matters* (New York: New York Univ. Press, 2017); Monica C. Schneider et al., "Power, Conflict, and Community: How Gendered Views of Political Power Influence Women's Political

Ambition," *Political Psychology* 37, no. 4 (2016): 515–531; Rachel Bernhard, Shauna Shames, and Dawn Langan Teele, "To Emerge? Breadwinning, Motherhood, and Women's Decisions to Run for Office," *American Political Science Review* 115, no. 2 (May 2021): 379–394; Melody Crowder-Meyer, "Baker, Bus Driver, Babysitter, Candidate? Revealing the Gendered Development of Political Ambition among Ordinary Americans," *Political Behavior* 42, no. 2 (2020): 359–384; Rachel Bernhard et al., "Beyond Ambition," *Politics, Groups, and Identities* 7, no. 4 (October 13, 2019): 815–816.

13. Crowder-Meyer, "Baker, Bus Driver, Babysitter, Candidate?"; Bernhard, Teele, and Shames, "Breadwinner Moms"; Rachel Silbermann, "Gender Roles, Work-Life Balance, and Running for Office," *Quarterly Journal of Political Science* 10, no. 2 (2015): 123–153.

14. Schneider et al., "Power, Conflict, and Community"; Holman and Schneider, "Gender, Race, and Political Ambition."

15. Tiffany D. Barnes, Victoria Beall, and Mirya R. Holman, "Pink Collar Representation and Policy Outcomes in U.S. States," *Legislative Studies Quarterly* 46, no. 1 (2021): 119–152; Tiffany D. Barnes and Gregory W. Saxton, "Working-Class Legislators and Perceptions of Representation in Latin America," *Political Research Quarterly* 72, no. 4 (February 15, 2019): 910–928.

16. International Women's Policy Research, "Status of Women in the States: Louisiana Factsheet" (Washington, D.C.: International Women's Policy Research, 2020), https://statusofwomen data.org/wp-content/themes/witsfull/factsheets/economics/factsheet-louisiana.pdf.

17. Mirya R. Holman, Jennifer L. Merolla, and Elizabeth J. Zechmeister, "Can Experience Overcome Stereotypes in Times of Terror Threat?," *Research & Politics* 4, no. 1 (January 1, 2017): 1–7; Crowder-Meyer, "Gendered Recruitment without Trying"; Nichole M. Bauer, "Untangling the Relationship between Partisanship, Gender Stereotypes, and Support for Female Candidates," *Journal of Women, Politics & Policy* 39, no. 1 (January 2, 2018): 1–25; Bernhard et al., "Beyond Ambition."

18. Melody Crowder-Meyer and Rosalyn Cooperman, "How Party Culture among Donors Contributes to the Party Gap in Women's Representation," *Journal of Politics* 80, no. 4 (2018): 1211–1224; Mirya R. Holman et al., "Terrorism, Gender, and the 2016 U.S. Presidential Election," *Electoral Studies* 61 (2019): 1–8; Nichole M. Bauer, "Running Local: Gender Stereotyping and Female Candidates in Local Elections," *Urban Affairs Review* 56, no. 1 (April 30, 2018): 96–123; Rachel Bernhard and Sarah F. Anzia, "Does Gender Stereotyping Affect Women at the Ballot Box? New Evidence from Local Elections in California" (paper presented at the American Political Science Association, August 31–September 3, 2017).

19. Heather L. Ondercin, "Is It a Chasm? Is It a Canyon? No, It Is the Gender Gap," *The Forum* 16, no. 4 (2018): 633–651; Heather L. Ondercin and Jeffrey L. Bernstein, "Context Matters: The Influence of State and Campaign Factors on the Gender Gap in Senate Elections, 1988–2000," *Politics & Gender* 3, no. 1 (March 2007): 33–53; Lilliana Mason, *Uncivil Agreement: How Politics Became Our Identity* (Chicago: Univ. of Chicago Press, 2018); Nathan P. Kalmoe and Kimberly Gross, "Cueing Patriotism, Prejudice, and Partisanship in the Age of Obama: Experimental Tests of US Flag Imagery Effects in Presidential Elections," *Political Psychology* 37, no. 6 (2016): 883–899.

20. Sarah A. Fulton and Kostanca Dhima, "The Gendered Politics of Congressional Elections," *Political Behavior,* March 26, 2020; Tracy Osborn, "Women State Legislators and Representation: The Role of Political Parties and Institutions," *State and Local Government Review* 46, no. 2 (June 1, 2014): 146–155.

21. Fulton and Dhima, "The Gendered Politics of Congressional Elections"; Nichole M. Bauer, "The Effects of Counterstereotypic Gender Strategies on Candidate Evaluations," *Political Psychology* 38, no. 2 (2017): 279–295; Nichole M. Bauer and Colleen M. Carpinella, "Visual Information and Candidate Evaluations: The Influence of Feminine and Masculine Images on Support for Female Candidates," *Political Research Quarterly* 71, no. 2 (2018): 395–407.

22. Susan J. Carroll and Kira Sanbonmatsu, *More Women Can Run: Gender and Pathways to the State Legislatures* (New York: Oxford Univ. Press, 2016); Kira Sanbonmatsu, *Where Women Run: Gender and Party in the American States* (Ann Arbor: Univ. of Michigan Press, 2006).

23. Women's representation data are from the Center for American Women in Politics; party seat data are from the National Conference of State Legislatures. CAWP, "State Fact Sheet—Louisiana"; National Conference of State Legislatures, "State Partisan Composition" (Washington, D.C.: National Conference of State Legislatures, 2020), https://www.ncsl.org/research/about-state-legislatures/partisan-composition.aspx.

24. Rebecca Kreitzer and Tracy Osborn, "The Emergence and Activities of Women's Recruiting Groups in the U.S." *Politics, Groups, and Identities* 7, no. 4 (2019): 842–852.

25. This program was created by the Center for American Women and Politics and is franchised in 24 states plus Puerto Rico.

26. This part of the training includes meeting pollsters, information on managing a campaign, understanding electoral law, and working with the media.

27. Julia O'Donoghue, "Campaign Funds Can Be Used for Child Care, Louisiana Ethics Board Rules in Reversal," *Times-Picayune,* February 16, 2019, https://www.nola.com/news/article_02e68e13-568a-50cd-a21b-ff85581fa108.html.

28. Elizabeth Crisp, "Louisiana Ethics Board: Campaign Funds Can't Cover Candidates' Child Care Costs," *The Advocate,* November 19, 2018, https://www.theadvocate.com/baton_rouge/news/politics/article_f158a2dc-ec46-11e8-b5ae-632d2ef013a2.html.

29. Julia O'Donoghue, "Campaign Money Can't Be Used for Child Care, Louisiana Ethics Board Rules," *Times-Picayune,* November 21, 2018, https://www.nola.com/news/article_7bb4324a-bb51-5390-9208-d5ceb9bea3b6.html.

30. Monica C. Schneider and Angela L. Bos, "The Application of Social Role Theory to the Study of Gender in Politics," *Political Psychology* 40, no. S1 (2019): 173–213; Erin C. Cassese and Mirya R. Holman, "Religion, Gendered Authority, and Identity in American Politics," *Politics and Religion* 10, no. 1 (2017): 31–56.

31. *The Louisiana Survey 2019,* Louisiana State University Reilly Center for Media and Public Affairs, https://pprllsu.com/wp-content/uploads/2019/05/Louisiana-Survey-2019-Report-Full-Final.pdf.

32. Anna Mitchell Mahoney, *Women Take Their Place in State Legislatures: The Creation of Women's Caucuses* (Philadelphia: Temple Univ. Press, 2018); Mirya R. Holman and Anna Mitch-

ell Mahoney, "Stop, Collaborate, and Listen: Women's Collaboration in US State Legislatures," *Legislative Studies Quarterly* 43, no. 2 (2018): 179–206, 9; Mirya R. Holman and Anna Mitchell Mahoney, "The Choice Is Yours: Caucus Typologies and Collaboration in U.S. State Legislatures," *Representation* 55, no. 1 (2019): 47–63; Tracy Osborn, *How Women Represent Women: Political Parties, Gender and Representation in the State Legislatures* (New York: Oxford Univ. Press, 2012).

33. Melissa Victoria Harris-Lacewell, *Barbershops, Bibles and BET: Everyday Talk and Black Political Thought* (Princeton, N.J.: Princeton Univ. Press, 2004); Katherine Tate, *What's Going On?: Political Incorporation and the Transformation of Black Public Opinion* (Washington, D.C.: Georgetown Univ. Press, 2010); Nadia Brown, *Sisters in the Statehouse: Black Women and Legislative Decision Making* (Oxford: Oxford Univ. Press, 2014).

34. *The Louisiana Survey 2019;* Mirya R. Holman, *Women in Politics in the American City* (Philadelphia: Temple Univ. Press, 2015); Bauer, "The Effects of Counterstereotypic Gender Strategies on Candidate Evaluations."

35. Tiffany D. Barnes, *Gendering Legislative Behavior: Institutional Constraints and Collaboration in Argentina* (New York: Cambridge Univ. Press, 2016); Barnes, Beall, and Holman, "Pink Collar Representation and Policy Outcomes in U.S. States."

36. *The Louisiana Survey 2019.*

37. Sarah Anzia and Christopher R. Berry, "The Jackie (and Jill) Robinson Effect: Why Do Congresswomen Outperform Congressmen?," *American Journal of Political Science* 55, no. 3 (2011): 478–493; Craig Volden, Alan E. Wiseman, and Dana E. Wittmer, "When Are Women More Effective Lawmakers Than Men?," *American Journal of Political Science* 57, no. 2 (2013): 326–341; Jeffrey Lazarus and Amy Steigerwalt, *Gendered Vulnerability* (Ann Arbor: Univ. of Michigan Press, 2018); Danielle M. Thomsen and Bailey K. Sanders, "Gender Differences in Legislator Responsiveness," *Perspectives on Politics* (2019): 1–14; Kenneth Lowande, Melinda Ritchie, and Erinn Lauterbach, "Descriptive and Substantive Representation in Congress: Evidence from 80,000 Congressional Inquiries," *American Journal of Political Science* 63, no. 3 (2019): 644–659.

38. "Bill to Raise Stripper Age Passes, after Outrage over Joke," wltv.com, May 18, 2016, https://www.wwltv.com/article/mb/news/local/bill-to-raise-stripper-age-passes-after-outrage-over-joke/202335653; Anna Mahoney, Meghan Kearney, and Carly Shaffer, "#MeToo in the Statehouse," in *Politicking While Female*, ed. Nichole Bauer (Baton Rouge: Louisiana State Univ. Press, 2020).

PART III

POLICY

THE ECONOMY OF LOUISIANA

GARY WAGNER AND
STEPHEN BARNES

Louisiana's economic and political systems are inherently connected. Important economic sectors support state and local tax revenues but can also wield influence to determine the laws and regulations that shape those industries and the state's long-term economic growth trajectory. Louisiana's economy has been heavily shaped by the state's natural resources, including oil and gas, agriculture, and its unique position at the mouth of the Mississippi River. Against a backdrop of increasing globalization and ever-greater integration of technology across the economy, Louisiana has made some progress to diversify and modernize but remains concentrated on industries with a long history in the state, which leaves it vulnerable to certain types of disruptions. This essay provides a brief overview of the Louisiana economy, with a focus on industries, events, and trends that helped define the state's economy today and will undoubtedly influence it for many years to come.

Most economic data are generally grouped into broad categories representing related activities called sectors or industries. This essay looks at how much of the state's economy was generated from these different sectors in the past and how this compared to the United States as a whole. This will illustrate the differences and similarities we share with the nation as well as how Louisiana's economic activity has evolved in the past half-century. Analyzing the unique combination of ingredients in Louisiana's economic gumbo provides context for thinking about how the economy has shaped politics and the public sector in Louisiana as well as how the political system can influence the state's future against a backdrop of broad economic trends.

* * *

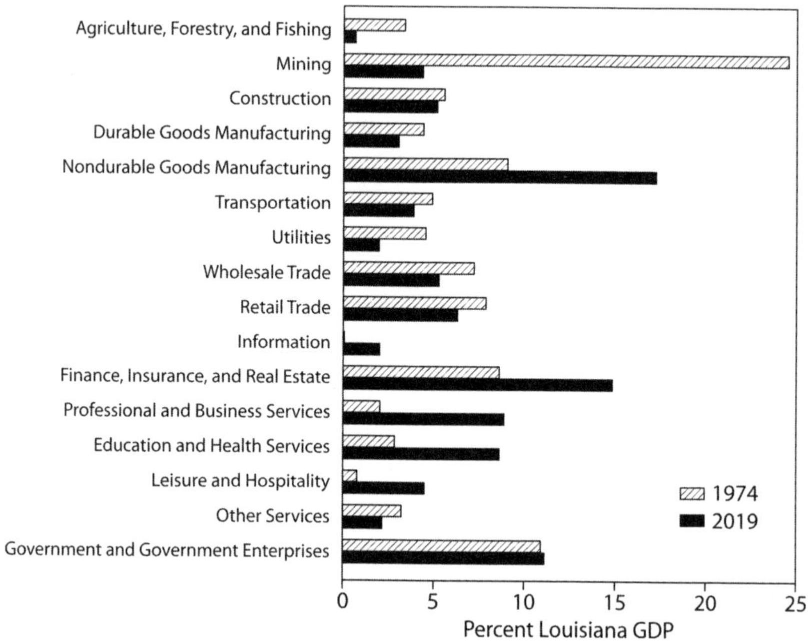

FIGURE 10.1. Louisiana Industry Mix, 1974 and 2019.

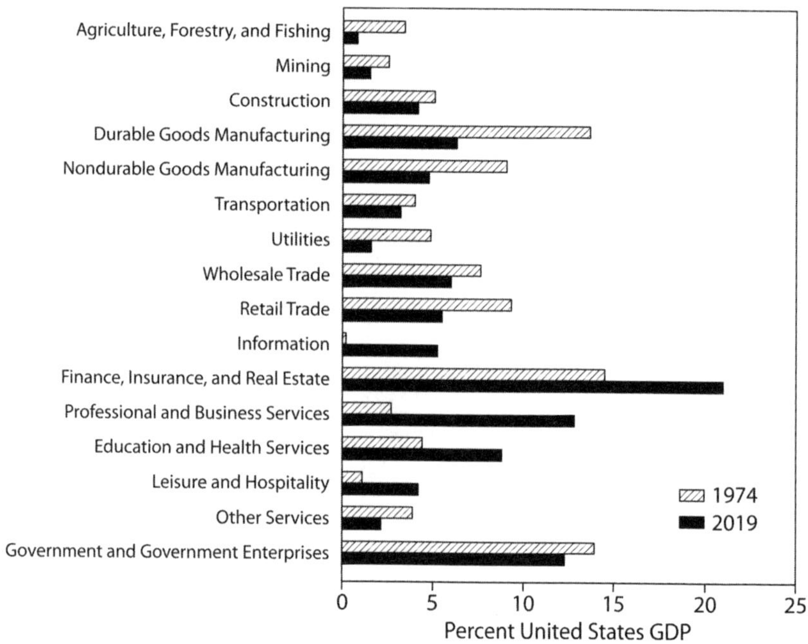

FIGURE 10.2. US Industry Mix, 1974 and 2019.

AN OVERVIEW OF LOUISIANA'S ECONOMY

Louisiana's economy is similar in many ways to that of other US states and market-based economies around the world, but it also is unique in several important ways. Figures 10.1 and 10.2 show the mix of goods and services produced in 1974 and 2019 within Louisiana and the United States, respectively.[1] These charts summarize the contribution of each sector to the economy based on Gross Domestic Product (GDP), which measures the total value of goods produced and services provided in a year. In 1974, Louisiana's total GDP amounted to just under $27 billion, which was just under 2 percent of the nearly $1.5 trillion national economy. The economies of both Louisiana and the nation have grown considerably over time; Louisiana now produces more than $263 billion worth of goods and services annually, a nearly ten-fold increase over the last forty-five years, while the US economy produces more than $21 trillion worth of goods and services annually in the United States, or nearly fifteen times the GDP in 1974.

Across many major sectors, such as agriculture, construction, transportation, and most services, the goods and services produced in Louisiana follow a similar pattern to those produced nationally. To illustrate how data presented in figures 10.1 and 10.2 should be interpreted, consider agricultural activity, which is shown to have accounted for approximately 3.4 percent of GDP in 1974 for both the United States and Louisiana, though the sector has dropped in relative importance to now represent only 0.8 percent of US GDP and 0.7 percent of Louisiana GDP. In other words, the United States and Louisiana economies had a similar focus on agriculture in 1974, but by 2019 that had declined significantly and was slightly less important in Louisiana relative to the United States. The sectors where Louisiana differs most from the nation—mining, manufacturing, and transportation—are what make the state's economy unique. The specific industries driving those differences include oil and gas, petroleum and chemical manufacturing, and pipeline and water transportation.

The most notable long-term difference between Louisiana's economy and that of the rest of the nation is seen in the *mining* sector, which includes the oil and gas industry. In total, this sector accounted for only 2.5 percent of US economic activity in 1974. In Louisiana, where almost all mining relates to oil and gas extraction, the sector accounted for 24.6 percent of the state's economy, by far Louisiana's largest sector at the time. That figure indicates that roughly one of every four dollars in Louisiana's economy was *directly related* to oil and gas extraction. We use the term *directly related* because economic activity in one industry or sector can spill over into other sectors as well, a phenomenon known as the multiplier effect. For example, oil and gas firms in Louisiana invest and expand in the state by purchasing equipment, machinery, or other technical expertise from other industries, so these investments spill over and create new economic activity in other industries. In the case of Louisiana's oil and gas industry, the Census Bureau has estimated that every $1.00 invested in the industry increases state GDP by roughly $1.60.[2] In the 1970s, this meant that Louisiana's oil and gas industry was likely responsible—directly and indirectly—for approximately 40 percent of the state's overall economy! Over time the importance of this sector has faded, and it represented less than 5 percent of Louisiana's economy in 2019.

The long history of oil and gas in the state has also influenced the mix of manufacturing activities. This long-term influence has led to a greater focus on petroleum refining and chemical manufacturing (which further process oil and gas) and the pipeline, machinery, and fabricated metal products manufacturing that provide supplies to oil and gas extraction. Overall, Louisiana's economy was much less dependent on manufacturing than was the United States' in 1974 (13.5 percent in Louisiana's economy compared to 22.7 percent in the United States). But Louisiana's manufacturing sector has seen a renaissance in recent years, with manufacturing in Louisiana growing at a time when it has fallen as a share of the national economy.

This discrepancy is explained by differences between durable goods manufacturing, or products that have a life expectancy of at least three years, such as automobiles, and nondurable goods manufacturing, or products that have a shorter life expectancy, such as paper products and chemicals. Manufacturing activity in the nation has been more focused on durable goods (13.6 percent of the economy versus 9.0 percent for nondurables in 1974), whereas manufacturing in Louisiana was much more heavily skewed toward nondurable goods (9.1 percent of the economy versus 4.5 percent for durables in 1974). Of these nondurable goods, Louisiana's economy is roughly three times more dependent on petroleum refining and chemical manufacturing than the United States. For example, chemical manufacturing accounted for only 1.8 percent of US GDP in 1974 but more than twice as much (4.1 percent of statewide GDP) in Louisiana. While industry-specific data for 2019 are not yet available, data from 2017 show that petroleum refining and chemical manufacturing made up only 2.5 percent of US GDP compared to 13.2 percent of Louisiana GDP.

While GDP provides a useful benchmark for quickly assessing the contribution of different sectors to the economy, it is worth noting that other measures of economic activity, such as jobs and income tied to each sector, are also important and should be considered to develop a more complete understanding of the economy. For example, these high-value sectors tend to pay relatively high wages but have become more capital intensive over time, with increasingly advanced technology enabling companies to produce more value added (or GDP) with fewer workers. Average annual salaries for the men and women employed in the oil and gas sector were (and remain) among the highest in the state. As table 10.1 shows, salaries averaged $11,333 in the mining sector in 1974 (the equivalent to almost $60,000 today) and were nearly 70 percent higher than the average annual salary in the state at the time. Several other key sectors also paid annual salaries well above the state norm, including nondurable manufacturing, which averaged more than $10,590 ($55,000 today). While these industries continue to pay relatively high wages, the number of jobs supported by some of these high-value industries has declined over time. For example, 10 percent of workers were employed in mining and nondurable manufacturing in 1974, but that has dropped to 5 percent of statewide employment in recent years.

As stated earlier, the nature of economic activity changes over time for a variety of reasons, including long-term changes in the tastes of consumers, technological innovations that disrupt markets by introducing new products and new production methods, and short-term shocks including natural disasters, like hurricanes and recessions. The national economy has shifted away from manufacturing and toward services. In particular, information; finance, insurance, and real estate; and professional and business services have

TABLE 10.1. Employment and Earnings by Sector, 1974 and 2019

	1974			*2019*		
	Employment	*Total Wages & Salaries*	*Average Wage & Salary*	*Employment**	*Total Wages & Salaries*	*Average Wage & Salary*
All-industry total	1,598,024	$10,795,628	$6,756	2,733,239	$104,343,254	$38,176
Agriculture, forestry, and fishing	76,910	$107,764	$1,401	50,817	$486,069	$9,565
Mining	61,368	$695,461	$11,333	62,571	$3,557,860	$56,861
Construction	111,452	$969,335	$8,697	212,255	$9,546,993	$44,979
Durable goods manufacturing	85,657	$803,659	$9,382	69,952	$4,326,569	$61,851
Nondurable goods manufacturing	104,523	$1,106,852	$10,590	76,447	$6,669,909	$87,249
Transportation and warehousing	74,508	$718,713	$9,646	123,547	$4,914,046	$39,775
Utilities	15,519	$165,140	$10,641	9,087	$833,374	$91,711
Wholesale trade	81,951	$786,347	$9,595	75,408	$4,792,913	$63,560
Retail trade	240,812	$1,135,752	$4,716	275,971	$6,810,205	$24,677
Information	22,133	$211,416	$9,552	29,944	$1,421,371	$47,468
Financial activities	95,210	$485,107	$5,095	231,887	$6,003,836	$25,891
Professional and business services	49,248	$247,976	$5,035	334,125	$12,883,274	$38,558
Education and health services	79,555	$460,416	$5,787	374,619	$15,001,141	$40,044
Leisure and hospitality	27,032	$111,602	$4,129	284,899	$5,980,484	$20,992
Other services	166,663	$581,855	$3,491	165,747	$3,644,454	$21,988
Government and government enterprises	305,483	$2,208,233	$7,229	355,963	$17,470,756	$49,080

Source: Bureau of Economic Analysis.

* Employment data are for 2018. Data for 2019 were not available until September 2020.

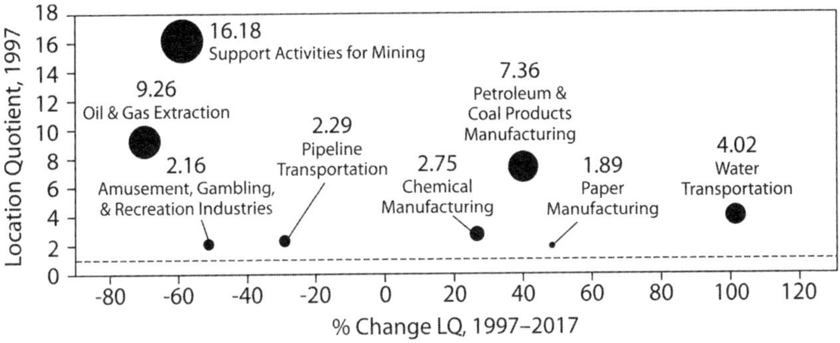

FIGURE 10.3. Industry Clusters in Louisiana: Change in Concentration, 1997–2017.

grown rapidly over the last forty-five years. While Louisiana has seen some growth in these areas, these sectors continue to be undersized. To show which industries have been gaining or shrinking in significance in the past generation, we calculate location quotients of specific industries using more detailed economic data available from the Bureau of Labor Statistics and examine how they have changed over time.[3] This information is shown in figure 10.3.

Figure 10.3 plots all of the industries in Louisiana with location quotients of 1.75 or higher in 1997 (along the y-axis) against the percentage change in its location quotient between 1997 and 2017 (along the x-axis).[4] The points are labeled with the 1997 location quotient, so we know the key drivers of the state's economy from twenty-five years ago. For example, pipeline transportation had a location quotient of 2.29 in 1997, so the industry was 2.3 times more concentrated in Louisiana than in the nation. The right quadrant of figure 10.3 shows the key industries in the state that have *expanded in importance* in the past twenty-five years, while the left quadrant shows the key industries that have *contracted in importance.*

The state's two most concentrated industries in 1997, oil and gas extraction and related support industries, both declined sharply in their relative importance to the state in the past twenty-five years. Oil and gas extraction had a location quotient of 9.26 in 1997, but its relative importance has dropped by 70 percent since that time. In contrast, the importance of industries such as chemical manufacturing, petroleum manufacturing, and water transportation has grown considerably in the past quarter-century. We will take

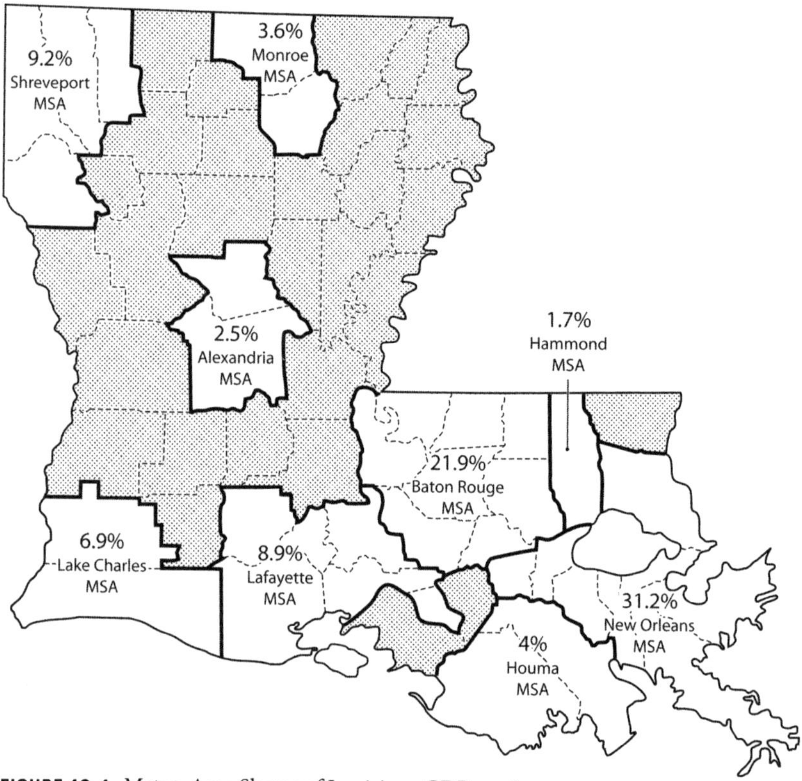

FIGURE 10.4. Metro-Area Shares of Louisiana GDP, 2018.

a closer look at the changing mix of economic drivers for the state later in the essay.

Although the focus to this point has been on major changes at the *statewide* level, it is helpful to keep in mind that the size and composition of economic activity in Louisiana also differs across different regions of the state. Figure 10.4 shows the share of statewide GDP that is generated within each of the state's nine metropolitan statistical areas (MSAs).[5] MSAs are often the most useful level of geography for exploring economic activity below the statewide level because they capture the geographic area where people who work in the region also generally live. The largest region in the state from an economic perspective is the New Orleans MSA. Economic activity in this eight-parish region accounts for roughly one-third of the value of goods and services produced in the state. After adding the Baton Rouge metro area, these two MSAs account for more than half of Louisiana's GDP. Shreveport–Bossier City and Lafayette are the next largest metro areas, accounting for 9.2 percent and 8.9 percent of state production, respectively. The next largest MSA is Lake Charles, which represents 6.2 percent of statewide GDP, but has grown rapidly in recent years thanks to a boom in industrial construction and expansion of chemical manufacturing in the area. In fact, Lake Charles was the fastest-growing MSA in the nation in 2016 and the third fastest in 2015.[6] The nine metro areas in the state, which encompass a total of thirty-five parishes, accounts for more than 90 percent of the value of goods and services produced within Louisiana.

In addition to variation in how much economic activity is concentrated in different parts the state, there is also wide variation in the type of activity that dominates local landscapes. For example, the hospitality and tourism sector in New Orleans is world-renowned and remains the major driver for the region. Tourism spending supports hotels, restaurants, and bars, but also a broader mix of retail spending and consumer services. Because many of these activities overlap with spending by residents, it is difficult to isolate the effects of tourism, but a location quotient for sectors important to tourism suggests that New Orleans has roughly twice as much economic activity in these sectors as would be expected for a city its size. New Orleans also has a strong education cluster, due to its above average concentration of colleges and universities, and a growing health care sector supported by the area's universities and a large Veterans Affairs hospital.

While the oil and gas industry has declined in relative importance nationally and in Louisiana in the past half-century, what remains in the state is concentrated in the Shreveport, Houma, and Lafayette MSAs. Relative to the United States, oil and gas location quotients for these areas are 17.25 (Shreveport), 10.45 (Houma), and 8.38 (Lafayette). The Houma and Lafayette regions primarily service rigs in the Gulf of Mexico, while Shreveport's focus is development of the Haynesville Shale play, supported by advances in fracking technology. These metro areas also have other important economic drivers, ranging from cybersecurity activities associated with Barksdale Air Force Base (Shreveport), water transportation (Houma), and blossoming health care and information technology firms (Lafayette). The Lake Charles and Baton Rouge metro areas are the bases of the state's refining and chemical manufacturing industries, discussed in more detail later in the essay.

The northern and central portions of Louisiana are home to the state's agricultural and forestry sectors. Both Alexandria and Monroe include notable activities in forestry and wood products manufacturing and have location quotients in this industry of 1.4 (Alexandria) and 3.2 (Monroe). These two regions also have the highest concentration of utilities-related activity in the state (location quotients above 2), with Cleco Power's Brame Energy Center driving Alexandria's activity and CenturyLink creating an outsized high-tech and communications presence in Monroe.

A CLOSER LOOK AT DECLINING INDUSTRIES: OIL AND GAS, AGRICULTURE

As noted previously, some of the state's major economic drivers have shifted since the 1970s. We use the term "declining industry" to indicate that, while economic activity in each industry may still be an important component of the state's economy, the industry's *relative* impact has decreased over time. The oil and gas sector and agricultural sector are two prime examples.

While nearly 40 percent of the state's overall economy was either directly or indirectly related to the oil and gas industry in the 1970s, in 2017 that figure stood at 4.3 percent (2.7 percent direct impact). Of course, the broad base of petroleum refining and chemical manufacturing that rely on oil and gas inputs benefit from local production, but with the vast array of pipelines across the state and access to global supplies via the state's port network and the Mississippi River, those industries are less dependent on local production today than was the case in the early years of development and expansion for those related sectors. One way to see the declining relative importance of the industry is to look at changes in direct industry employment over time. Figure 10.5 shows the number of direct oil and gas jobs in the state since 1975 alongside the price of oil.[7] The price of oil per barrel is measured on the left y-axis, and the number of industry jobs (in thousands) is measured on the right y-axis.

As the (annual average) in oil prices increased from $7.67 a barrel in 1975

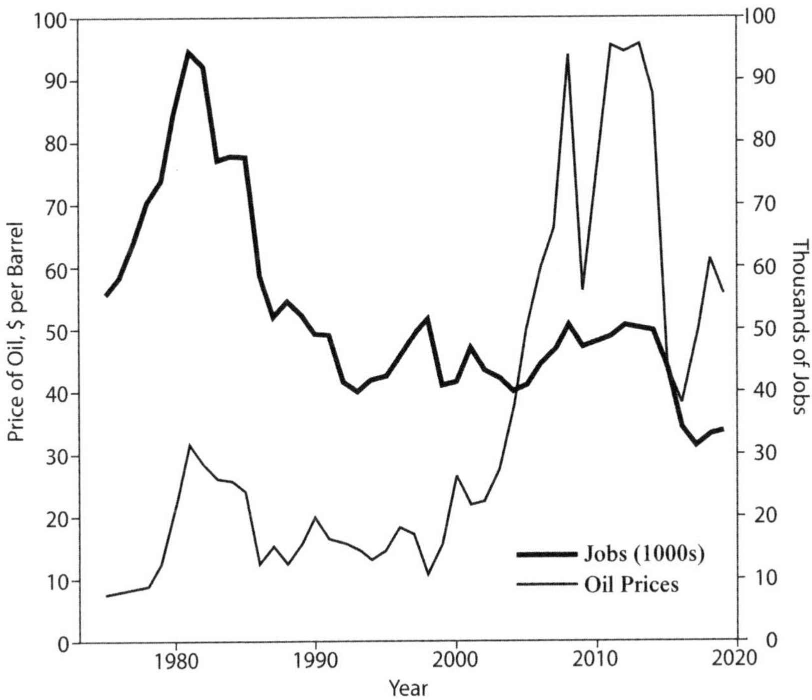

FIGURE 10.5. Oil Prices and Oil and Gas Jobs in Louisiana, 1975–2019.

to more than $31 a barrel in 1981 (an increase of 315 percent), oil and gas jobs in the state increased in lockstep with oil prices. By 1981, almost ninety-five thousand men and women in the state were directly employed in the industry (an increase of 70 percent since 1975). When oil prices collapsed in 1986, falling from an annual average price per barrel of $24 dollars in 1985 to just $12 per barrel, oil and gas employment fell 25 percent in 1986 and another 12 percent in 1987. This event precipitated the worst recession the state had experienced in generations, as unemployment ballooned to more than 13 percent in Louisiana. The difference between the breakeven price of oil (the per-barrel cost of extracting the oil) and the price at which it sells on the open market is what drives industry activity. If oil prices fall below the breakeven price, which is exactly what happened in 1986, it is no longer profitable for producers to extract oil, so they may shutter wells, lay off workers, and even file for bankruptcy. The producers that remain in business following price shocks are the firms that innovate, become more efficient, and lower their breakeven price points.

As oil prices stabilized, direct industry employment never returned to pre-1986 levels, but it did remain stable between forty thousand and fifty thousand workers from 1990 until 2014, as new horizontal drilling technology became the norm in the Gulf of Mexico. Rather than just drilling straight down from a single platform rig, horizontal drilling allows producers to boost the output from existing rig structures at a substantially lower cost than drilling a new directional well.

The most recent industry disruption began in the mid-2000s as hydraulic fracturing (otherwise known as fracking) became commonplace. The technique, which is aimed at extracting oil and natural gas from shale rock, had a much lower breakeven price than traditional extraction methods, and it had a profound influence on the industry and Louisiana. As figure 10.6 shows, the growth of fracking led to a situation in which the number of inland rigs exceeded the number of traditional offshore rigs in the state. Shreveport's oil and gas industry began to flourish, and Lafayette's and Houma's began to suffer. From 2005 to 2010, inland rigs increased by sixty while offshore rigs fell by forty-five. However, it should be noted that the level of economic activity tied to a rig varies considerably, with some land-based rigs requiring small investments and fewer workers and offshore development in the Gulf of Mexico sometimes requiring much larger investments and hundreds of workers to support a single rig. When oil prices fell sharply in 2014 (see figure 10.5), active rigs and employment dropped yet again. Industry employment statewide shrank by almost 40 percent between 2014 and 2017, and the total active rig count in the state fell below 50 for the first time in decades. Industry employment today is only one-third of the level it was in the 1980s. Moreover, Louisiana was home to roughly 20 percent of all active rigs in the nation in the 1980s (Texas had the largest share at around 30 percent). The recent disruptions from fracking and price shocks have reduced the state's share of all active rigs to around 5 percent, while Texas's share has grown to almost 50 percent.

The state's agricultural sector, which has long been a vital piece of the state's cultural identity, has also declined in relative economic importance over the years, following generally in line with broad economic trends. De-

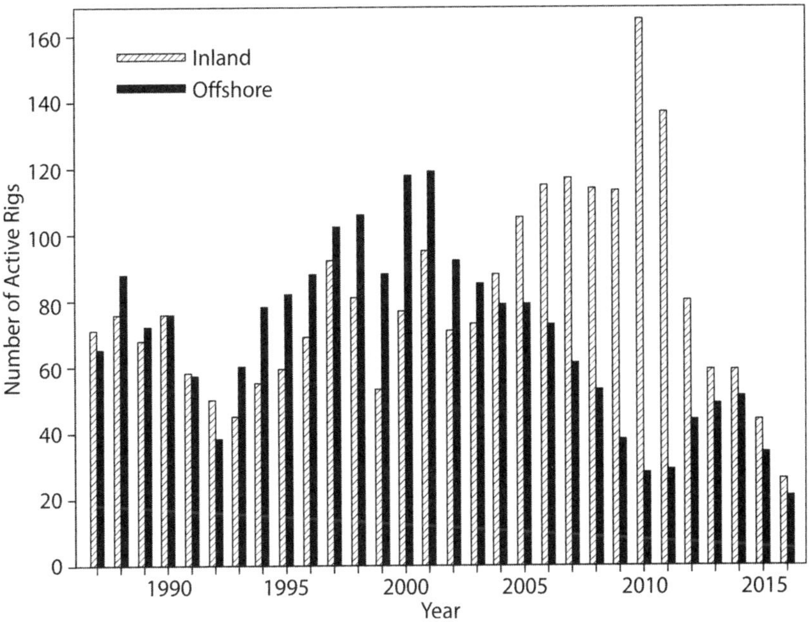

FIGURE 10.6. Inland and Offshore Rig Count in Louisiana, 1987–2016.

spite Louisiana always being one of the nation's top soybean, rice, and seafood producing states—if not *the* top seafood producing state for certain types of catch—the overall agricultural and fishing industry employment has declined from roughly sixty-five thousand people in the 1970s to around twenty thousand today. Of these twenty thousand people, upwards of fifteen thousand people are directly employed in commercial fishing. Much like oil and gas, mechanization and other productivity-enhancing advancements have permitted farms and fisheries in Louisiana and other states to generate the same or even greater output with fewer employees. The decline in agriculture has been both a driver of and a response to the long-run trend of migration to cities, where economic opportunities have grown more rapidly. While labor markets have adjusted to some extent, this broad trend has certainly left pockets of high unemployment and poverty in rural parts of the state. In terms of GDP, Louisiana's agricultural sector now accounts for less than 1 percent of the state's total output, which ranks the state around thirtieth in the nation.

A CLOSER LOOK AT EXPANDING INDUSTRIES: CHEMICAL MANUFACTURING, TRANSPORTATION, HEALTH SERVICES

Fortunately for Louisiana, some of the state's major economic drivers have performed well over time and helped to support an overall path of growth since the 1970s. Similar to the previous discussion on declining industries, "expanding industry" is used here to indicate that the relative importance has increased over time and it now serves as a source of growth and promise for the future. Chemical manufacturing, transportation, and health services are prime examples.

Louisiana's history in the oil and gas industry supported the development of one of the state's other large and rapidly growing sectors, chemical manufacturing. Louisiana currently has both the second largest refining capacity of any US state and is home to one of the largest refineries in the United States (ExxonMobil in Baton Rouge).[8] Aside from its own direct contribution to the economy, the petroleum refining industry produces distillates that provide a steady stream of inputs to another key industry, chemical manufacturing. As figure 10.3 demonstrated, Louisiana's strength in chemical manufacturing expanded considerably in the past twenty-five years as the state's skilled workforce and access to inputs (including regional production and an extensive pipeline network) gave it a distinct advantage in attracting additional investments to expand existing plants and build entirely new chemical manufacturing and liquified natural gas (LNG) export facilities.

The chemical manufacturing industry went through a major transformation in the late 1990s to early 2000s as global competition intensified and rising exchange rates made it increasingly difficult for domestic manufacturers to sell products on the global market. Companies reduced headcounts and shifted to a greater reliance on subcontractors to operate and maintain their facilities. More recently, however, the industry has experienced a renaissance as abundant, low-cost natural gas once again established a strong advantage for domestic producers, including Louisiana. Since 2010, capital investments in the state tied to low-cost and abundant natural gas, which is the primary feedstock of chemical manufacturing, are rapidly approaching the $100 billion mark. In addition to more traditional chemical manufacturing in the

Baton Rouge region, a wave of new LNG export facilities are being developed. As of March 2020, two facilities were operating in the Lake Charles area (Cheniere/Sabine Pass LNG and Sempra-Cameron LNG), four more facilities were under active construction, and five additional projects are approved but not yet under construction.[9] This investment has boosted overall employment in the Lake Charles MSA, and in the construction sector more specifically, to the point that year-over-year job gains in the region has ranked it among the top twenty-five metro areas in the nation on multiple occasions since 2011.

In addition to chemical manufacturing, the health care sector has grown rapidly across the US economy and in Louisiana, mirroring the general aging of the population. The sector accounted for around 2 percent of state gross domestic product in 1974 but has grown to approximately 8 percent today. The nature of health care work makes it very labor intensive, so the health and social assistance sector in Louisiana is the state's largest private sector employer, with almost 320,000 workers. To put these figures into context, the health care industry employs ten times as many people as the oil and gas industry and is now responsible for generating almost three times as much gross domestic product for the state. While health care is often thought of as a supporting industry, several clusters of specialized care within the state offer the potential to attract patients to Louisiana and support health and medical research, driving future economic growth.

The final sector that has grown considerably in relative importance in the state's economy is water transportation. Louisiana's early development was defined by unique access to water along the coast and most notably the Mississippi River. This sector includes passenger and cargo transportation from ships, barges, and boats. Occupations in the sector are not just limited to water vessel pilots and personnel, but also encompass cargo handlers, vessel repair and maintenance workers, and even ship engineers and designers. The industry is four times more concentrated in Louisiana than in the United States, and the relative importance of this sector to Louisiana's economy doubled over the past quarter-century (see figure 10.2).

The Port of South Louisiana is the largest tonnage port in the western hemisphere.[10] The Port of New Orleans remains one of the twenty largest ports in the nation in cargo tonnage, benefiting from rail connectivity to six of the seven major railroad operators in the United States (called Class I railroads). In addition to activity on the Mississippi River, the Lafayette and Houma metro areas contribute considerably to the state's water presence via their offshore support services connected to oil and gas production in the Gulf of Mexico. All in all, there are almost three hundred firms operating in this sector around the state to provide services to the state's more than thirty ports and other facilities.

A LOOK AHEAD

While Louisiana's history remains rooted in its proximity to the Mississippi River and the Gulf of Mexico, which has yielded both bountiful seafood and energy resources, the economic landscape of the state has changed markedly in the past half-century. The oil and gas industry no longer dominates the economy, as the shifts toward energy efficiency, alternative fuel sources, and other technological innovations have opened the door for new industries to grow in importance. These include water transportation, petrochemicals, and health care services. Each of these industries is well-positioned to capitalize on future growth opportunities. Beyond those industries that have demonstrated the strongest near-term growth opportunities based on the state's existing strengths, Louisiana should also look to expanding information and professional and business services. To make the most of Louisiana's long-term growth opportunity, the state will need to identify emerging trends and make strategic investments that can build on historic strengths to grow in new ways as it continues to adapt in a changing economic environment.

NOTES

1. Older economic data were typically classified by the Standard Industrial Classification (SIC) System, while more recent economic data are typically classified by the North American Industry Classification System (NAICS). To make comparisons over such a long period of time, SIC codes were grouped into the closest NAICS grouping, but the matches are not perfect and are used here only to illustrate broad patterns in the economy.

2. The US Bureau of Economic Analysis (BEA) generates multiplier estimates for more

than 360 industries down to a county or parish level. The estimates are derived from their Regional Impact Modeling System, or RIMS II.

3. A location quotient is a widely used measure of industry concentration. It is a simple ratio that is equal to the share of economic activity in Louisiana's economy in each sector, divided by the share of the same sector in the US economy. For example, if 5.7 percent of economic activity in Louisiana is generated by chemical manufacturing and 1.8 percent of economic activity in the United States is generated from the same industry, Louisiana's chemical manufacturing location quotient would be equal to 3.17 (= 5.7/1.8). If Louisiana and the nation shared the exact same industry mix, then every industry location quotient in Louisiana would be equal to 1. In other words, if an industry's location quotient is greater than 1, this indicates that economic activity in that industry is more highly concentrated in Louisiana than in the nation. Conversely, a location quotient below 1 reveals that activity in that specific industry is less concentrated in Louisiana than in the nation.

4. As noted previously, consistent groupings of industry data are not available over long time horizons. Detailed industry data from more recent years cannot be aligned with earlier data, so figure 10.1 is limited to the period from 1997 to the present because federal statistical agencies only began using the current North American Industry Classification System (NAICS) in 1997 to group economic activity together.

5. Metropolitan statistical areas (MSAs) are defined by the White House Office of Management and Budget and include collections of counties or parishes that are strongly economically linked and where the largest city in the region has a population of at least fifty thousand. The counties or parishes within an MSA can change over time as the relationships between counties or parishes change.

6. Bureau of Economic Analysis, https://www.bea.gov/news/2017/gross-domestic-product-metropolitan-area-2016 and https://www.bea.gov/news/2016/gross-domestic-product-metropolitan-area-2015 (accessed 7/15/2020).

7. The most robust measure of employment for detailed industries is the Quarterly Census of Employment and Wages, which began in 1975. So, the timing of this graph does not align exactly with the essay's frame of reference starting with the 1974 Louisiana constitution.

8. US Energy Information Administration, https://www.eia.gov/petroleum/refinerycapacity/table1.pdf (accessed 5/1/2020).

9. Federal Energy Regulatory Commission, https://cms.ferc.gov/media/north-american-lng-export-terminals-existing-approved-not-yet-built-and-proposed-1.

10. Port of South Louisiana, http://portsl.com/ (accessed 7/15/2020).

THE COAST

Federal and State Relations in the Midst of a Crisis

MARK DAVIS

Historically, Louisiana's attitude toward environmental protection and the federal government has reflected populist politics as well as the bona fide concerns of a small state with little regulatory experience. Louisiana was also dominated by extractive industries, such as sulfur mining, shell dredging, timbering, and oil and gas. In Louisiana, the axiom has long been that what is good for the environment cannot be good for business. In Louisiana politics, calling someone an environmentalist has rarely been a compliment.[1] The list of items on the so-called radical environmental agenda has included climate change and wetland protection, despite Louisiana's profound connections to both. The one notable exception to this tendency toward hyperbole has been coastal restoration, which is Louisiana's most home-grown environmental initiative, arguably because both the values and problems of the coast are seen as being more directly intertwined with the interests of communities, business, and private property rights. Looking forward, it seems clear that those sorts of connections are not confined to the coast and will become more evident across the state, forcing and forging new relationships between environmental stewardship, politics, and law.[2]

Focusing on Louisiana's coast, this essay will explore the state's complex and often confounding relationship with its natural and human environments and how those have been shaped—and are being reshaped—by politics and law. This essay is organized into several sections—Dominion, Coastal Louisiana, Levees, Oil and Gas, and Coastal Restoration.

* * *

A MATTER OF DOMINION: LAW, POLITICS, AND THE ENVIRONMENT

The relationship between nature and humankind is complicated, as are the relationships between people with respect to the bounty and burdens of the natural world. With perspectives ranging from the reverential to the purely utilitarian, it is no surprise that those perspectives—and the differences between them—are often expressed through politics, laws, and policies. For most of the history of Louisiana and our nation, those politics, laws, and policies have been decidedly skewed in favor of putting nature's resources into the service of human society. Shaped by deep-seated notions of "dominion," in which nature was a realm to conquer, not protect, wetlands were viewed as wastelands. Draining them was not an act of destruction in the dominion view, but of "reclamation," a term that nonsensically presupposes an underlying usefulness to land if it is reordered as providence or God intended.

COASTAL LOUISIANA: A CASE STUDY IN ENVIRONMENTAL POLITICS AND LAW

Coastal Louisiana is an example of how that dominion philosophy, translated into law and political agendas, shaped the world we now live in. Simply put, it took enormous expenditures of time, dollars, and labor to wreck the estuaries and wetlands of Louisiana's coast and bring them to the point that their survival and that of the human and natural communities they host are in doubt. That destruction required a supporting political and legal structure. Ironically, the same can be said for massive efforts now being mounted by Louisiana and the federal government to save Louisiana's coastal wetlands and barrier shorelines.[3]

Coastal Louisiana is a place of immense value and rare beauty. Few places on Earth can lay claim to such a rich and diverse array of natural resources. The interwoven waterways, forests, marshes, and estuaries make up a web of renewable resources of astounding economic, cultural, and ecological value. Judging by the state's "Sportsman's Paradise" moniker, its distinctive cuisine, and its arts and literature, one could easily conclude that respect for the intrinsic values of the state's natural bounty is indelible. But a look at the disappearing coast, the polluted air, water, and soil, and the disparity in how the benefits of Louisiana's environmental wealth and the burdens of its degradation are shared tells a very different story.

If ever there was a place where the environment is well loved but poorly served, Louisiana is it. But it is not enough to just point out the inconsistencies and say, "Well, that's Louisiana." The real issues are how did it come to be, and what lessons have been learned? There are no simple answers to those questions, but the pervasive roles of politics and law are inescapable. Exploring those roles so they can be better appreciated is the aim of this essay.

The state government, federal government, and private sector have all contributed to the degradation of Louisiana's coast. At the time of statehood, Louisiana's coastal wetlands covered nearly seven thousand square miles, or 4.5 million acres. The federal government retained ownership of those lands despite Louisiana's statehood. The federal Swamp Land Acts of 1849 and 1850 transferred those wetlands to Louisiana to facilitate their "reclamation." This reflected the view that Louisiana's wetlands were wastelands fit only to be drained, ditched, and leveed so that they could be developed.

LEVEES: THE PARADOX OF FLOOD PROTECTION AND COASTAL FLOODING

To understand Louisiana's environment today, it is important to understand the roles that levee building played in the state's development. Louisiana's southern Interstates 10 and 12 owe their existence to the Mississippi River and the deposition and transport of its sediments. Ironically, the river that created that land also made it unsuitable for development. Persistent river floods prompted European settlers to erect levees to protect their homes and communities. Without the levees constructed along the Mississippi River, life as we now know it in south Louisiana would not be possible. It is a second irony that those levees are significant contributors to the collapse of Louisiana's coast. The coastal ecosystems were built and replenished by river waters and sediments. The separation of the river from the coastal systems via levees triggered the collapse of those ecosystems due to subsidence, erosion, and encroaching salt water from the Gulf.

Through leveeing, draining, and filling, Louisiana's coast was transformed. But it came at a cost in terms of flooding, land loss, collapsing fisheries, and doubts about the insurability and fiscal viability of coastal communities. Those costs were not unforeseen; indeed, the warning signs were there for years, going back to the late nineteenth century.[4] It was obvious to some observers that Louisiana's practice of reclamation (draining, ditching, and diking) was a failure and that the state's policies were "killing the goose that laid the golden egg."[5] To others, like the US Department of Agriculture and other governmental agencies, it was convenient to believe and espouse that the coast was in equilibrium.[6] So, those practices continued due to the lack of a supporting legal framework and the political will to change them. This paradox of flood protection that leads to flooding, land loss, and collapsing fisheries exemplifies the tensions between state and federal policies and between science and official policy.

The political and technical consensus that produced today's Mississippi River levee system did not come easily, nor has it evolved smoothly. The current federally engineered system of levees and spillways was not a given. In fact, today's system is more the product of previous failures than it is the result of thoughtful planning. The process of levee building began at the time of European settlement and was mostly the handiwork of state, local, and even private initiatives. By the start of the twentieth century, the river was leveed for a thousand miles on each side. There were robust debates about what that system should look like, but the view that prevailed was one that preferred levees to all other options.[7]

It was only in 1928, following the historic 1927 flood and the failure of the levees-only concept, that the levee system was federalized.[8] Since then, the system has been tested but has not failed. But even with success at preventing river flooding there has still been some flooding, since those levees have been so clearly linked to the ongoing collapse of Louisiana's coastal wetlands, as noted above. By the 1930s, the 4.5 million acres of coastal wetlands that existed when Louisiana joined the Union in 1812 had shrunk to 3.2 million acres. By 2010, less than 2 million acres remained. Despite voices pointing to the problem and its causes, the situation was not acknowledged or acted on by state or federal authorities until the late 1980s. At that time, the governor's office created what has evolved into the Coastal Protection and Restoration Authority. In 1990, Congress, led by Louisiana Democratic senators John Breaux and Bennett Johnston, working closely with Rhode Island's pro-environmental Republican senator John Chaffee, enacted the Coastal Wetlands Planning, Protection and Restoration Act (CWPPRA) as a companion to Louisiana's new law. The relationship between Louisiana's senators and Senator Chaffee, who chaired an influential committee, highlights the importance of the interplay between Louisiana politics and national politics.

OIL AND GAS: THE INTERPLAY OF WETLANDS, WATER, AND ENERGY

In the twentieth century, a combination of political and economic drivers that developed the state's oil and gas resources drove further destruction of the wetlands—many of which were concentrated in the state's coastal region. Revolutionary developments in transportation and military thinking in the first quarter of that century transformed life in America and put petroleum at the heart of America's notions of progress and security. Fueling that progress created immense pressure to find new oil and gas fields and bring the fuel to market. Finding those in Louisiana transformed the state's landscape, economy, and politics in ways that continue to compromise the state's environment. Culturally and politically, the relationship between the state and the oil and gas industry was fraught with tension, mistrust, and opportunism. Governor Huey Long famously used popular distrust of the new industry and its environmentally destructive ways to extract concessions in the form of severance taxes and royalties. This arrangement propelled both the industry's development and Long's populist agenda and political ambitions.

The industry's influence on the environment persists today, and oil and gas interests have become the largest group of landowners in coastal Louisiana. That was not by happenstance. As noted earlier, the federal government divested itself of Louisiana's wetlands in the mid-nineteenth century. The state then sold most of those lands to private persons and companies that acquired large tracts of land for the purpose of harvesting the natural resources associated with them. Originally timber, furs, and bird plumage were emphasized, but the twentieth century saw oil and gas (and in places sulfur) become the dominant drivers.

Today, roughly 80 percent of Louisiana's coastal wetlands are owned by oil and gas developers. The reason for this is rooted in Louisiana property law, which favors unified ownership of surface and subsurface rights.[9] This dynamic has given the industry an amplified voice in state and local politics and has led many of those landowners to put the extraction of minerals ahead of the stewardship of the wetlands and has fueled resistance to laws and regulations governing economic activity in coastal waters and wetlands.[10]

The symbiotic relationship between industry and government, while enduring, is also changing as energy markets and the coast change. Oil and gas continue to play an outsized role in Louisiana, but its ability to provide good-paying jobs and monies to the state treasury have dwindled as new sources of energy have ascended. Landowners and local governments, even if traditionally sympathetic with the industry, now sometimes see their interests and those of oil and gas diverging. This has led to a series of lawsuits by local governments and landowners against some members of the oil and gas industry seeking compensation for damages to coastal wetlands attributable to oil and gas exploration and production. Those lawsuits have been occasionally successful and predictably polarizing, with the industry repeatedly seeking judicial, legislative, and political protection from them. While the legal and financial outcomes have been mixed, the political fallout has been more clear. Opposition or support for those suits, often with little consideration of their merits, became a political litmus test in the 2019 gubernatorial race between Governor John Bel Edwards (pro) and challenger Eddie Rispone (anti). These simplistic characterizations make for crisp, polarized politics, but they do little to illuminate the actual rights and responsibilities at stake, much less encourage the types of discussions and compromises that are the hallmarks of good governance.

A similar pro/anti dichotomy was seen after the 2010 Deepwater Horizon disaster that killed eleven rig workers and saw more than 200 million gallons of oil spill into the Gulf of Mexico. Many of the practices that compounded the tragedy were not confined to the Macondo well or British Petroleum (BP).

The failure to plan for such a disaster was not an accident; it was a product of industry practices supported by federal policy and an iron triangle of shared state, federal, and industry interest in getting as much revenue as quickly as possible from beneath the Gulf.[11]

A sharp line quickly emerged between the White House and Louisiana's oil and gas industry when the Obama administration declared a temporary moratorium on oil and gas drilling in the deep Gulf in order take collective stock of what went wrong and what changes might be in order. Making the case that the industry should not be punished for the bad acts of one company, oil and gas industry representatives working with then Governor Bobby Jindal organized a campaign to portray the Obama administration as being anti-oil and politically motivated.[12] While it is highly doubtful that either the moratorium or the coordinated pushback did much to change the arc of oil and gas activity in the Gulf—those were already being reshaped by legal and economic forces—there is little doubt that the partisan politics sharpened after the Deepwater Horizon event.[13]

COASTAL RESTORATION: CITIZEN ACTION AND THE POLITICS OF ENVIRONMENTAL STEWARDSHIP

The Deepwater Horizon disaster revealed deep differences and divisions between the numerous agencies and stakeholders with an interest in the use and stewardship of the Gulf and coastal Louisiana, but it did not create them. The checkered and chaotic relationship between Louisiana, the federal government, and the environment has worked against a coherent approach to the use and stewardship of natural resources, much less an approach focused on the ongoing resilience and sustainability of those resources. Given the dominion roots of property law and environmental law, that should not be surprising. The evolution of environmental law has been characterized by the addition of new perspectives and priorities to the mix rather than by any fundamental reordering of rights, duties, and priorities. It is perfectly natural to try to balance those things, to simultaneously protect and exploit, but at the end of the day conflict is baked into environmental law and management.

When the carrying capacity of the environment is reached or surpassed, a new paradigm is needed to address ecological devastation. That is what is happening in coastal Louisiana, which is home to perhaps the largest fish and wildlife habitat collapse on the planet. By the 1980s, environmental laws required permits to damage or destroy an acre of wetlands, but the systemic collapse of more than thirty square miles a year was not within the mission of any state or federal agency to address, much less stop. Stepping up to those challenges is not the sort of thing government is good at. In coastal Louisiana, the impetus for change was informed by broad-based citizen action.

In the 1970s, the work of scientists like Sherwood Gagliano, which challenged the contemporary perception of a "coast in balance," began to gain an audience and civic understanding.[14] These scientists concluded that Louisiana's coast was disappearing fast. Without radical changes to coastal management and new regulations reflecting the natural processes that had built it, the coast would cease to be. Unsurprisingly, their conclusions garnered little interest in governmental circles. In part, that was because most state and federal authorities thought they did not have the jurisdiction to act. Fishermen, landowners, environmentalists, and some local governments saw the web of life, the tax bases, and their future on the line. Coalescing into the Coalition to Restore Coastal Louisiana, they issued "Here Today, Gone Tomorrow" in 1987 as a call to action and framework for melding science, law, and politics to forge a more hopeful future for the coast.

This brand of civics- and science-driven politics was not typical in Louisiana, but it worked. In 1989, the state enacted Act 6, which made coastal restoration a state priority and funded it with a share of state oil and gas royalties and severance taxes.[15] The legislation put the new Governor's Office of Coastal Activities in charge of a multiagency effort and created the position of executive assistant to the governor to lead it. The decision to vest this responsibility in the governor's office was a pragmatic one. Article 4 of Louisiana's constitution limits the number of executive branch agencies, and there was no room for a new one. Just as compelling was the understanding that Louisiana is a "strong governor" state, especially then, and that it would take the imprimatur of the governor to make coastal restoration a true priority. On paper this seemed to settle the matter, but without the clear support of the executive, the Governor's Office of Coastal Activities often found it challenging to hold its own against other executive branch agencies that were also headed by persons appointed by the governor. It took years and Hurricanes Katrina and Rita to secure the real investment of gubernatorial power in the office, but the seeds had been planted. Following this legislation and state investment, the Coalition to Restore Coastal Louisiana worked to persuade Congress to enact the Coastal Wetlands Planning, Protection and Restoration Act (CWPPRA) in 1991, creating a federal counterpart to Act 6. The bones of the coastal restoration effort were then in place.

The birth of this restoration effort in the early 1990s coincided with an extremely polarizing effort to revamp the wetlands protection provisions of the federal Clean Water Act, an effort led in large part by Louisiana's congressional delegation at the behest of the oil and gas industry. In Louisiana, antipathy for regulatory protection for wetlands contrasted with wide support for the restoration effort. This reflected the belief that restoration was a public works program rather than regulatory, despite the clear connections between wetland conservation and restoration. By the end of the 2010s, the naive notion that coastal restoration was possible without conflict, controversy, and litigation would be laid to rest as the impacts on fisheries and mineral ownership became more clear. In the end, the Clean Water Act remained as it was, but the significant support for restoring Louisiana's wetlands that had been built up in the passage of CWPPRA had been eroded. More importantly, time was lost that Louisiana's degrading coast could ill afford to lose. To be sure, coastal restoration planning and projects continued, but now in a more polarized and politicized way.

Since then, as demonstrated by the CWPPRA program and the state's development of its Master Plan for Coastal Protection and Restoration, Louisiana and the federal government have devoted years and millions of dollars to developing plans to stem the loss of the state's coastal wetlands. Those plans are elaborate and complex, but, at their core, they all depend on restoring riverine flows to the coast. The federal government has provided most of the dollars for Louisiana's coastal restoration and protection program, but those dollars all come from the same oil and gas development that burdens Louisiana's environment. The investment of time, money, and water in coastal planning is not usually justified by reference to abstract environmental values; rather, it is justified by the services that the ecosystem provides to the communities, cultures, and economies that rely on it for storm buffering, water filtration, and fisheries production, among other things. In short, coastal restoration is about more than just nature and ecology, which would never generate sufficient support for action, it is about the survival of human communities, cultures, and economies. This atypically broad and comprehensive approach to the challenge grew out of a broad-based civic movement instead of the jurisdictional lens of any governmental agency.

The power of that kind of thinking proved itself following Hurricanes Katrina and Rita and the Deepwater Horizon oil spill in 2010. Each of those tragedies brought into sharper focus the interdependence of human and natural communities of the coast. That holistic view of the coast and the need to be better stewards of it were foundational to Governor Blanco's lawsuit against Minerals Management Service (MMS) to force a fresh look at the impacts of outer continental oil and gas development on coastal Louisiana.[16] Not only did MMS agree to postpone an offshore lease sale and revise its National Environmental Policy Act compliance, but the suit reinvigorated efforts to pass the Gulf of Mexico Energy Security Act (GOMESA), which greatly increased the sharing of outer continental shelf revenues with the state. A key feature of GOMESA was the dedication of revenues to coastal restoration and protection.

That set the pattern for the RESTORE Act, passed after the Deepwater Horizon spill. Again, the demonstrated need coupled with widely supported restoration plans provided the basis for directing fines and penalties to the state for use in coastal restoration and protection. If there was ever a question that state-centric environmental policy can be good politics and good economics, the RESTORE Act is strong evidence that it can. This is also strong evidence that the center of gravity for developing environmental policy has shifted from the federal level back to the state level.

At this point, Louisiana's vast but quickly disappearing coast demands a multifaceted approach if it has any hope of surviving. It will take a mix of conservation, wetland and hydrologic restoration, flood protection, and community adaptation on a massive scale to begin to address the issues facing the coast. Aside from its undisputed ecological importance, this "working coast" is the home of millions of residents who are literally witnessing the ground disappear beneath their homes and feet.[17] In short, coastal restoration does not mean recreating a lost coast or even keeping the coast. At best, it means restoring limited functional sustainability, although with each passing day less is possible. That means hard choices must be made and that there will be winners and losers regardless of what course is taken. The choice of courses is and will remain acutely political at both the state and federal levels.

All state and federal plans to save coastal Louisiana call for using the forces that built the coast, especially river water and sediments. Louisiana is "water rich" with an abundance of rivers, streams, and aquifers. In a time of growing water scarcity, that abundance should bode well for Louisiana's coast and the state's overall prospects for growth and prosperity. But Louisiana is not the master of many of those water resources. Many of them are shared with other states or are subject to federal control or oversight. That is especially so for the Mississippi, Red, Atchafalaya, and Sabine rivers. Louisiana's plans for sustaining its coast depend on rivers that are available and fit to use, both in terms of water quantity and quality. Louisiana's plans are compelling, but other states and the nation have compelling plans and priorities of their own for those waters. Unfortunately, those plans and priorities frequently conflict with one another. Navigation, public and industrial water supply, agriculture, flood control, and public and private water rights all have claims—legal and political—to those waters. There is also the matter of reconciling coastal restoration efforts with important federal laws, such as the Endangered Species Act and the Marine Mammal Protection Act, which take precedence over state law. Contending with all of this and the needs and desires of neighboring states will force legal and political reckonings of a sort that must become more commonplace as communities across the nation come to terms with the forces reshaping the physical, cultural, and political landscapes.

Overlaying all of these hopes and plans for coastal restoration and protection is the problem of climate change and sea level rise. The tug between politics and science can be seen in the state's various coastal master plans. Climate science has always informed those plans, but the leanings of a particular administration can be seen in the plans' language. The 2007 master plan released by Governor Blanco contains an entire section on the threats and uncertainties posed by climate change, while the 2017 master plan drafted during the Jindal administration avoids any such direct discussion, though it does reference the issue and climate science in several places.[18]

That rhetorical waxing and waning reflect deep divisions in public opinion about the issue, especially in powerful business sectors, such as the oil and gas industry. In the case of industry, state-based companies and trade associations expressed open hostility to the scientific legitimacy of climate change as an issue, even as large numbers of those organizations openly embraced it.[19] As a result, Louisiana adopted the practice of saying as little as possible about climate change while also acknowledging it in its coastal planning. As the voices of other business sectors that must contend with climate change become more prominent, the politics will likely change as well. That is already beginning to happen, and there is evidence that even long-standing skeptics of climate change are taking a more pragmatic approach.[20]

As change comes to America's coasts and discussions of coastal restoration, adaptation, and retreat become less abstract, the interplay between state and federal interests and jurisdictions will be reinvented. The political and civic dimensions of this reinvention can draw from the lessons taught by Louisiana's coastal restoration experience. Key among those lessons is the fact that good science and good intentions will not be enough to compensate for bad politics, law, and policy. The state's reluctance to consider raising public revenues for essential coastal projects and its reflexive enthusiasm for "regulatory relief" to spur economic growth starkly illustrate the tension that underlies environmental law and policy in the state.[21] The road ahead will be a hard one without a fuller public discussion about the reasons for and benefits of environmental protection and a greater realization that, while social and economic sectors wax and wane, a supportive and resilient environment is essential to the state's future prosperity and sustainability.

NOTES

1. See, for example, Alan Neuhauser, "Jindal Declares Climate Change a 'Trojan Horse,'" *US News,* September 16, 2014, https;//www.usnews.com/news/articles/2014/09/16/louisianas-bobby-jindal-declares-climate-change-a-trojan-horse.

2. An example of how this is beginning to happen is the Louisiana Watershed Initiative, which promotes watershed-scale flood management. This program was created in the wake of floods driven by extreme rain events in 2016.

3. See, for example, Louisiana's extensive program for coping with and responding to coastal land loss as described in plans produced by the Louisiana Coastal Protection and Restoration Authority, https://coastal.la.gov/. With regard to the federal role, in 1991 Congress enacted the Coastal Wetlands Planning, Protection and Restoration Act in large part to engage with Louisiana in efforts to stem coastal land loss. For a discussion of the legal and political constraints on implementing those plans, see Mark S. Davis, John Driscoll, and Harry Vorhoff, "Financing the Future," *Tulane Institute on Water Resources Law and Policy,* August 18, 2014, http://docs.wixstatic.com/ugd/32079b_a814e210f6b547e4a1affab6618a479a.pdf.

4. Elmer Lawrence Corthell, "The Delta of the Mississippi River," *National Geographic* 8 (1897): 354.

5. Percy Viosca Jr., "Louisiana Wetlands and the Value of Their Wildlife and Fishery Resources," *Ecology* 9, no. 2 (1928): 216–229.

6. Jack Davis, *The Gulf: The Making of an American Sea* (New York: Liveright Publishing, 2017), 496.

7. See, for example, Mark Twain, *Life on the Mississippi* (New York: Bantam Books, 1976), 139–142.

8. For a more complete discussion of how the Flood Control Act of 1928 brought the Mississippi River levee system under federal control, see John M. Barry, *Rising Tide: The Great Mississippi River Flood of 1927 and How It Changed America* (New York: Simon and Schuster, 1998).

9. In most other states, surface estates and subsurface mineral estates are severable, which means they can be owned by different people.

10. Oliver A. Houck, "The Reckoning: Oil and Gas Development in the Coastal Zone," *Tulane Environmental Law Journal* 28, no. 2 (2015): 185–296.

11. Mark S. Davis, "Lessons Unlearned: The Legal and Policy Legacy of the BP Deepwater Horizon Spill," *Washington and Lee Journal of Energy, Climate, and the Environment* 3, no. 2 (2012): 155–175.

12. See, for example, Sal Perricone, "Rally Recollections," *The Hayride,* July 22, 2010, https://thehayride.com/2010/07/rally-recollections/.

13. This model for action was not the invention of Louisiana coastal advocates, but rather an extension of social change practices with deep roots in the civil rights, labor, and conservation movements.

14. Davis, *The Gulf,* 500–501.

15. Act 6, Louisiana Legislature General Session, 1989, https://www.seagrantfish.lsu.edu/pdfs/lcl/legislative/OCTOBER%201989.pdf.

16. See Ryan M. Seidemann and James G. Wilkins, "Blanco v Burton; What Did We Learn from Louisiana's Recent OCS Challenge?," unpublished paper, 2007, https://digitalcommons.pace.edu/cgi/viewcontent.cgi?article=1046&context=pelr.

17. See, for example, Michael D. Blum and Harry H. Roberts, "Drowning of the Mississippi Delta Due to Insufficient Sediment Supply and Global Sea-Level Rise," *Nature Geoscience* 2 (June 28, 2009): 488–491, https://www.nature.com/articles/ngeo553.

18. "Louisiana's Comprehensive Master Plan for a Sustainable Coast," Coastal Protection and Restoration Authority of Louisiana, June 2, 2017, https://coastal.la.gov/wp-content/uploads/2017/04/2017-Coastal-Master-Plan_Web-Book_CFinal-with-Effective-Date-06092017.pdf.

19. Oil and gas companies with broader constituencies than Louisiana were acknowledging the problem of climate change in the early to mid-2000s. Shell Oil was explicitly supporting a cap and trade approach to reducing greenhouse gas emissions in 2009.

20. In 2020, Governor John Bel Edwards created a Climate Initiatives Task Force with the support of much of the Louisiana oil and gas industry. Lori Leblanc, "Oil and Gas Industry Leads the Way in Carbon Capture," *Business & Industry Connection Magazine*, May 6, 2020, https://www.bicmagazine.com/industry/refining-petchem/oil-and-gas-industry-leads-the-way-in-carbon-capture/.

21. The term regulatory relief is often used to describe the rollback of environmental laws and regulations in order to encourage economic development. The impetus for regulatory relief is often tied to economic slowdowns like that associated with the COVID-19 crisis. The reliance on things like the RESTORE Act are indicative this problem. As welcome and beneficial as the funding was, there is no hiding from the fact that it took a staggering disaster to generate it. That is cruel serendipity, not purposeful finance. Electoral politics in Louisiana and many other places are still dominated by a "no more taxes" philosophy that is divorced from the fact that some things demand revenues and that the failure to find ways of generating them will come with dire consequences. See "Financing the Future—Turning Coastal Restoration and Protection Plans into Realities: The Cost of Comprehensive Coastal Restoration and Protection," Tulane Institute on Water Resources Law and Policy, August 18, 2014, docs.wixstatic.com/ugd/32079b_a814e210f6b547e4a1affab6618a479a.pdf.

POVERTY AND THE LOUISIANA SAFETY NET IN THE TWENTY-FIRST CENTURY

JAN MOLLER

Louisiana, unique among states, has a tradition of providing charity health care that started before America was even a country. The first Charity Hospital opened in New Orleans in 1736, financed by a grant from a French shipbuilder, Jean Louis, who specified in his will that he wanted a hospital built in New Orleans to provide care for the indigent.

Several versions of the hospital sprung up over the years. But the hospital that generations of New Orleanians knew as "Big Charity" was erected on Tulane Avenue in 1938. The twenty-story limestone Art Deco building stood as the centerpiece of a statewide network of ten public hospitals that had no equivalent anywhere in the country. It is the place where generations of Louisiana doctors did their postgraduate training, and where New Orleanians of every race and class had gone to be treated for everything from sore throats to gunshot wounds—often at no out-of-pocket cost.

Beyond its imposing physical footprint in downtown New Orleans, the hospital also stood as a symbol of Louisiana's historic commitment to providing an adequate social safety net. It is a legacy that dates back to the Huey Long era, one that Louisiana stubbornly clung to even as America's health care system evolved through the decades and federal welfare policies upended the relationship between low-income families and the government.

But over a two-decade span starting in the mid-1990s, Louisiana's safety net was fundamentally transformed. Part of this was due to the political shifts at the state capitol, where conservatives seized control of the legislature and Governor Bobby Jindal made the state a laboratory for ideas he hoped would vault him into the presidency. Part of the change came due to Hurricane

Katrina, which wreaked physical devastation on South Louisiana but also brought federal reconstruction money that was used to build a new teaching hospital to replace Big Charity. Changes in federal policy played another huge role, as federal overhauls of traditional welfare programs and Medicaid funding filtered down to the state level.

Today, Louisiana's health care system for the poor is almost unrecognizable. The centralized statewide charity system is gone, replaced by a series of public-private partnerships where the state contracts with private hospitals to provide indigent care.

More people than ever before have health insurance, thanks to the expansion of Medicaid in 2016 by Governor John Bel Edwards. After years of having one of the nation's highest uninsured rates, Louisiana now has a lower rate than the national average. There are more clinics in more neighborhoods where people can get the care they need without waiting for hours in a hospital emergency room.

But other parts of the safety net have frayed. Needy families in Louisiana have a harder time getting cash assistance to meet their basic needs than anywhere else in the country. There are two Louisiana residents living in prison for every person living in public housing. Louisiana's investments in public health have declined over the past decade, and the number of children being served by state-subsidized childcare services has plummeted.

Through these changes, some things in Louisiana have remained fairly constant: the percentage of the population living near the poverty line, and the poor health outcomes that result from not being able to afford the basic necessities of life. The official poverty rate in Louisiana has hovered around 18–20 percent for many years, among the highest rates in the nation. But that only tells part of the story. A better measurement comes from the United Way's ALICE report (Asset Limited, Income Constrained, Employed), which found that nearly half (48 percent) of all Louisiana households do not earn enough to make ends meet each month.[1]

For Black Louisianans, the situation is even more dire. Nearly one in three Black Louisianans live below the federal poverty line, and almost half of all Black children are being raised in poverty.[2] The news is even worse when it comes to health, where Louisiana has consistently ranked at or near the bottom of national indicators. The annual America's Health Rankings, put out each year by the United Health Foundation, ranks Louisiana forty-ninth—right ahead of Mississippi—on the list of healthy states. The Pelican State has never ranked higher than forty-seventh in the thirty-year history of the rankings. If ever a state needed a stronger safety net, it is Louisiana.

This essay will cover the major changes to Louisiana's public safety net in the first two decades of the new millennium, and the political forces that made them happen. At the center of that change is the dismantling of the statewide charity hospital system, which was replaced by an expansion of Medicaid eligibility and the transition to a managed care delivery system. It will also cover Louisiana's decision to end most cash assistance for needy families, and the persistence of poverty in a state that is rich in resources.

THE BATTLE OVER "BIG CHARITY"

By the time the new millennium rolled around, the Charity system was showing its age. The flagship New Orleans hospital was in dire need of a facelift, and other hospitals in the network were in even worse physical shape. The maintenance backlog topped $1 billion, and operating funds were in equally short supply. Still, there was little political appetite to overhaul a system that had served as the primary health care provider for generations of poor Louisianans—even as the rest of the country had evolved over the previous decades.

Almost everywhere else around the country, the creation of Medicare and Medicaid in 1960s meant that public hospitals had to restructure themselves to start competing with private hospitals for these patients. But that never happened in Louisiana, where a "two-tiered" health care system evolved: a private one for people with insurance, including Medicare, and a public system for the nine hundred thousand or so Louisianans who were uninsured or underinsured.

The arrangement was a lucrative one for private hospitals, which were able to focus almost entirely on treating patients with private insurance or Medicare, without having to absorb the cost of providing uncompensated care to the uninsured. In the years before Hurricane Katrina, the average private hospital in America delivered twice as much uncompensated care as those in Louisiana. Yet this "two-tiered" system was not particularly good for either group. As the consulting firm PricewaterhouseCoopers would later note, the system was "embedded in the practice patterns of health care professionals in the state, and accentuates the problem; private paying patients are admitted to private hospitals by the same physicians who admit nonpaying patients to public hospitals."[3]

Freed from the financial burden of having to treat the uninsured, Louisiana's private hospital industry built far more beds than were needed. The charity system, forced to rely almost entirely on taxpayer support, often found itself struggling financially to survive, despite the clear need. Its outpatient clinics and emergency rooms were typically packed with patients, and its occupancy rates were well above those of most private hospitals.

While the quality of care in the charity system was generally top-tier, the Louisiana State University administrators who ran the system had to fight annually against cuts to the hospitals' operating budgets. And while the private hospitals kept building, the charity system could never get the money it needed to upgrade its hospitals in a way that could attract private-pay patients and create a "healthier" payer mix.

The public debate over charity hospitals changed on August 29, 2005, when Hurricane Katrina destroyed the inadequate flood walls that protected New Orleans and water flooded the flagship hospital in New Orleans and shut its doors. Almost immediately after the storm, top LSU System officials made it clear that they saw it as an opportunity to replace the aging building with a modern teaching hospital that could serve as the hub of a new bio-sciences district in New Orleans. The state may have lacked the money and the willpower to rebuild the charity system, but state leaders quickly realized that Louisiana would reap billions of dollars in reconstruction funding through the Federal Emergency Management Agency, which could cover most of the cost.

While LSU and then-Governor Kathleen Blanco wanted a modern teaching hospital, many of the doctors who worked in the hospital—along with community activists in New Orleans—saw these efforts as a threat to Charity's historic mission of providing care for the indigent. Many of the doctors had spent weeks after the storm cleaning the hospital and getting it ready to see patients again—only to later be barred from the building while being forced to treat their patients in a temporary field hospital.[4]

By March 2006, six months after the storm, more than three hundred former hospital workers and activists participated in a "Rally to Save Charity Hospital." A few weeks later, the New Orleans City Council weighed in with a resolution, passed unanimously, demanding that the hospital be reopened.[5] The battle that began in early 2006—between activists and preservationists who wanted to rebuild the hospital and restore the charity system and state officials who wanted a modern teaching hospital—would continue for more than four years, with politicians of both parties staking their claims on different sides.

Stuck in the middle was FEMA, which had originally determined that the storm damage to the hospital only amounted to $126 million—far below the full replacement value that the state was seeking. Years of appeals would follow. The issue did not get resolved until Louisiana's Senator Mary Landrieu got language inserted into a 2009 spending bill that set up a binding arbitration process.

In January 2010, the federal arbitrator finally ruled that Louisiana was owed $475 million—nearly the full amount it was seeking—that it could use toward building a new hospital. The decision meant that New Orleans would soon get a state-of-the-art facility. But major decisions still lay ahead, including who would operate the new hospital—and whether Louisiana's statewide charity system model would survive intact.

THE BOBBY JINDAL ERA

By the time the hospital financing issue was settled, Louisiana had undergone a political and economic transformation. A new governor had been elected, and the state legislature was about to turn majority Republican for the first time since Reconstruction. The state's economy, which had soared after Katrina as reconstruction dollars poured into the state and energy prices spiked, had crashed—and so had the state's budget.

Gone was Governor Kathleen Blanco, an early champion of the teaching hospital whose popularity plunged after the public soured on her leadership after Katrina and who declined to seek reelection in 2007. In her place was Bobby Jindal, an Ivy League–educated conservative Republican who had risen to prominence when then-Governor Mike Foster picked him to lead the state's Health Department in 1996 when he was just twenty-four years old.

As a young health secretary, Jindal had championed the legislation in the late 1990s that handed control of the charity hospital system to Louisiana State University, under the theory that it made sense to combine public health care and medical education under a single entity. As governor, Jindal continued the Blanco administration's push for the new teaching hospital, which LSU was supposed to own and operate. That's where their similarities ended. Jindal had very different ideas about the government's role in health care delivery. While he understood that federal and state tax dollars were necessary to provide safety net care, he wanted as much of that care as possible turned over to the private sector.

The job of carrying out that vision fell to Alan Levine, a veteran hospital administrator who billed himself as an acolyte of former House speaker Newt Gingrich. Levine was a star in conservative policy circles and shared Jindal's belief in a private, free-market approach to health care. Just as the wonky, fast-talking Jindal was a sharp contrast to the grandmotherly Blanco, Levine differed in both tone and substance from the man who led the Health Department for most of Blanco's tenure, Dr. Fred Cerise. A physician by training, Cerise had come up through the charity system, serving as the top administrator at Earl K. Long Medical Center in Baton Rouge before joining the administration. A New Orleans native, Cerise believed passionately in the charity system and thought it should be strengthened, not abandoned.

By the time Jindal took office, Cerise had moved from the Health Department to a newly created position at LSU, where he oversaw both the charity hospital system and the state's medical schools in New Orleans and Shreveport. As Cerise settled in at LSU, Levine first set his sights on overhauling the way Louisiana paid doctors, hospitals, and other providers through the Medicaid program. For decades, Louisiana had relied on a traditional "fee for service" model, where health care providers that participate in Medicaid sent bills directly to the state.

Jindal and Levine thought Louisiana should follow the lead of other states, including Florida, that relied on a "managed care" model where the state contracts with private insurance companies that get paid a flat monthly per-patient premium and serve as a middleman between patients and providers. Managed care systems are attractive to politicians because the risk of higher-than-expected health care costs are shifted from government to private insurance companies. But they are often disliked by doctors and other health care providers, who prefer being paid directly for the services they provide.

In late 2008, nearing the end of his first year in office, Jindal unveiled his proposal: The Louisiana Health First plan. This plan set up pilot programs in a few major markets, where an estimated 380,000 low-income people, mainly children, would be steered into private managed care networks that would be given new flexibility to vary the benefits that Medicaid patients traditionally received. Another part of the plan involved expanding Medicaid eligibility to anyone earning 50 percent or less of the federal poverty levels, with people in the Lake Charles region being covered at up to 200 percent of the poverty line. In exchange for expanding coverage, the Jindal administration wanted forgiveness for nearly $800 million that Louisiana owed the federal government for prior misspending in the Medicaid program.[6]

The proposed coverage expansion was a sea change for Louisiana, where Medicaid eligibility had historically been highly restricted. While people with disabilities, elderly people in nursing homes, and pregnant women could get covered, it was practically impossible for nondisabled adults to get on Medicaid, no matter how little they earned. For them, the only options were the charity system or an emergency room visit to a private hospital that could result in bills they could never hope to pay.

Because of the debt forgiveness component, Jindal's Health First plan needed federal approval. But America had just elected a new president, Barack Obama, who would take office two months later and had his sights set on more ambitious reforms—not just for Louisiana but for the whole nation. The Health First plan would never get approved. But the public debate over expanding Medicaid coverage was just getting started.

* * *

JINDAL VERSUS OBAMA

The Patient Protection and Affordable Care Act—known to most people as Obamacare—became federal law on March 23, 2010, after passing Congress without a single Republican vote. Among the law's key provisions was an expansion of Medicaid coverage to any adult with a household income below 138 percent of the federal poverty line—or about $30,000 per year for a family of three. To make the expansion affordable for states, which share the cost of Medicaid with the federal government, the law called for the federal government to cover the full cost of the expansion population for the first three years, starting in 2014. After that, states would start paying a share, but never more than 10 percent. That was a dramatically better deal for states than the traditional Medicaid program, where Louisiana generally bore 30 to 40 percent of the cost (the percentage varies each year).

But Obama had lost Louisiana by 19 points to Senator John McCain, and his signature health care law was unpopular in a state where Tea Party sentiment was strong. Jindal's own presidential ambitions were an open secret, and an easy way for him to enhance his popularity was to oppose Obamacare at every turn.

The Health First initiative was quickly forgotten, as the debates in Baton Rouge turned to the massive budget shortfalls that had sprung up as a result of the Great Recession and a series of ill-advised tax cuts. While Hurricanes Katrina and Rita had devastated much of South Louisiana, the 2005 storms also gave birth to an economic boom as massive amounts of federal aid flowed to Louisiana at the same time that oil prices hit record highs. The economic boom had produced record tax revenues, and legislators in Baton Rouge had suddenly found themselves with billions of dollars in annual budget surpluses.

Although everyone knew the boom was temporary, legislators could not resist the urge to pass permanent tax cuts. In her final session as governor in 2007, Blanco had signed more than a dozen tax cut measures, including the restoration of a lucrative income tax deduction that state voters had eliminated as part of a 2002 tax reform plan. Jindal followed suit in 2008 by signing another, even larger income tax cut that also reversed changes that voters had approved just a few years earlier.

By 2010, the post-Katrina budget surpluses had become billion-dollar shortfalls. At first the damage to the state budget was offset by federal aid, but budget cuts soon became unavoidable. Jindal flatly ruled out any tax increases, meaning the only way for the state to address the problem was through budget cuts and, increasingly, gimmicks.

The hardest hits fell on Louisiana's colleges and universities, which would end up sustaining the second-biggest cuts in state support in the country.[7] To make up for the loss of state support, campuses began raising student tuition, which would nearly double at most universities over the next decade. But it did not stop with colleges. To fill other gaps, Louisiana began making creative use of the federal dollars the state receives each year for public assistance. For decades, federal law had guaranteed cash assistance to low-income families with children that needed help making ends meet. Promising to "end welfare as we know it," President Bill Clinton signed a 1996 law that transformed the federal welfare program into an annual block grant that gave states broad flexibility on how to use the money.

No state made more use of the new flexibility than Louisiana.[8] Welfare caseloads began dropping dramatically—from more than seventy thousand in 1996, the year before the new law took effect, to fewer than seven thousand by 2015. Instead of being used for the core goals of welfare reform—direct cash assistance, child care assistance, and programs that help families join the workforce—Louisiana used its block grant to pay for programs previously financed with state taxpayer dollars, such as child welfare services and the popular LA 4 pre-kindergarten program for at-risk children.

A particularly sad casualty was Louisiana's Child Care Assistance Program (CCAP), which subsidized childcare services for low-income families so their parents could go to work. In 2007, before the budget cuts began, the program served more than forty thousand children from low-income families—all with federal dollars. But as the state began using its block grant to fill other holes, the childcare caseload fell dramatically to just over twelve thousand.

As education services were straining under budget cuts, health care had been mostly unaffected. That would change dramatically in 2012, at the start of Jindal's second term in office. Having abandoned his Health First plan, Jindal moved forward with a plan that left eligibility unchanged but which brought most of the program under a new managed care model. Called Bayou Health, the plan was unveiled the previous year by Levine's successor as Louisiana's health secretary, Bruce Greenstein. It required nondisabled Medicaid patients to enroll in one of five private health insurance plans that contracted with the state. Unlike the earlier proposal, this one did not require federal approval, just approval from a legislative budget committee. Nor did it call for expanding Medicaid coverage. Instead, it would simply require about eight hundred thousand low-income Louisianans to get Medicaid coverage through a health insurance plan.

But Jindal was just getting started. In the summer of 2012, two things happened that would dramatically change Louisiana's model for health care delivery. The first came in late June, when the US Supreme Court upheld the Obamacare law as constitutional, but with a key caveat: Chief Justice John Roberts, who wrote the 5–4 opinion, said the law could not require states to expand their Medicaid programs. Instead, it would be optional. Within hours of the court's ruling, Jindal announced that Louisiana would not be expanding Medicaid on his watch, even though more than four hundred thousand low-income adults without health insurance stood to benefit.

The second came a few weeks later, in early July, when Congress reached a budget agreement that sharply lowered the federal government's contribution to the state's Medicaid program.[9] For Louisiana—which had just completed its legislative session and approved a balanced budget for the July 1 start of its fiscal year—it meant that the health care part of that budget was suddenly $523 million out of balance.[10] The ink was barely dry on the budget, and already it was facing a severe mid-year cut.

Although the publicly owned charity hospitals were a relatively small part of the overall Medicaid budget, which mostly consisted of payments to private hospitals, doctors, nursing homes, and pharmacies, Jindal quickly decided that most of the cuts—$319 million worth—would come from the public hospital system.

Jindal, however, did not just want to cut the hospitals. He wanted to turn over their operations to private management. His plans became clear in August, when Cerise—Blanco's former health secretary who was then running the hospital system for LSU—was called into a meeting with Levine, his successor at the Health Department who by then was running a private hospital system in Florida.[11]

Cerise had proposed that the budget cut be spread out among different Medicaid providers instead of concentrated on the public hospitals. And he saw the Medicaid expansion, set to take effect in 2014, as a financial shot in the arm for the system. What Levine and the Jindal administration had in mind was something totally different.

While he was still Louisiana's health secretary, Levine had succeeded in closing Earl K. Long Medical Center, the Baton Rouge hospital that Cerise had led before heading the Health Department.[12] The hospital was located in a mostly Black and impoverished part of north Baton Rouge, and its closure meant residents now had to trek to the private Our Lady of the Lake Regional Medical Center in the whiter, more affluent southern part of the parish. "The Lake," as it is known around Baton Rouge, had been the first charity hospital to enter into a public-private partnership with the state, where it would get extra funding from the state to take on indigent patients.

Levine's vision—carried out by his successor Greenstein—would soon carry the day. And Cerise, the most vocal opponent of privatization, would be deposed from his job overseeing the hospital system by the LSU Board of Supervisors, which Jindal controlled during his second term thanks to his ability to appoint its members.

Over the next few months, the Jindal administration would enter into problematic no-bid contracts involving nine of the ten state hospitals, including the gleaming $1.1 billion flagship teaching hospital that was under construction in New Orleans. Instead of the hospital being owned and operated by the state through LSU, it would now be managed by Louisiana Children's Medical Center, a nonprofit hospital. Three of the state hospitals, in Baton Rouge, Pineville, and Lake Charles, would be permanently closed. The deals were hastily put together, so much so that some of the contracts had blank pages when the LSU Board was asked to sign off.[13]

Besides fulfilling Jindal's hope of privatizing the hospitals, the deals came with a political bonus: they called for the private operators to lease the hospitals from the state, and to make the lease payments up front. The front-loaded payments totaled more than $300 million, cash that the administration was able to use to mitigate the effects of the Medicaid cuts.

But this maneuver also meant that the state was pushing the job of sustaining the new partnerships to future years. By using a lump-sum lease payment to cover ongoing state operating costs, Jindal was not solving the budget problem but instead putting it off.

Jindal's refusal to expand Medicaid, meanwhile, was making less and less sense as the state's budget problems continued to deepen. If there was one issue that had traditionally cut across party lines at the capitol, it was the need to maximize the dollars Louisiana gets from the federal government; yet, here the state was deliberately forgoing billions of dollars per year that could have been used to finance health care services.

LOUISIANA EXPANDS MEDICAID

By the time the 2015 governor's race came along, all four major candidates—Republicans Scott Angelle, Jay Dardenne, and David Vitter and Democrat John Bel Edwards—agreed that Louisiana should expand Medicaid. The only difference was in how to implement the expansion. Edwards wanted a "straight" expansion, which could be accomplished by simply telling the federal government that Louisiana was expanding coverage. The three Republicans were advocating a more complicated approach that involved striking a deal with the federal government by adding provisions such as the work requirements favored by conservatives.

When voters surprised the political pundits by choosing Edwards over the favored Vitter, the fate of expansion was clear. Edwards signed an executive order to expand coverage on his first full day as governor. With the stroke of a pen, more than four hundred thousand low-income adults became eligible for no-cost health coverage starting July 1, 2016.

Addressing the structural budget deficits that Jindal left behind would take additional time and effort, requiring more than two years and seven legislative sessions before a tax compromise was struck in the spring of 2018. By then, Louisiana's uninsured rate had fallen to historic lows. The following year the legislature started reinvesting in some of the programs that had been cut, with new money for childcare subsidies and higher education.

As Louisiana entered the third decade of the new century, the safety net was still frayed and imperfect. The poverty rate was still among the highest in the nation, and nearly half of all Black children lived below the poverty line. But two decades of hurricanes and political upheaval had changed how low-income people access care and government benefits.

Nowhere is that change more evident than in New Orleans, the state's economic and cultural hub, where a sparkling new, privately managed hospital carries out the twin missions of medical education and safety net care, while networks of community clinics serve the primary care needs of the population that once flocked to Charity. As for the Art Deco hospital that Huey Long built in the 1930s? In the fall of 2019, after years of dithering, the LSU Board finally decided to turn it into apartments.

While much has changed in Louisiana politics in the first two decades of the twenty-first century, a few things remain true: The governor remains the state's most powerful elected official and the driving force behind most policy decisions involving health care and welfare policy. But the government safety net that the governor oversees looks very different than it did at the turn of the century. The expansion of Medicaid eligibility in 2016 has brought historic gains in health coverage and billions of new federal dollars into Louisiana's health care system. The coverage expansion has given more low-income families greater access to health care than ever before. But other programs that support families have seen deep cuts. College tuition has spiraled as state funding has decreased, and fewer poor families have access to subsidized childcare services or cash assistance.

Underlying these changes is a fundamental shift away from the public safety net programs—symbolized by the charity hospital system—that prevailed in Louisiana for generations. Instead the state has embraced the privatization approach that has swept across southern states in recent decades, a trend that shows no sign of ending anytime soon.

NOTES

1. Stephanie Hoopes et al., "ALICE: A Study of Financial Hardship in Louisiana," Louisiana Association of United Ways, 2018, https://issuu.com/louisianaassociationofunitedway/docs/18uw_alice_report_la_-_used_for_iss?e=22574709/66844506.

2. Stacey Roussel and Neva Butkus, "Poverty Drops (Slightly) in Louisiana," Louisiana Budget Project, September 2019, https://www.labudget.org/wp-content/uploads/2019/09/Census-Poverty-Data-2018-2.pdf.

3. PricewaterhouseCoopers, "Report on Louisiana Healthcare Delivery and Financing System," 2006, https://www.braf.org/braf-research/2016/2/29/report-on-louisiana-healthcare-delivery-and-financing-system.

4. Adam Nossiter, "Dispute Over Historic Hospital for the Poor Pits Doctors against the State," *New York Times,* December 17, 2005 https://www.nytimes.com/2005/12/17/us/dispute-over-historic-hospital-for-the-poor-pits-doctors-against-the.html?searchResultPosition=9.

5. Brad K. Ott, "Avery C. Alexander, Charity Hospital in New Orleans: A Timeline since Its Forced Closure after Hurricane Katrina," *A Katrina Reader,* February 1, 2007, http://katrinareader.cwsworkshop.org/avery-c-alexander-charity-hospital-new-orleans-timeline-its-forced-closure-after-hurricane-katrina.html.

6. Jan Moller, "Jindal's Health Secretary Alan Levine Pushes Hard for Healthcare Reform," *Times-Picayune,* December 18, 2008, https://www.nola.com/news/article_a1ce0f8d-34c6-5042-9502-e6d41eb2df78.html.

7. Michael Mitchell, Michael Leachman, and Matt Saenz, "State Higher Education Cuts Have Pushed Costs to Students, Worsened Inequality," Center on Budget and Policy Priorities, October 24, 2019, https://www.cbpp.org/research/state-budget-and-tax/state-higher-education-funding-cuts-have-pushed-costs-to-students.

8. Grace Reinke, "TANF at 20: Failing Louisiana's Poor," Louisiana Budget Project, August 2016, https://www.labudget.org/wp-content/uploads/2016/08/TANF-Report.pdf.

9. Bill Barrow, "Jindal Administration Announces Steep Medicaid Cuts; LSU Hospitals Hit Hard," *Times-Picayune,* July 14, 2012, https://www.nola.com/news/politics/article_54429bd4-4f9c-5003-a683-bf42d52b42b6.html.

10. Don Gregory and Alison Neustrom, "A New Safety Net: The Risk and Reward of Louisiana's Charity Hospital Privatizations," Public Affairs Research Council of Louisiana, December 2013, http://parlouisiana.org/wp-content/uploads/2016/03/A-New-Safety-Net-The-risk-and-reward-of-Louisiana-s-Charity-hospital-privatizations.pdf.

11. Jeff Adelson, "Response to Medicaid Cuts Divided LSU, Bobby Jindal Administration," *Times-Picayune,* August 3, 2012, https://www.nola.com/news/politics/article_79514610-dbd2-5d8c-8f9e-065c1127d076.html.

12. Andy Kim, "Louisiana Governor Bobby Jindal's Evolving Leadership," *Governing,* October 2010, https://www.governing.com/topics/politics/louisiana-governor-bobby-jindal-evolving-leadership.html.

13. Melinda Deslatte, "Louisiana Reaches Settlement to Pay $5M, not $190M, for Jindal-Era LSU Hospital Deals," Associated Press, July 6, 2017, https://www.theadvocate.com/baton_rouge/news/politics/article_866578ce-626d-11e7-8d4d-63938e02929d.html.

LOUISIANA CRIME AND JUSTICE IN THE TWENTY-FIRST CENTURY

CHASE J. EDWARDS
MICHELLE N. JEANIS
AND DAVID N. KHEY

Louisiana has a long, storied, and complex history regarding crime and responses to the crime problem. With violence in urban spaces a recognized social problem, data revealed that the Louisiana cities of Shreveport, Baton Rouge, and New Orleans ranked among the most violent in the nation. Even as incarceration patterns separated the United States from all other industrialized nations, Louisiana led all other states in incarcerating its citizens. Some of this can be explained by an examination of social conditions, political pressures and statecraft, and demographic shifts, all of which are examined here. This essay describes crime in Louisiana, how the state has historically responded to crime, and the emerging innovations focused on reducing the incarceration rate and the carceral state.

THE CURRENT SCOPE OF THE CRIME PROBLEM IN LOUISIANA

It is widely known that the state of Louisiana has historically and consistently struggled with crime and disorder. Recent statistics suggest that lawlessness is a prominent feature of our society, including both nonviolent and violent crime in Louisiana.[1] Specifically, nonviolent/property crimes (including burglary, larceny theft, and motor vehicle theft) occur in Louisiana at a rate of 3,366.8 per 100,000 residents, much higher than both the southern region crime rate (2,609.9) and the national crime rate (2,362).[2] This trend has remained consistent across recent years and reflects a slight increase in the Louisiana nonviolent crime rate, compared to a decrease at the national level. Although an overall decrease in nonviolent crime occurred over the last decade, 2017 saw a notable increase in the crime rate.

Violent crime in Louisiana is even more concerning. According to the Uniform Crime Report, Louisiana is ranked as one of the most violent states in the nation. Louisiana saw an increase in both murder/nonnegligent manslaughter (12.4 per 100,000) and rape (39.9) in 2017. While instances of rape are lower than the national average (41.7), the homicide rate remains significantly higher in Louisiana, compared to the national rate of 5.3. In addition, although decreasing since 2016, both robbery (114.4) and aggravated assault (390.3) rates remain higher than the national average. Viewed over the decade, Louisiana experienced a significant drop in violent crime; however, rates remain significantly higher than the national average and have increased in recent years.

New Orleans ranks fourth in the nation for rate of murders, a troubling statistic that has plagued the city for approximately three decades. Although New Orleans is often blamed for the high violent crime and homicide rate in Louisiana, this criticism is not entirely accurate. Cities such as Baton Rouge, Monroe, and Shreveport all have significantly higher homicide rates than the national average, suggesting that Louisiana's crime (and particularly violent crime) problem is not a regional issue but rather a state-wide symptom of larger structural and societal problems. In addition, racial disparities remain consistent in both official arrests and victimization statistics.[3] For example, Black males in Louisiana are most at risk for homicide and comprise a larger portion of arrests for both violent and nonviolent crime.[4]

CONTRIBUTING FACTORS

There are many factors that contribute to the crime problem in the United States generally and Louisiana specifically. Macro-level factors, such as concentrated disadvantage, neighborhood and community risk factors, poorly performing education systems, systematic racism within the justice system, and harsh penalties for minor offenses, all increase the likelihood of delinquency and adult offending.[5] Individual-level factors, such as poverty, familial abuse/neglect, substance use/abuse, and various environmental and biological risk factors, also work to increase risk for offending.[6] These macro-level factors combine with individual-level risk factors and greatly increase the likelihood of offending and contribute to the high crime rate.[7] Generally speaking, all of these macro- and individual-level factors are consistently found in the southern region of the United States and Louisiana specifically.

Louisiana also has significant substance use and abuse issues, particularly related to opioids and marijuana use.[8] For example, in 2018, for every 100 persons there were 79.4 opioid prescriptions, which is far higher than the national average of 51.4 and places Louisiana into the top five states for opioid prescriptions. Furthermore, a large portion of arrests in Louisiana reflect substance use-related crimes, such as possession of marijuana.[9] This rate of substance use and dependence in Louisiana is one of the many factors that contribute to the high crime rate.

Louisiana ranks among the ten poorest states, and minorities are particularly likely to be poor in Louisiana. Many studies have established a connection between high crime rates and high poverty rates.[10] Population density is also associated with high violent and property crime, which is reflected in the four cities with the highest rates of violent crime in Louisiana.[11] One factor that contributes to the lethal nature of violence in Louisiana is the use of firearms as weapons of choice for crimes. Specifically, the overwhelming weapon of choice when committing homicides in Louisiana is guns; 460 out of 566 murders/nonnegligent manslaughters used some form of firearm to commit the offense.[12] This reliance on firearms when committing crimes increases the likelihood of lethal violence and contributes to the high rate of homicide in Louisiana.[13] Taken together, poverty, population density, and the use of firearms contribute to the crime problem in Louisiana, a problem that governing bodies have long sought to address.

ARRESTS AND INCARCERATION

Louisiana historically attempted to curtail the crime problem by utilizing incarceration in a variety of ways, with a heavy reliance on long-term incarceration of offenders. Louisiana incarcerates citizens at a rate higher than all other industrialized nations and the United States generally, making it the prison capital of the world.[14] Typically held in state prisons, Louisiana citizens are incarcerated at a rate of 1,052 per 100,000, which is substantially higher than the national rate of 689.[15] Louisiana has held this high incarceration ranking for years, usurped briefly by Oklahoma in 2017.[16] Louisiana residents are not equally likely to experience incarceration. Minorities, particularly Black Louisianans, are far more likely to be incarcerated than white citizens. Furthermore, although Louisiana is only comprised of 32 percent Black residents, over 60 percent of arrestees are Black.[17] It is difficult to determine if Black residents are committing more crime than white residents in Louisiana; however, a growing body of research suggests that this racial disparity in incarceration does not reflect a racial disparity in committing crimes, but rather pervasive racial bias in the justice system. For example, research on marijuana use suggests near equal use by Black and white citizens, but unequal arrests for marijuana usage for Black individuals.[18] Further research is needed to disentangle the relationship between race, crime, and incarceration in the United States generally and Louisiana specifically.

CRIMINAL JUSTICE REFORM IN LOUISIANA'S FUTURE

Like nearly every other aspect of Louisiana culture, the criminal justice system is continuing to trend toward one that more closely resembles the rest of the United States. However, these changes likely will not be linked to the same national trends that have brought about reform in other states. Louisiana's path to criminal justice reform will be plagued by resistance to change and politicians who fear being perceived as "soft on crime." Further, it remains easier to pass a new law than to change an existing one, particularly when the criminal justice establishment (for example: sheriffs, district attorneys, judges) dissents. Several factors limit reform, including conservative attitudes about individual responsibility, attitudes toward race, "tough on crime" policies, and one-party domination.[19]

Louisiana has a long and ignoble relationship with the prison industry dating back to the nineteenth century. The Louisiana State Penitentiary, the first state penitentiary built in the Trans-Mississippi region, operated as a government entity for less than a decade before it was leased to the McHatton, Pratt, and Ward Company in 1844.[20] The company opened a factory using imprisoned men to make cheap clothing for sale to plantation owners for their slaves. The memoir of a prisoner transferred to this new industrial operation noted that the company immediately "laid aside all objects of reformation and re-instated the most cruel tyranny, to eke out the dollar and cents of human misery."[21] With surprisingly little change, the modern-day equivalent can be seen in what is now called Prison Enterprises, a division of the Louisiana Department of Public Safety and Corrections that runs production facilities in eight prisons throughout the state. Prisoners are paid well below the federal minimum wage while churning out everything from cleaning products to road signs for a variety of government and private customers.[22]

The money generated by Prison Enterprises is returned through the state government and helps pay for the costs of running the Louisiana prison system. Two Louisiana prisons on the other hand—Allen Correctional Center and Winn Correctional Center—are run strictly for profit by GEO Group and LaSalle Corrections, respectively. Ignoring the general question of whether confinement of citizens is an inherently governmental function, evidence is mounting that private prisons are prone to many problems, including inadequately trained guards,[23] reduced oversight, and lengthier prison sentences.[24] Furthermore, when factors other than the pure cost of the initial contract are factored in, Saleh Mamun and his colleagues showed that private prisons are actually 1.5 percent more expensive over a twenty-five-year time span and 3 percent more expensive over forty years.[25] For these and a variety of other reasons that range from fiscal to ethical, other states have decided to end their use of private prisons.[26] Louisiana will likely follow suit, mostly due to these fiscal rather than humanitarian or constitutional considerations.

Cracks have slowly started to show in the for-profit model in Louisiana. In mid-2017, GEO Group threatened to cancel its contract with the state because of lost revenue. A year before, Louisiana cut its costs by downgrading the status of its private facilities from "prisons" to "jails," which, under the contract, reduced the amount paid to the contractor from $31.51 per day to $24.39 per day.[27] The company took less than a year to deem the contract unprofitable. While overall state spending on corrections is trending downward, local sheriffs are finding it harder to win property or sales tax renewals for prison construction and maintenance that, for decades, were little more than a rubber stamp formality at the ballot box.[28] With citizens less willing to bear the costs of mass incarceration, lawmakers will be forced to reevaluate whether every crime should come with a stiff penalty.

Pressured by fiscal reality and citizen interest groups, reform has blossomed in the last decade. In 2017, the legislature and Governor John Bel Edwards passed and signed into law a number of bills designed to reduce incarceration rates, strategically lower penalties for certain crimes, explore alternatives to incarceration, and remove the barriers to reentry for individuals transitioning from prison back to their communities.[29] Many of these reforms include evidence-based approaches to reduce recidivism. For example, reentry court programs have adapted the adult drug court framework—a post-conviction alternative sentencing program for individuals with substance use disorder caught up in the criminal justice system—to aid their transition.[30] Programming for release begins while incarcerated—individuals receive vocational training by licensed and trained inmate instructors, substance abuse education, GED education, and much more. After transitioning back to the community, program participants receive a broad array of services, including substance use disorder treatments, case management, employment placement assistance, and other services in a phased-down approach that takes five years until graduation. Results have been impressive; only 20 percent of one jurisdiction's reentry court clients returned to prison, compared to the more typical 39.9 percent rate for individuals who did not receive programing and were released to the same catchment area within twenty-four months.[31] This particular program has become one of a few growing model programs for the state—defying the inertia of a tough-on-crime approach that has been emblematic of Louisiana for more than a century.

THIS REFORM WILL NOT COME EASY

Reformation of the criminal justice system will largely depend on the willingness and effectiveness of the Louisiana legislature, whose inability to institute transformative reform, even with the overwhelming momentum of justice, history, and public opinion behind it, was highlighted with the 2018 reform of jury verdicts. The requirement of jury unanimity has been present in the common law since the fourteenth century and was incorporated into Louisiana law from its founding until the constitutional convention of 1898.[32] In that year, the state constitution was changed to require agreement among only nine out of twelve jurors to find someone guilty. To be clear, this means that while the state must prove someone's guilt "beyond a reasonable doubt," three jurors could swear to the nine others that they *know* the defendant is innocent because they themselves saw him on the other side of the city at the moment the crime was committed, and the defendant would still be sentenced to life without the possibility of parole based on the opinion of the remaining nine.[33] The 1974 constitution raised this standard to ten out of twelve, but the effect remained the same.

Such was the case of Evangelisto Ramos, who was charged with second-degree murder and exercised his right to a jury trial. Upon deliberation, ten of the twelve jurors found that the state had proven its case beyond a reasonable doubt. Two jurors found the opposite. Nonetheless, Ramos was sentenced to life in prison without the possibility of parole. The reasons for this are no secret, and they are available in the *Congressional Record*.[34] They were even the subject of a contemporaneous examination by Amasa Eaton in the *Harvard Law Review* in 1899, wherein the author quotes the president of the Louisiana constitutional convention thus:

> We have not drafted the exact Constitution we should have liked to have drafted; otherwise we should have inscribed in it, if I know the popular sentiment of this State, universal white manlihood suffrage and the exclusion from the suffrage of every man with a trace of African blood in his veins. We could not do that on account of the Fifteenth Amendment to the Constitution of the United States . . . What care I whether the test we have put be a new one or an old one? What care I whether it be more or less ridiculous or not? Doesn't it meet the case? Doesn't it let the white man vote, and doesn't it stop the negro from voting, and isn't that what we came here for? (Applause.)[35]

Therefore, when Louisiana Attorney General Jeff Landry, backed by the powerful Louisiana District Attorneys Association, sent his top lawyer to the US Supreme Court in October of 2019, there was no question that the law they were fighting to preserve was the essence of systemic racism. When the Court reversed the conviction of Mr. Ramos, it did not spare Louisiana its ire or sugarcoat this history, stating that we cannot allow "our shared respect for rational and civil discourse, [to] supply an excuse for leaving an uncomfortable past unexamined."[36]

The systematic racism built into this jury scheme succeeded in exacerbating the disparate treatment of white and Black Louisianans. Although Black people make up one-third of Louisiana, they make up two-thirds of the prison population and three-fourths of those serving life without parole. When the *Times-Picayune* analyzed six years of jury trial verdicts, the newspaper's analysis "found that 40 percent of trial convictions . . . came over the objections of one or two holdouts. When the defendant was black, the proportion went up to 43 percent, versus 33 percent for white defendants."[37]

As tragic as these cases are, they pale in comparison to the tens of thousands of felony cases that have been resolved through plea bargain every year because defense lawyers rightfully calculated the risk/reward scenarios when recommending whether their clients should take a "deal." After all, while it is possible to convince a juror to vote not guilty, getting three jurors to do so is far more difficult. And it is unlikely that an assistant district attorney would try charges so weak as to allow three not guilty votes. These tens of thousands of newly minted felons contribute to overcrowded prison populations and suffer from 1,266 separate disenfranchisements of citizenship, known as "collateral consequences," that prevent them from finding adequate employment, housing, and education.[38]

The most curious aspect of the recent repeal of nonunanimous juries is that while the *Ramos* case wound its way through the court system a constitutional amendment was placed on the ballot for voters to decide whether to add a right to a unanimous jury to the Louisiana constitution. The proposition was supported by a wide variety of groups, from Americans for Prosperity to the American Civil Liberties Union, and voters passed it by a 2-to-1 margin. Thus, the newly adopted constitutional amendment requires a unanimous verdict for all *future* cases, and the *Ramos* decision impacts sentences that have already been imposed. The impact of these two changes will be both immediate (the amendment) and slow (*Ramos*) and will result in a new normal for Louisiana criminal justice in years to come. This momentous shift in policy may be a sign of a seismic shift in public opinion regarding criminal justice reforms, which may put additional pressure on reform resisters to adjust their tactics after years of having public opinion on their side.

At the time of this writing, the Ramos verdict does not retroactively impact verdicts. In fact, a related decision by the Supreme Court during the following judicial session—*Edwards v. Vannoy*—leaves this decision to Louisiana and Oregon, the two remaining states that had allowed for nonunanimous jury decisions into the twenty-first century. Immediately after the verdict, the Louisiana Supreme Court affirmed its decision not to make any retroactive changes, relying instead on prosecutors to decide on whether any relief should be pursued on a case-by-case basis. In a related case, the Louisiana Supreme Court had affirmed that the cutoff for retroactivity would be to those individuals who were convicted by a nonunanimous jury who have not yet exhausted their appeals afforded to them by law.

For those convicted who are impacted by *Ramos*, these individuals will have their convictions vacated, resulting in their immediate release from prison under certain circumstances. Sometimes those tried of crimes have received multiple convictions from their trial, some unanimous while others nonunanimous. In these cases, the nonunanimous decisions that resulted in conviction are vacated with the possibility that a prosecutor may seek to retry this element of the original case, while the unanimous decisions remain intact. If time served for the intact decision has not been completed, these individuals will remain in prison. Also, if a prosecutor decides to retry a case after someone is released under *Ramos* relief, they could petition the court to remand this person to jail without bail if they can argue they are a public safety threat or a flight risk.

* * *

LEGISLATORS AT REST TEND TO STAY AT REST

If voters and special interest groups on both sides of the political spectrum agreed on changing the 120-year-old law ending nonunanimous juries, why did the legislature resort to a constitutional amendment? The legislature could have, instead, amended the Louisiana Code of Criminal Procedure to require unanimity. Looking for cover, legislators passed the controversial issue to the voters. Even for those who have no qualms about our current criminal justice system, its roots, or the human consequences of its operation, Louisiana can no longer afford to be the prison capital of the world.

In order to move toward a criminal justice system that is more equitable and more affordable, several major reforms will be required. One change Louisiana might consider is ending partisan elections for judges, a practice that inclines the public to think of the justice system in partisan terms. Judges could be appointed based on merit (however measured). A further change might extend the term in office for district court judges from six to ten years, like the appellate judges and justices of the Louisiana Supreme Court. Once judges are insulated from public backlash by longer tenure, Louisiana should focus on sentencing reform. The current system gives an extraordinarily large range for each crime. For instance, someone convicted of manslaughter could be sentenced to zero days or thirty years at hard labor.[39] These wide sentencing ranges expand the discretion of individual prosecutors and create unequal and prejudicial effects. Wide ranges also have a drastic effect on sentencing negotiations during plea bargaining.

Since the vast majority of cases never go to trial, the sentence that any given defendant receives is dependent on the negotiation between the defense counsel and the prosecutor. High potential maximums have an anchoring effect in negotiations, meaning that the fact that someone *could* get forty years in prison for a crime, even if no judge in the state would sentence that defendant to forty years, means that the settlement will be correspondingly higher.[40] As referenced in the opening of this essay, constituents are influenced by their perceptions of the prevalence of violent crime, and those perceptions are influenced by powerful lobbyists such as the Louisiana District

Attorneys Association and the Louisiana Sheriffs' Association. These lobbying groups frequently espouse the need to "get tough on crime" without any evidence that doing so achieves the goal of a safer society.

Ideally the Louisiana legislature would stop creating reactive crime legislation for every special interest group (for example, theft of copper for the utility companies, theft of alligators and crawfish for farmers) and laws narrowly crafted to address ephemeral trends in behavior (for example, battery of a teacher, battery of a school bus driver). The general battery laws are quite broad; those who break them can be sentenced to anything from probation or a fine to a significant amount of time behind bars. When judges are deciding the appropriate sentence for someone convicted of a crime, they can already consider a wide variety of factors, including the roles of the assailant and the victim. These laws make the criminal codes and statutes needlessly complicated.

Ironically, Louisiana could simplify the criminal code by returning to its roots in civil law. The codes written by Napoleon were designed on the premise that any person of average intelligence should be able to read and understand the laws that govern his or her life and society. A simplified sentencing system, administered by impartial judges placed above the fray of political opinion, would help Louisiana shed the expensive, inefficient, ineffective, and often unjust criminal justice system that the state has worn like an albatross for over two hundred years.

NOTES

1. "Table 8: Louisiana, Offenses Known to Law Enforcement by City, 2018," *Uniform Crime Report (UCR)*, US Department of Justice, Federal Bureau of Investigation, https://ucr.fbi.gov/crime-in-the-u.s/2018/crime-in-the-u.s.-2018/tables/table-8/table-8-state-cuts/louisiana.xls (accessed July 1, 2020).

2. Crime rates are calculated by dividing the total number of reported crimes by the total population in the area, then multiplied by 100,000. This method allows for comparisons across areas of different sizes.

3. Frank R. Baumgartner and Tim Lyman, "Race-of-Victim Discrepancies in Homicides and Executions, Louisiana 1976–2015," *Loyola Journal of Public Interest Law* 17 (2015): 129; Southern

Poverty Law Center, "Racial Profiling in Louisiana: Unconstitutional and Counter-Productive," 2018, https://www.splcenter.org/sites/default/files/leg_special_report_racial_final.pdf.

4. Prison Policy Initiative, "Louisiana Profile, 2018," https://www.prisonpolicy.org/profiles/LA.html.

5. Mohammed Imran, Mosharrof Hosen, and Mohammad Ashraful Ferdous Chowdhury, "Does Poverty Lead to Crime? Evidence from the United States of America," *International Journal of Social Economics* 45, no. 10 (2018): 1424–1438; Augustine J. Kposowa, Kevin D. Breault, and Beatrice M. Harrison, "Reassessing the Structural Covariates of Violent and Property Crimes in the USA: A County Level Analysis," *British Journal of Sociology* 46, no. 1 (1995): 79–105; Stephen G. Tibbetts, *Criminological Theory: The Essentials* (Thousand Oaks, Calif.: Sage Publications, 2018).

6. Jayajit Chakraborty and M. Martin Bosman, "Measuring the Digital Divide in the United States: Race, Income, and Personal Computer Ownership," *Professional Geographer* 57, no. 3 (2005): 395–410; Barney Warf, "Contemporary Digital Divides in the United States," *Tijdschrift voor economische en sociale geografie* 104, no. 1 (2013): 1–17.

7. See Tibbetts, *Criminological Theory,* for an overview of correlates of offending.

8. Centers for Disease Control and Prevention, "Opioid Prescribing Rate Maps," 2006–2018, https://www.cdc.gov/drugoverdose/maps/rxrate-maps.html.

9. Southern Poverty Law Center, "Racial Profiling in Louisiana."

10. Imran, Hosen, and Chowdhury, "Does Poverty Lead to Crime?"; Kposow, Breault, and Harrison, "Reassessing the Structural Covariates"; US Census Bureau, "Quick Facts: Louisiana," https://www.census.gov/quickfacts/LA.

11. Kposow, Breault, and Harrison, "Reassessing the Structural Covariates."

12. *Uniform Crime Report (UCR).*

13. Martin Kaste, "Violent Crime Stays Flat Nationally, Louisiana Still Leads States for Murder," National Public Radio (2018).

14. Prison Policy Initiative, "Louisiana Profile, 2018," April 29, 2019, https://www.prisonpolicy.org/profiles/LA.html.

15. Ibid.

16. Ibid.

17. Southern Poverty Law Center, "Racial Profiling in Louisiana."

18. Ibid.

19. Alexander Love, "Arrested Development: Political Barriers to Modern Pretrial Reform" (undergraduate thesis, College of William & Mary, 2019), Paper 1307, https://scholarworks.wm.edu/honorstheses/1307.

20. Shane Bauer, *American Prison: A Reporter's Undercover Journey into the Business of Punishment* (New York: Penguin Books, 2019).

21. Ibid.

22. Even the universities that employ many of the authors of this book take advantage of low-cost office and dorm room furniture produced by prison labor.

23. Melissa A. Kowalski, "Hiring and Training Requirements for Correctional Officers: A Statutory Analysis," *Prison Journal* 100, no. 1 (2020): 98–125.

24. Christian Dippel and Michael Poyker, "Do Private Prisons Affect Court Sentencing," *UCLA Anderson Review* (2018).

25. Saleh Mamun, Xiaoxue Li, Brady P. Horn, and Janie M. Chermak. "Private vs. Public Prisons? A Dynamic Analysis of the Long-Term Tradeoffs Between Cost-Efficiency and Recidivism in the US Prison System," *Applied Economics* 52, no. 41 (2020): 4499–4511.

26. Anthony J. Williams, "The Road to Private Prison Divestment: Inside the University of California Student Campaign," *Boom: A Journal of California* 6, no. 2 (2016): 98–103.

27. Julia O'Donoghue, "Louisiana Private Prison Company Quitting Its Contract after Budget Cuts," *Times-Picayune*, August 12, 2017, https://www.nola.com/news/politics/article_3ab210cf-1bc8-5377-b65a-3ae2fb8f2a23.html.

28. Two specific examples include the half-cent sales tax to fund public safety that failed to pass in Lafayette Parish in December 2018 and various sales tax renewals (three failed attempts) to fund the 22nd Judicial District Court and jail in St. Tammany Parish that expired in 2018. Both jurisdictions faced significant shortfalls that resulted in reductions in capacity and/or programming. The resulting impact on crime and recidivism is yet to be studied in both jurisdictions.

29. "Louisiana's Big Step on Justice Reform," editorial, *New York Times*, July 19, 2017, https://www.nytimes.com/2017/07/19/opinion/louisiana-justice-prison-reform.html?mcubz=3.

30. J. Mitchell Miller and David N. Khey, "Fighting America's Highest Incarceration Rates with Offender Programming: Process Evaluation Implications from the Louisiana 22nd Judicial District Reentry Court," *American Journal of Criminal Justice* 42, no. 3 (2017): 574–588.

31. David Khey and Jada Hector, "Process and Outcome Evaluation of the 22nd Judicial District Court of Louisiana—Reentry Court Program," Final Report, Grant No. TI026706, Substance Abuse and Mental Health Services Administration, December 15, 2019.

32. Louisiana is famously not a common law state, but neither is it a pure civil law jurisdiction. Commonly referred to as bijural, the state retains portions of its civil law heritage for some areas of law while simultaneously operating under common law principles for others. Sales, leases, property rights, torts, contracts, and successions (estates) are solidly civil law topics and are weighted double on the Louisiana Bar Exam. However, several topics, including criminal law and evidence, are based on common law principles.

33. Many men were sentenced to death under this rule as well. However, federal case law eventually bifurcated the verdict in a death penalty case into separate votes on guilt and punishment. Unanimous verdicts were required to impose the death penalty, but defendants could be found guilty and sentenced to life without parole with a nonunanimous verdict.

34. 31 Cong. Rec. S1019 (January 26, 1898) (statement of Mr. Chandler speaking on "Service on Juries in Louisiana").

35. Amasa M. Eaton, "The Suffrage Clause in the New Constitution of Louisiana," *Harvard Law Review* 13, no. 4 (1899): 279–293.

36. *Ramos v. Louisiana*, 590 U. S. (2020), footnote 44.

37. Jeff Adelson, Gordon Russell, and John Simerman, "How an Abnormal Louisiana Law Deprives, Discriminates and Drives Incarceration: Tilting the Scales," *The Advocate,* April 1, 2018, https://www.theadvocate.com/baton_rouge/news/courts/article_16fdoece-32b1-11e8-8770-33eca2a325de.html.

38. "Collateral Consequences Inventory," The Council of State Governments, https://niccc.csgjusticecenter.org/database/results/?jurisdiction=252&consequence_category=&narrow_category=&triggering_offense_category=&consequence_type=&duration_category=&page_number=1 (accessed July 1, 2020).

39. Louisiana Rev Stat § 14:31.

40. Russell D. Covey, "Plea Bargaining and Price Theory," *George Washington Law Review* 84 (2016): 923–937.

THE POLITICS OF RACIAL MEMORY IN LOUISIANA

RICK A. SWANSON

Questions of racial equity exploded on the US political scene in 2020 after George Floyd, a Black man in police custody, was killed by a white officer by kneeling on Floyd's neck for over eight minutes. The widespread national protests after this event included opposition to public statues that celebrate slave owners or those who fought for slavery during the Civil War. In response, cities are increasingly removing Confederate flags and monuments from public spaces, and renaming schools or streets currently named after slave owners or Confederates. Yet this movement has received a backlash from many whites who resent what they call the "erasing" of their history and heritage. Thus, how the past is symbolically represented has become part of today's racially focused political struggle in the United States, including in Louisiana.

In this essay, I first provide an overview of the history of racial oppression in Louisiana. I next explain how southern whites hid that history through textbooks and monuments. Using the dispute over Confederate monuments as the focal point, I conclude by discussing how representations of racial history have become entangled in identity politics.

SLAVERY THROUGH JIM CROW

The evils of slavery are well documented. Under Louisiana Law, the Code Noir, or "Black Code," allowed lifelong theft of enslaved people's labor, rape of enslaved women, selling of enslaved family members including children, and torture or murder of those who resisted enslavement. Even wanton cruelty went largely unchecked.[1] By 1860, enslaved people of African descent made up 47 percent of the population of Louisiana, and 29 percent of free households in Louisiana enslaved at least one person.[2]

The majority of wealth in most rural parishes in Louisiana was the value enslavers had in "ownership" of people. Even most nonenslavers benefitted from slavery. Businesses and their employees sold goods and services to enslavers, and all citizens used government services such as roads paid for by taxes on enslavers based on the assessed value of their slaves.

Given the economic dependence of every white Louisianan on slavery, the 1860 election of Abraham Lincoln—a US president who vowed to limit slavery—led white Louisianans to secede and help form the Confederate States of America. Louisiana's top political leaders, religious ministers, and newspaper editors all asserted that secession was about slavery.[3]

As we shall see shortly, *after* the war most southern whites argued that secession was not about slavery. Yet the seceding states which offered an explanation *before* the war said it *was* to preserve slavery.[4] Confederate vice president Alexander Stephens explained that the founding principle of the Confederacy was not just preserving slavery, but the broader principle of white supremacy.[5] As Stephens told the Virginia Secession Convention, "The great truth, I repeat, upon which our system rests, is the inferiority of the African."[6]

A four-year-long civil war then occurred between the United States and the Confederacy. During the war, US forces liberated tens of thousands of enslaved Louisianans. Approximately twenty-five thousand formerly enslaved Black Louisiana men joined the Union army, while approximately fifty thousand white Louisiana men joined the Confederate army.

After the US victory in the Civil War in 1865 and the abolition of slavery, the period of southern "Reconstruction" occurred from 1865 to 1877. New amendments to the US Constitution, federal legislation, and a new Louisiana constitution all attempted to provide Black Louisianans with racial equality. Yet most Louisiana whites still violently opposed this. White supremacist terrorist groups across Louisiana murdered Black political leaders and Black voters and committed large-scale massacres of Blacks.[7] After 1876, the federal government ended any enforcement of civil rights in Louisiana.[8] Using systematic terrorism to regain political control, Louisiana whites then reinstated white supremacy by law. They prohibited Black voting, instituted a thorough system of racial segregation, and implemented many practices to keep the Black population economically and socially subservient. In short, although southern whites had lost their war to keep slavery, they won the larger war to maintain white supremacy. It would not be until 1960s federal civil rights legislation that racial equality under law would occur in Louisiana.

Having regained political control after Reconstruction, southern whites created a fictional southern history they called the "Lost Cause."[9] In this narrative, and as portrayed in "southern" history textbooks, the Confederacy's fight was noble but doomed to fail due to the north's superior resources. Other key elements of this invented mythos were that slavery was rare and benevolent, and that secession and the "War Between the States" was not about slavery, but about unspecified "states' rights." Most Union leaders were vilified. The fact that 125,000 Black southerners fought for the Union was erased. Anti-Black Reconstruction violence was portrayed as rare, minimal, and justified. Defenders argued this practice punished Black criminals and also ended government led by unintelligent and corrupt Blacks.[10] Moreover, anti-Black racial oppression in the South since Reconstruction was ignored, minimized, or defended in these "southern" histories.

THE LOST CAUSE IN LOUISIANA TEXTBOOKS

The entrenchment of Lost Cause ideology in the South developed over time. In the decades immediately following the Civil War, the all-white Louisiana State Board of Education approved history textbooks—including one written by a former Confederate congressman—that taught that southern whites had fought for slavery during the Civil War and for white supremacy during Reconstruction.[11] By the turn of the century, however, southern whites demanded textbooks that consistently told only Lost Cause dogma. White "southern heritage" groups such as the United Confederate Veterans (UCV), Sons of Confederate Veterans (SCV), and the United Daughters of the Confederacy (UDC) led this effort in Louisiana and across the South.[12]

In Louisiana, a UCV reunion in 1901 publicly resolved "No histories or other school books, which may treat of questions involving the respective merits or demerits of the North or South, should be taught in Southern schools, unless written by one in thorough sympathy and affiliation with the South and its people."[13] White-owned Louisiana newspapers endorsed this effort.[14] Note that the phrase "the South and its people" implicitly refers only to *white* people—the UCV did not want textbooks written "in sympathy and affiliation" with southern *Blacks*.

The Louisiana UCV, SCV, and UDC became de facto members of the Louisiana State Board of Education Textbook Committee. They gave lists to the Board of Education superintendent and the governor of material they deemed appropriate and inappropriate, including lists of approved publishers.[15] Only texts that defended slavery, secession, war by southern whites, and anti-Black Reconstruction violence passed the pro-Confederate litmus test.[16] Prohibited history books told the truth: the conditions of enslavement were horrible, and secession and the Civil War were caused by the southern white desire to preserve slavery.[17] Textbooks could not portray the Union cause or leaders in a positive light, nor portray the Confederate cause or leaders in a negative light. Describing or depicting anti-Black oppression by southern whites was "offensive in its treatment of the negro question" and would give children "a cruelly unjust opinion of the south."[18] Acknowledging Black intelligence was disallowed.[19] State Superintendent Harris assured the UDC it would only approve textbooks that were "fair and just to the South.'"[20] Again, by "South" Harris clearly meant southern *whites*. Even the Louisiana attorney general helped lead the drive to purge Louisiana textbooks of historical accuracy.[21]

By the 1930s, scholars documented the skewed nature of southern school textbooks.[22] Yet national textbook publishers, unwilling to lose the substantial profits from the sizeable southern market, had long since complied with southern white requests to alter facts and avoid topics.[23] For the next half-century, at least through the early 1960s, the Louisiana State Board of Education approved history textbooks that espoused only Lost Cause doctrine.[24]

THE LOST CAUSE AND LOUISIANA MONUMENTS

During this same period, southern white heritage groups, led by the UDC, promoted white supremacy in other ways. In Louisiana, schools and streets were named for Confederate leaders, and Confederate-related monuments were erected. This undertaking peaked between 1900 and the mid-1930s but occurred both before and after this period.[25] No Black man ever fought as a member of the Louisiana state militia or the Confederate army; both Louisiana and Confederate law prohibited such. Nor was any monument erected to the twenty-five thousand Black Louisiana Civil War veterans who fought for the United States. Thus, Lost Cause monuments honored the white race exclusively, and some monuments admitted such. In 1920, whites placed a monument in Grant Parish honoring three white "heroes" who died "fighting for White supremacy" during the Colfax massacre.[26] In 1932, the white leaders of New Orleans added a plaque to a city monument celebrating the murderous defeat of the racially integrated New Orleans police force by a white supremacist militia in 1876. The plaque declares that the end of Reconstruction "recognized White supremacy and gave us our state."[27]

Even if Lost Cause monuments did not say they were celebrating the victory of white supremacy, it was understood. Speaking to Confederate veterans at the 1910 annual convention of the Louisiana UCV, Louisiana governor Jared Y. Sanders Sr. explained that Confederates had fought for a single unified cause throughout the Civil War and Reconstruction: "I shudder to think of the awful curse that damaged the South from 1860 until 1876, and I love to glory in the manhood that against the triumphant government itself gritted its teeth, and said, by the eternal gods, this Southland is ours and our children's and by the eternal we will redeem it and give it back to the White people where it belongs."[28] Louisiana newspapers likewise praised Confederates because they achieved "the triumph of the rule of intelligence and White supremacy over the Africanization of Louisiana" and were able "to establish the supremacy of the White race on a firm basis."[29]

LOUISIANA VIEWS ON CONFEDERATE MONUMENTS TODAY: IDENTITY POLITICS

The rewriting of history by the Lost Cause movement had substantial, long-term effects on how Louisianans perceive and portray their racial past. The 1960s civil rights movement did not entirely stop southern whites from building Lost Cause monuments or pushing the Lost Cause narrative in textbooks. Also, publishers are still catching up in providing accurate southern history in textbooks.[30] Moreover, Lost Cause textbooks were still used by Louisiana students in the 1950s and 1960s. Fifteen-year-old students in 1960 were 55 years old at the turn of the millennium. These adults were thus peaking as community leaders and opinion influencers. Many were teachers; some were teachers of teachers. Unless they received accurate history education in college or were avid history readers on their own, they knew only the fictional Lost Cause version of Louisiana history, and so taught it to their children and students.

Given how Lost Cause doctrine succeeded in permeating historical thought in Louisiana (and the nation), it is unsurprising that a 2016 poll showed that 73 percent of Louisianans opposed removing Confederate monuments.[31] Yet polls show significant divisions on this issue by age, race, and party. As textbook accuracy has improved over time, so has the understanding of southern history among younger age groups. This has translated into an age gap in attitudes toward Confederate symbols. A national 2017 survey found 40 percent of adults under the age of thirty strongly favored removing Confederate monuments, whereas only 12 percent of adults over the age of sixty-five did.[32] This age gap is present in Louisiana as well, especially among white Louisianans: A 2016 survey showed 21 percent of white Louisianans aged eighteen through twenty-nine favored removing Confederate monuments compared to only 4 percent of white Louisianans aged fifty to sixty-four.[33]

Louisiana polls also reveal significant racial differences. Racially segregated schools still existed throughout much of Louisiana until the early 1970s. Students in white schools were not just taught the Lost Cause; they were influenced by the racial attitudes of their parents and teachers, most of whom supported racial segregation. On the other hand, students in Black schools were more likely to learn Black history as they were taught by Black teachers, who themselves were overseen by Black principals. Black children also could have learned about Black history through oral history from their parents and grandparents. These historical realities might help explain why a 2016 survey of Louisianans showed a plurality of 47 percent of Blacks favored removing Confederate monuments, in contrast with an 88 percent majority of white Louisianans who opposed it.[34] Black support for such monuments might have been expressed out of fear of objecting to the monuments (as occurred in the past), or perhaps exposure to Lost Cause narratives led them to believe the Confederacy did not fight for slavery. Regardless, the racial disparities in attitudes toward such monuments explains, in large part, why the first monument removal in Louisiana occurred in New Orleans, which had a 60 percent majority Black population at the time.[35]

Yet if support for Confederate symbols was based on support for the Confederacy, one would expect that primarily only *southern* whites would support these monuments. This is not the case, however. A 2017 poll found 54 percent of whites nationwide and 75 percent of Republicans nationwide (comprised predominantly of whites) opposed removing Confederate monuments.[36]

This national white opposition can be explained in part by the growing feeling of resentment among whites.[37] Faced with increasing multiculturalism and a decreasing share of the population, whites are increasingly asserting a white identity that presents themselves as being under attack.[38] For example, one 2017 national poll showed 55 percent of whites believe whites are discriminated against in the United States today (such as in job-seeking), with higher percentages among whites of lower and moderate incomes.[39] A 2017 survey found:

> More than six in ten (61%) of White residents of the South-east . . . say discrimination against White people has become as big a problem as discrimination against Black people and other minorities, compared to 51% of Whites living outside these regions who share this view. . . . Whites in the Southeast . . . are also more likely than Whites in other parts of the country to believe they are being asked to make sacrifices that benefit minority groups (42% vs. 32%, respectively), and that government pays too much attention to the problems of minorities (48% vs. 42%, respectively).[40]

In 2018, per-capita income in Louisiana was 15 percent below the national average.[41] Because white resentment appears higher among lower-income whites, this could help explain why opposition to removing Confederate monuments is 34 points higher among whites in Louisiana than in the rest of the nation.[42] Indeed, Gaines M. Foster, a historian who has studied the Lost Cause movement, concludes that for many whites—not just in the South but nationally—Confederate history is no longer important as a representation of the Confederacy itself. Instead, flags, monuments, and other representations of the Confederacy have become "symbol[s] of multiple grievances, including resentment over the increased—if not fully equal—status of African Americans, the power and influence of economic and cultural elites, and a perceived loss of traditional values."[43]

In short, there is an increasing match between Louisiana opinion and national opinion regarding symbols of southern white heritage. Confederate symbols have become entangled in arguments over our national racial identity: should we promote racially diverse multiculturalism in the United States, or should we preserve and perpetuate the nation's predominantly white European heritage?

This cultural clash was displayed when New Orleans began removing its Confederate monuments. Opposition involved not just lawsuits and protests, but death threats.[44] White objectors, using Lost Cause arguments, insisted the monuments celebrated neither slavery nor white supremacy, but merely "southern heritage"—in other words, *white* southern heritage—which they believed was being attacked. Other racially diverse movements in Louisiana opposing Confederate monuments have also generated intense white opposition.[45]

This cultural battle also occurred in the Louisiana legislature in 2017. A bill passed the House that would have limited the removal or relocation of Confederate monuments. The bill's sponsor stated that slavery did not cause the Civil War. The legislative Black Caucus pointed out otherwise. On a "largely party-line vote," the House passed the bill. The Black Caucus left the chamber in protest, with members calling the vote "disgusting" and "the worst thing I've ever seen done in this building." The head of the Black Caucus declared that the vote represents "a deep-seated belief in White supremacy." Yet white Republican members who voted for the bill said they were flooded with calls from white constituents to protect Confederate monuments.[46] The bill failed in the Louisiana Senate, but a revealing moment came during the House Committee hearing on the bill. All the witnesses testifying in support of the bill were white. One of them declared, "I don't care if we have White supremacy carved in stone."[47]

Clearly, a significant divide persists on how Louisiana's violent racial past should be remembered. A political shift on this issue appears to be happening involving identity politics, but the long-term future of this change remains to be seen.

NOTES

1. Works Progress Administration Federal Writer's Project, *Slave Narratives: A Folk History of Slavery in the United States from Interviews with Former Slaves* (Washington, D.C.: Library of Congress, 1941); Ronnie W. Clayton, *Mother Wit: The Ex-Slave Narratives of the Louisiana Writers' Project* (New York: Peter Lang Publishing, 1990); Joe Gray Taylor, *Negro Slavery in Louisiana* (Baton Rouge: Louisiana Historical Association, 1963).

2. 1860 US Census.

3. *Pointe Coupee Democrat,* August 18, 1860; *Opelousas Courier,* August 25, 1860; Plaquemine *Gazette and Sentinel,* August 25, 1860; *Plaquemine Gazette and Sentinel,* November 17, 1860, December 1, 1860; *Plaquemine Gazette and Sentinel,* December 1, 1860; *Opelousas Courier,* November 3, 1860, English language edition; *Plaquemine Gazette and Sentinel,* November 11, 1860; *Alexandria Constitutional,* December 1, 1860; *Alexandria Constitutional,* January 19, 1861; *Baton Rouge Sugar Planter,* December 1, 1860; *New Orleans Daily Crescent,* December 24, 1860; *New Orleans Daily Crescent,* December 3, 1860; *New Orleans Daily Crescent,* December 11, 1860; *Congressional Globe,* December 31, 1860, 217; *New Orleans Daily Crescent,* January 7, 1861; *Western Sentinel* (Winston, N.C.), January 18, 1861; *The South-Western* (Shreveport, Louisiana), February 27, 1861.

4. *New Orleans Daily Crescent,* February 1, 1861; *Official Journal of the Proceedings of the [Secession] Convention of the State of Louisiana* (New Orleans: J. O. Nixon, Printer, 1861), 9–11; South Carolina: *Richmond Enquirer,* December 28, 1860; Georgia: *Journal of the Public and Secret Proceedings of the [Secession] Convention of the People of Georgia* (Milledgeville, Ga.: Boughton, Nisbet and Barnes, State Printers, 1861), 104–113; Mississippi: *Nashville Union and American,* February 6, 1861; Texas: *Dallas Herald,* February 13, 1861.

5. *Nashville Union and American,* March 28, 1861 (reprinting from the *Savannah Republican*); *Memphis Daily Appeal,* March 29, 1861; *Baltimore Daily Exchange,* March 28, 1861.

6. *Richmond (Va.) Enquirer,* November 5, 1861.

7. Charles Lane, *The Day Freedom Died: The Colfax Massacre, the Supreme Court, and the Betrayal of Reconstruction* (New York: Holt, 2008); LeeAnna Keith, *The Colfax Massacre: The Untold Story of Black Power, White Terror, and the Death of Reconstruction* (Oxford: Oxford Univ. Press, 2008); C. Dier, *The 1868 St. Bernard Parish Massacre* (Charleston, S.C.: History Press,

2017); Matthew Christensen, *The 1868 St. Landry Massacre: Reconstruction's Deadliest Episode of Violence* (unpublished dissertation, University of Wisconsin-Milwaukee, 2012); John Ficklin, *History of Reconstruction in Louisiana to 1868* (Baltimore, Md.: Johns Hopkins Press, 1920).

8. Ella Lonn, *Reconstruction in Louisiana after 1868* (New York: G. P. Putnam's Sons, 1918); Joe Gray Taylor, *Louisiana Reconstructed, 1863–1877* (Baton Rouge: Louisiana State Univ. Press, 1974).

9. *Opelousas Courier,* March 26, 1904; *Lafayette Advertiser,* January 23, 1907; *Weekly Iberian,* June 25, 1921.

10. Charles Reagan Wilson, *Baptized in Blood: The Religion of the Lost Cause, 1865–1920* (Athens: Univ. of Georgia Press, 2009); David W. Blight, *Race and Reunion: The Civil War in American Memory* (Cambridge, Mass.: Harvard Univ. Press, 2001); Caroline E. Janney, *Remembering the Civil War: Reunion and the Limits of Reconciliation* (Chapel Hill: Univ. of North Carolina Press, 2013); Gaines M. Foster, *Ghosts of the Confederacy: Defeat, the Lost Cause, and the Emergence of the New South* (New York: Oxford Univ. Press, 1987).

11. See approved textbooks' coverage of slavery, secession, the Civil War, and Reconstruction in the *Weekly Thibodeaux Sentinel,* June 27, 1885; *St. Tammany Farmer* (Covington, Louisiana), April 17, 1886; John Dimitry, *Lessons in the History of Louisiana* (New Orleans: A. S. Barnes, 1877); George F. Holmes, *New School History of the United States* (New York: University Publishing Company, 1886); *Weekly Thibodeaux Sentinel,* January 8, 1888; February 9, 1901; February 8, 1890; Henry E. Chambers, *A School History of the United States* (New Orleans: University Publishing Company, 1898); Henry Edward Chambers, *A Higher History of the United States* (New Orleans, La.: F. F. Hansell and Bro., 1899); *New Iberia Enterprise,* August 24, 1901; J. L. M. Curry, *Civil History of the Government of the Confederate States* (Richmond, Va.: B. F. Johnson Publishing Company, 1901); J. L. M. Curry, *The Southern States of the American Union* (Richmond, Va.: B. F. Johnson Publishing Company, 1895).

12. James M. MacPherson, "Long-Legged Yankee Lies: The Southern Textbook Crusade," in *The Memory of the Civil War in American Culture,* ed. Alice Fahs and Joan Waugh (Chapel Hill: Univ. of North Carolina Press, 2004).

13. *Lafayette Gazette,* August 10, 1901.

14. Ibid.; *St. Mary Banner,* January 27, 1906; *Shreveport Caucasian,* September 24, 1911.

15. *Bossier Banner,* April 13, 1916.

16. *Rice Belt Journal,* September 19, 1913; Nathaniel Wright Stephenson, *An American History* (Boston: Ginn, 1913); *Bogalusa Enterprise,* September 7, 1916; Harry F. Estill, *The Beginner's History of Our Country* (Dallas, Tex.: Southern Publishing Company, 1912); *Rice Belt Journal,* August 31, 1917; Lawton B. Evans, *The Essential Facts of American History* (Chicago: Sanborn, 1914); Harriet Magruder, *A History of Louisiana* (Boston: Heath, 1909).

17. See, for example, David H. Montgomery, *The Beginner's American History* (Boston: Ginn, 1899), 212–213; John Fiske, *A History of the United States for Schools* (Boston: Houghton Mifflin, 1895), 345–371; James Baldwin, *Barnes's Elementary History of the United States* (New York: American Book Company, 1908), 283–344; Charles Carleton Coffin, *Building the Nation* (New York: Harper and Brothers, 1882), 282–290; 305–313, 387–388, 399–406, 418–424; David H. Montgomery, *The Student's American History* (New York: Ginn, 1905), 436–437.

18. *Woman's Enterprise,* September 16, 1921.

19. *Thibodeaux Sentinel,* February 13, 1909.

20. *Bossier Banner,* April 13, 1916; *Woman's Enterprise,* September 16, 1921.

21. *Shreveport Caucasian,* March 18, 1909; *Thibodeaux Sentinel,* June 13, 1908.

22. Lawrence D. Reddick, "Racial Attitudes in American History Textbooks in the South," *Journal of Negro History* 19, no. 3 (July 1934): 225–265.

23. *Opelousas Courier,* April 1, 1905.

24. The lists of approved textbooks for this time period are available in the Louisiana Department of Education Textbook Adoption files, 1950–1979, Accession P1986-259, Box 1, Louisiana State Archives, Baton Rouge, Louisiana. See the approved textbooks' coverage of slavery, secession, the Civil War, Reconstruction, and civil rights in: Eugene C. Barker and Henry Steel Commager, *Our Nation* (Evanston, Ill. Row, Peterson and Company, 1950; Everett Augspurger and Richard A. McLemore, *Our Nation's Story* (Chicago: Laidlaw Brothers, 1956); Henry W. Bragdon and Samuel P. McCutchen, *History of a Free People* (New York: MacMillan, 1956); Paul F. Boller and E. Jean Tilford, *This Is Our Nation* (St. Louis: Webster Publishing Company, 1961); David Saville Muzzey, *A History of Our Country* (Boston: Ginn and Company in Boston, 1948); Leon H. Canfield and Howard B. Wilder, *The Making of Modern America* (Cambridge, Mass.: Houghton Mifflin, 1950).

25. Southern Poverty Law Center, *Whose Heritage: Public Symbols of the Confederacy,* 2016, 25–26.

26. *Colfax Chronicle,* August 28, 1920.

27. "City of New Orleans Begins Remove of Divisive Confederate Statutes Commemorating 'Cult of the Lost Cause,'" City of New Orleans, April 17, 2017, https://www.nola.gov/mayor/news/archive/2017/042417-pr-city-of-new-orleans-begins-removal-of-di/.

28. *St. Landry Clarion,* October 8, 1910.

29. *Bossier Banner,* September 26, 1907; *Shreveport Caucasion,* September 15, 1907; *Woman's Enterprise,* October 1, 1922; see also *St. Mary Banner,* September 19, 1914.

30. Southern Poverty Law Center, *Teaching Hard History: American Slavery* (Atlanta: Southern Poverty Law Center, 2018).

31. LSU Manship School of Mass Communication, Reilly Center for Media and Public Affairs, *The Louisiana Survey 2019,* April 8, 2016, https://pprllsu.com/wp-content/uploads/2016/04/Louisiana-Survey-2016-Report-Seven-FINALv2.pdf.

32. HuffPost/YouGov survey, August 15–16, 2017, http://big.assets.huffingtonpost.com/tabs HPConfederateFlag20170815.pdf.

33. LSU Manship School of Mass Communication, Reilly Center for Media and Public Affairs, *The Louisiana Survey 2019,* raw data provided by Michael Henderson.

34. *The Louisiana Survey 2019;* HuffPost/YouGov survey.

35. 2010 US Census.

36. Huffpost/Yougov survey.

37. Katherine J. Cramer, *The Politics of Resentment: Rural Consciousness in Wisconsin and the Rise of Scott Walker* (Chicago: Univ. of Chicago Press, 2016); Arlie Russell Hochschild,

Strangers in Their Own Land: Anger and Mourning on the American Right (New York: New Press, 2018).

38. Ashley Jardina, *White Identity Politics* (Cambridge: Cambridge Univ. Press, 2019).

39. "Majority of White Americans Say They Believe Whites Face Discrimination," NPR, October 24, 2017, https://www.npr.org/2017/10/24/559604836/majority-of-White-americans-think-theyre-discriminated-against.

40. "Attitudes on Child and Family Wellbeing," Public Religion Research Institute, September 18, 2017, https://www.prri.org/wp-content/uploads/2017/09/PRRI-Family-Wellbeing.pdf.

41. "Louisiana per Capita Personal Income Grew Faster Than National Average," *Acadiana Advocate,* November 15, 2019, https://www.theadvocate.com/baton_rouge/news/business/article_3199f432-07cf-11ea-afd3-a70670c902a8.html.

42. *The Louisiana Survey 2019;* HuffPost/YouGov survey.

43. Gaines M. Foster, "Today's Battle over the Confederate Flag Has Nothing to Do with the Civil War," *Zocalo Public Square,* October 23, 2018, https://www.zocalopublicsquare.org/2018/10/23/todays-battle-confederate-flag-nothing-civil-war/ideas/essay/.

44. Mitch Landrieu, *In the Shadow of Statues: A White Southerner Confronts History* (New York: Penguin, 2019).

45. "Upcoming Court Date in Ongoing Confederate Monument Court Battle Reset," *Shreveport Times,* December 24, 2019, https://www.shreveporttimes.com/story/news/2019/12/24/upcoming-court-date-ongoing-confederate-monument-court-battle-reset/2734160001/; "Court Hearing on 1980 Mouton Statue Agreement Delayed," *Acadiana Advocate,* January 21, 2020, https://www.theadvocate.com/acadiana/news/article_d3e0a7f8-3bd8-11ea-8160-3fc60c6ce28f.html.

46. "Louisiana Black Caucus Condemns 'Disgusting' Vote by House to Block Removal of New Orleans Monuments," *New Orleans Advocate,* May 15, 2017, https://www.nola.com/article_814d139e-0694-5554-8cd3-9fe0d137db5e.html; "Legislative Black Caucus Says Confederate Monument Vote Exposes 'Deep-Rooted Belief in White Supremacy,'" *Baton Rouge Advocate,* May 16, 2017, https://www.theadvocate.com/baton_rouge/news/politics/legislature/article_c3ec9214-3a44-11e7-a2b8-df666da8d331.html.

47. "Bill to Stop Confederate Monument Removals, Put Power in 'People's Hands' Passes Committee," *Baton Rouge Advocate,* May 3, 2017, https://www.theadvocate.com/baton_rouge/news/politics/legislature/article_06f5be64-3004-11e7-9e40-c7745579a325.html.

CONCLUSION

Louisiana's Post-Carnival Politics

CHRISTIE L. MALOYED

Long known for its carnival-style politics, Louisiana entered the political mainstream in the twenty-first century. The distinct political culture that distinguished the state for over a century gave way to national political and partisan trends. The spectacle of retail politics once defined Louisiana campaigns—from candidates tossing beads to revelers from Mardi Gras parade floats to stump speeches at the Shrimp and Petroleum Festival. Today's political campaigns, by contrast, are dominated by elite fundraising events, outside spending by political action committees, and social media advertising. Institutional reforms, including legislative term limits and ethics legislation, have reduced both the governor's and legislators' power, ultimately empowering special interest groups and lobbyists. The heyday of free-flowing oil and gas revenues has ended, taking with it some, but not all, of the corruption that used to typify Louisiana politics. Today, Louisiana must depend on funding generated through individual and business taxes and federal largesse that comes with spending limits. Once a distinct political outlier, especially among southern states, Louisiana's politics have become more, if not entirely, conventional.

Historically, the state's geographic, racial, and religious makeup contributed to Louisiana's unique gumbo-style politics. Three distinct cultural and ethnic groups defined the political cleavages and fueled competition: white evangelical Protestants in the north, white Catholics in the south, and Blacks throughout the state. In the twenty-first century, however, national trends have permeated politics in the Pelican State, redefining and undermining the precarious balance of power. Partisan realignment, ideological polarization, outside money in elections, and national and global economic and climatic crises have contributed to a poisoned policy process. Local newspapers have folded, and those that survived often replaced local staff and coverage with nationally syndicated content. State and local candidates now campaign on national issues like the Second Amendment or the US president rather than local economic, social, or infrastructure issues. Louisiana's distinct ethnic, religious, and regional coalitions have been overshadowed by the emergence of strong national partisan identities.

Long after other southern states switched to Republican control, Louisiana remained a Democratic outlier in the late 1990s and early 2000s. Following the national Tea Party movement in 2010, however, multiple elected officials switched their party registration from Democrat to Republican, contributing to Republicans winning control of both houses in the 2011 election. Republican registration has grown steadily, and Democratic growth is unlikely given the out-migration of college graduates, relatively small urban centers, and a slow-growing Hispanic population. Among Louisiana residents, politics has become hyperpartisan. Members feel a stronger tie to their party and hold unfavorable views of other parties. Voters are more divided over partisanship than ideology. The split over policy issues is mild among voters, but they choose from a slate of ideologically divided candidates. Without some realignment of the national parties, this trend will persist.

In divorcing from its colorful past, Louisiana politics matured in ways that can help the state move beyond its reputation as a "banana republic" that is tolerant—even indulgent—of corruption. But Louisiana's new professionalized form of politics brings to the state the same dysfunction seen on the national stage: gridlock, distrust in government, and perilous levels of polarization. The essays gathered in this volume recognize these challenges and point toward opportunities to leverage the state's cultural and economic strengths to build a better Louisiana. The following sections offer actions to take and reforms to implement in institutions, politics, and policy to invest in a better future for Louisiana's citizens.

* * *

INSTITUTIONS

The Louisiana constitution looms large over all other political discussions in the state. Beyond its unwieldy length and frequency of amendment, the document is overly complicated with narrowly tailored restrictions. These restrictions prevent state government from operating under broader grants of authority that would allow a more flexible decision-making approach. Health care and higher education bear the brunt of these limitations, as they are the two significant areas whose funding is not constitutionally protected. Louisiana voters deserve the opportunity to reexamine these fiscal restrictions, enshrined in the constitution since the 1980s and 1990s. In recent years, good governance groups have built support for constitutional reform, including the Public Affairs Research Council, the Council for a Better Louisiana, and the Committee of 100. The legislature could achieve this through the normal amendment process or a constitutional convention to allow an open discussion about our state's priorities. Louisiana needs a constitution that gives the legislature more fiscal agility and avenues for political compromise.

The balance of power in Baton Rouge has tipped in recent years, with conservative lawmakers expanding the authority of the legislative branch at the expense of gubernatorial control. The 2019 reelection of Democratic governor Jon Bel Edwards underscored the partisan tension in Baton Rouge, not only between the governor and the Republican-controlled state legislature but across the state itself. Historically the governor wielded formidable formal and informal powers, from crafting the budget to hand-picking legislative leadership. But the legislature asserted its independence, from first dismissing the governor's preferences for speaker of the House in 2016 to calling itself into special session in the summer of 2020. While balanced power between branches is healthy, the legislature's recent attempts to curtail the governor's emergency powers during the COVID-19 pandemic could ultimately handicap state efforts at effective crisis management down the road.

The many crises Louisiana has faced in the twenty-first century have underscored state and local governments' interdependence. Local governments have been especially strained by the volatility, from localized flooding and storm damage to regional surges during the pandemic. The state can support local government by offering greater autonomy and predictability, especially in fiscal affairs. Many local governments want to incentivize economic development, but they want input in the process. Governor Edwards's executive action giving local taxing authorities a say in the Industrial Tax Exemption Program offered an important step toward increased local control. Similarly, a centralized sales and inventory tax collection program would support local business development, but local governments need assurances that those tax dollars will return to their home parishes. To strengthen local businesses and the governments' ability to innovate, the state government needs to streamline the local taxing process.

POLITICS

Though recent, Louisiana's conversion to Republicanism has been thorough. In 2021, Republicans held substantial majorities in both legislative chambers, all but one federal office, and all statewide offices except the governorship. Democrats' electoral success has primarily been held to urban centers and majority-minority districts. Robust parties and partisan competition provide the foundation for vibrant democracies, and bipartisan cooperation provides the basis for successful policymaking. Unfortunately, the national trend of hyperpartisanship has trickled down to state and local politics. Even though Louisiana voters are only mildly split on many policy issues, the distrust of other parties exaggerates the differences and hampers opportunities for compromise. Louisiana's political parties are more ideologically moderate than those in other states; however, they are more racially polarized. The deeply partisan split results in the election of candidates who are more ideologically polarized than the constituents whom they represent.

For most of the twentieth century, Louisiana pursued a populist political agenda funding social safety net programs by taxing petrochemical industries. But Hurricane Katrina and the Great Recession pushed Louisiana to the political right. Governor Jindal successfully spearheaded dramatic budget cuts gutting social welfare programs. By the 2016 election of President Trump, right-wing populism permeated US politics at all levels. State and local campaigns frequently used national slogans like "Drain the swamp" and "Fake news." Increasingly, politically and racially polarizing policy debates over immigration, policing, and election integrity made their way to the state capital. Given the decline of local newspapers and state and local news coverage, the domination of national political trends in Louisiana seems almost inevitable.

The challenges posed by rising hyperpartisanship and declining local news are among the most serious for effective governance. Though hyperpartisanship is not unique to Louisiana, there are three areas where the state can protect itself from the worst effects. First, Louisiana should protect its jungle primary system, which supports voter engagement and dampens ideological extremism. Compared to other states, Louisiana substantially exceeds voter turnout rates for primary elections, meaning more voters from diverse political perspectives select candidates. Partisan primaries drive turnout down and overrepresent the views of the most ideologically extreme voters and candidates.

Second, Louisiana should seek to further reduce the number of elections held each year. Historically, municipalities held elections off-cycle from federal elections to limit national influence in local contests. Local elections often have less than 10 percent turnout, and those who participate are typically among the most partisan and ideologically polarized. Continuing to hold off-cycle elections empowers those with money and resources. The decision to hold high-cost, low-turnout elections is a choice to privilege the voices of a small segment of voters. The state can reduce costs, decrease polarization, and increase trust by limiting the number of off-cycle elections.

Third, Louisiana can support the recruitment and training of more women candidates. Women in office are more likely to work across partisan lines and compromise. Diverse groups offer more innovative policy solutions, and women in office are more successful in meeting their policy goals. Louisiana consistently ranks in the bottom fifth of all states for the share of women in the state legislature. Working toward gender parity in state and local government will help stave off the worst effects of the increasingly partisan and polarized politics.

POLICY

For decades, the oil and gas industry's boom-and-bust economics perpetuated a political cycle of investment and austerity. During boom times, the state supported populist projects to expand infrastructure, education, and welfare programs, but then severely cut those investments during downturns, never quite getting ahead for falling behind. In the last decade, Louisiana's shift toward right-wing populism reoriented the state's fiscal policy toward ending "big government." It favored privatization and tax reductions. In practice, this meant defunding social safety net programs, such as childcare benefits, the charity hospital system, and low-cost college tuition.

Louisiana's economic and political future is particularly vulnerable to external shocks. With the intensification of weather events—from hurricanes to flooding to polar vortex freezes—the state depends on national emergency funds to rebuild. Moreover, the COVID-19 pandemic has underscored the state's reliance on federal aid, narrowly avoiding deep budget cuts in 2020 and 2021 by using federal relief funds to plug holes.

Two issues loom large over discussions of Louisiana's future: the coast and the economy. Louisiana is losing ground—with barrier islands disappearing at an astonishing rate over the last century. The loss of land due to erosion, subsidence, and sea level rise puts the coastal region at greater risk from climate change and hurricanes. The costs associated with restoration attempts are staggering, totaling in the billions, and require federal support. The Coastal Master Plan aims to slow the loss of land and rebuild where possible. In 2020, Governor Edwards additionally formed a Climate Initiatives Task Force with representatives from the public, private, and academic sectors to tackle these issues.

Climate forecasting is an inexact science, but historically the forecasts have gotten worse rather than better whenever they are revised and updated. Because of rising seas and longer storm seasons, state government can expect substantial numbers of displaced residents, significant reductions in property values, and new gaps in the availability of insurance coverage in the coming years. It is unclear whether local governments will be able to cope with the resulting increase in demand for services and simultaneous decrease in revenues with which to provide them. To forestall the worst outcomes, the state needs a sustained effort that takes seriously the problems of climate change, supports local governments, and seeks partnerships with coastal residents and industries.

The fate of Louisiana's coast has been bound up with off-shore drilling. The relative decline of the oil and gas industry remains politically polarizing among state legislators, with some Republicans, especially those representing southern parishes, urging continued investment. Meanwhile, economic sectors, including chemical manufacturing, health care, and water transportation, have expanded with additional growth opportunities in professional and business services. The 2020 coronavirus pandemic shifted some professional and technical sectors toward remote work, a trend that may persist for years to come. Louisiana's vibrant culture and low cost of living can make it an attractive place to live. But the state must actively seek out and support emerging industries to attract and retain a talented workforce.

While debates over the economy, taxing, and spending have been mired in partisan disagreement, one bright spot of bipartisan compromise has been criminal justice reform. Spearheaded by a broad coalition of political, religious, and community leaders, the 2017 reform package supported evidence-based approaches that are successfully reducing recidivism rates. Building on this success, Louisiana should consider additional reforms that will continue to increase equity and reduce costs. Institutional reforms include ending the partisan judicial election and extending the terms of district judges. These changes would insulate judges from the political pressures associated with campaign contributions and public backlash against unpopular decisions. Moreover, the state should consider sentencing reform. Too often, defendants agree to plea bargains with longer sentences than a judge would issue. These reforms would provide economic savings as well as reduce the racial disparities in Louisiana's criminal justice system.

The killings of George Floyd, Breonna Taylor, Ahmaud Arbery, among so many others, sparked an ongoing racial reckoning in the summer of 2020. Organizers in Louisiana cities, including New Orleans, Baton Rouge, and Lafayette, joined nationwide demonstrations and protests to demand police reforms. Louisiana confronted how it symbolizes its past heritage, with cities discussing removing Confederate monuments and other symbols from public spaces.

In Lake Charles, only weeks after the Calcasieu Police Jury voted to keep their "South's Defenders Monument" on their courthouse grounds, Hurricane Laura toppled the statue.[1] The story made for an easy punch line in national news coverage. But in Louisiana, it is a stark reminder that political, social, racial, economic, and environmental issues are inexorably bound together. The essays included in *The Party Is Over* underscore the connection between our institutional, political, and policy choices. The state cannot effectively tackle criminal justice issues without reckoning with the dismantling of the social safety net over the last decade. To the degree that its coastline can be salvaged, the state must envision new directions for its economy. Without constitutional reform that allows for budget flexibility, hyperpartisan gridlock will perpetuate legislative stalemates.

Louisiana stands at a tipping point. The era of carnival-style politics has ended, but dysfunctional national-style politics threatens to replace it. The recent criminal justice reforms reflect the best of Louisiana's gumbo-style political heritage, bringing together richly diverse coalitions to work across partisan lines. The initiatives and reforms suggested above can help Louisiana overcome gridlock and build on the best of its political heritage while meeting the challenges of a new century.

NOTES

1. Grace Pateras, "Hurricane Laura Damaged a Lake Charles Confederate Monument, After Parish Officials Voted to Keep It," *Lafayette Daily Advertiser,* August 27, 2020.

SELECTED BIBLIOGRAPHY ON LOUISIANA POLITICS

Alford, Jeremy. *The Last Constitution: Louisiana's Greatest Political Generation and the Document that Defined Them All*, edited by Clancy DuBos. Baton Rouge: CC73 Publishing, 2020.

Baker, Liva. *The Second Battle of New Orleans: The Hundred-Year Struggle to Integrate the Schools.* New York: Harper Collins Publishers, 1996.

Bridges, Tyler. *Bad Bet on the Bayou: The Rise of Gambling in Louisiana and the Fall of Governor Edwin Edwards.* New York: Farrar, Straus, and Giroux, 2001.

Bridges, Tyler, and Jeremy Alford. *Long Shot: A Soldier, a Senator, a Serious Sin, an Epic Louisiana Election.* Baton Rouge, La.: Lisburn Press, 2016.

Brinkley, Allen. *Voices of Protest: Huey Long, Father Coughlin, and the Great Depression.* New York: Knopf, 1982.

Conaway, James. *Judge: The Life and Times of Leander Perez.* New York: Knopf, 1973.

Faircloth, Adam. *Race and Democracy: The Civil Rights Struggle in Louisiana, 1915–1972.* Athens: Univ. of Georgia Press, 1995.

Gill, James. *Lords of Misrule: Mardi Gras and the Politics of Race in New Orleans.* Jackson: Univ. Press of Mississippi, 1997.

Jeansonne, Glen. *Leander Perez: Boss of the Delta.* Baton Rouge: Louisiana State Univ. Press, 1977.

Kane, Harnett T., and Sam H. Jones. *Louisiana Hayride.* Gretna, La.: Pelican, 1990.

Kurtz, Michael, and Morgan Peoples. *Earl K. Long: The Saga of Uncle Earl and Louisiana Politics.* Baton Rouge: Louisiana State Univ. Press, 1990.

Liebling, A. J. *The Earl of Louisiana.* Baton Rouge: Louisiana State Univ. Press, 1970.

Maginnis, John. *Cross to Bear.* Baton Rouge: Darkhorse Press, 1992.

———. *The Last Hayride.* Baton Rouge: Gris Gris Press, 1984.

Mann, Robert. *Legacy to Power: Senator Russell Long of Louisiana.* New York: Paragon House, 1992.

Martin, Michael. *Russel Long: A Life in Politics.* Jackson: Univ. Press of Mississippi, 2014.

Parent, Wayne. *Inside the Carnival: Unmasking Louisiana Politics.* Baton Rouge: Louisiana State Univ. Press, 2004.

Rose, Douglas, ed. *The Emergence of David Duke and the Politics of Race.* Chapel Hill: Univ. of North Carolina Press, 1992.

Sindler, Allan P. *Huey Long's Louisiana: State Politics, 1920–1952.* Baltimore, Md.: Johns Hopkins Univ. Press, 1968.

Sullivan, Jas M., and Jonathan Winburn. *The Louisiana Legislative Black Caucus: Race and Representation in the Pelican State.* Baton Rouge: Louisiana State Univ. Press, 2011.

Van Meter, Matthew. *Deep Delta Justice: A Black Teen, His Lawyer, and Their Groundbreaking Battle for Civil Rights in the South.* New York: Little, Brown, 2020.

Vidrine, Clyde C., *Louisiana Political Hijinks: "I Ain't Talkin', But—."* Baton Rouge, La.: Claitor's Pub. Division, 1985.

Williams, T. Harry. *Huey Long.* New York: Bantam Books, 1970.

CONTRIBUTORS

JEREMY ALFORD is an author and independent journalist based in Baton Rouge. The author of *The Last Constitution* and coauthor of *Long Shot,* Alford is a regular contributor to the *New York Times* and has appeared as an analyst-source on CNN, Fox, MSNBC, and C-SPAN. He is the editor and publisher of LaPoliticsWeekly.com and *The Tracker,* Louisiana's leading trade publications for elected officials, campaign professionals, and donors. Alford was the recipient of grants from the Pulitzer Prizes and Andrew W. Mellon Foundation in 2019 to write about late Governor Kathleen Blanco, and the Center for Public Broadcasting in 2010 to produce a series on the Deepwater Horizon oil spill.

STEPHEN BARNES is the director of the Kathleen Blanco Public Policy Center at the University of Louisiana at Lafayette and an associate professor of economics in the B. I. Moody III College of Business. He also serves as the independent economist on the Louisiana Revenue Estimating Conference, a forecasting panel that sets income projections used to create the state budget. Barnes previously spent ten years in the Department of Economics at LSU, including serving as the director of the Economics & Policy Research Group. He has led studies on many topics related to the Louisiana economy, including topics in the economic fields of public, labor, and health.

PEARSON CROSS is an associate professor of political science and has served as the associate dean of the College of Liberal Arts at the University of Louisiana at Lafayette. His research focuses on state and local politics, with expertise on Louisiana. He hosts a weekly radio program on Louisiana politics, *Bayou to Beltway,* on Lafayette's NPR affiliate station, KRVS 88.7 FM.

MARK DAVIS is a research professor at Tulane University Law School and the Eugenie Schwartz Professor of River and Coastal Studies at the Tulane ByWater Institute. He also serves as the director of the Institute on Water Resources Law and Policy at the Tulane University Law School, the Tulane Center for Environmental Law, and the Tulane ByWater Institute.

CHASE J. EDWARDS is an assistant professor of business law at the University of Louisiana at Lafayette, where he holds three endowed research professorships and teaches courses in white-collar crime, cybersecurity, negotiations, and law for entrepreneurs. He is a former project manager and contract negotiator for the National Security Agency and National Reconnaissance Office. He earned his MBA as an NRO Advanced Academic Fellow at the US Naval Postgraduate School and earned a law degree at Louisiana State University.

BEVERLY MOORE HAYDEL is the president/CEO of Sequitur Consulting in Baton Rouge. Her work focuses primarily on public policy, governmental relations, and management consulting. Prior to founding Sequitur, Haydel served as the director of Civic Leadership Initiatives at the Baton Rouge Area Foundation. Haydel received her undergraduate degree from Harvard University and her law degree from Stanford Law School. Following several years practicing law in Washington, she returned home to Louisiana in 2013 to serve as a policy advisor to former governor Bobby Jindal.

MICHAEL HENDERSON is an assistant professor of political communication at Louisiana State University's Manship School of Mass Communication. He studies public opinion, campaigns, and elections. Additionally, he is the director of the school's *Louisiana Survey*, an annual poll of political attitudes among residents of Louisiana.

MIRYA HOLMAN is an associate professor of political science at Tulane University, with joint appointments in environmental studies and the Tulane Law School. She is an expert on gender and politics, urban politics, and political behavior. She has published widely in these areas, including her book, *Women* *in Politics in the American City,* and her coedited volume, *Good Reasons to Run.* She is the author or coauthor of more than fifty articles.

MICHELLE N. JEANIS is an assistant professor of criminal justice at the University of Louisiana at Lafayette. Jeanis's primary research interests include missing persons, youth runaways, and the representation of crime and victimization in the media.

DAVID KHEY is an associate professor of criminal justice at the University of Louisiana at Lafayette. His research focuses on criminology, criminal justice, and forensic science. His current research projects investigate drug policy, drug control, and evidence-based criminal justice programming, including reentry services. He has presented research on drug and alcohol use/abuse and provided policy analysis to local and state officials, including an invitation to address the Florida Governor's Office Drug Policy Advisory Council in 2007. Khey is an active member of the American Society of Criminology, American Academy of Forensic Sciences, and Southern Criminal Justice Association.

ANNA MITCHELL MAHONEY is an administrative assistant professor of women's political leadership at the Newcomb Institute at Tulane University. In 2016, she became the director of research for the institute. Anna's research is centered on women's representation and gendered institutions, which is explored in her book, *Women Take Their Place in State Legislatures: The Creation of Women's Caucuses* (Temple University Press, 2018). She has published articles in *Politics & Gender, Representation,* and *Legislative Studies Quarterly.*

CHRISTIE L. MALOYED is an associate professor of political science at the University of Louisiana at Lafayette. Her research focuses on civic education, religion and politics, and state and local government. Maloyed has published in the *Journal of Church and State,* the *History Teacher,* and the *Journal of Political Science Education* as well as in various edited volumes. She contributes regular columns on state and local politics for Lafayette's independent digital news magazine, *The Current.*

ROBERT MANN holds the Manship Chair in Journalism at the Manship School of Mass Communication at Louisiana State University. He has written books about the US civil rights movement, the Vietnam War, American wartime dissent, and the 1964 presidential election. Before joining the LSU faculty, he served as the communications director to Governor Kathleen Blanco; the state director and press secretary to US Senator John Breaux of Louisiana; press secretary to US Senator Russell Long of Louisiana; press secretary for the 1990 reelection campaign of US Senator J. Bennett Johnston; press secretary to the 1992 and 1998 Breaux reelection campaigns; and press secretary to the 2003 Blanco campaign.

JAN MOLLER is the director of the Louisiana Budget Project, which monitors and reports on state government spending and how it affects Louisiana's low- to moderate-income families. He is an award-winning journalist formerly with the *New Orleans Times-Picayune*'s state capital bureau, where he covered the state budget, health care policy, higher education, and races for Louisiana governor and US Senate seats. Before moving to Louisiana in 2003, he covered local and national politics at the *Las Vegas Review-Journal* and worked as a reporter and editor in Washington, D.C., primarily with the syndicated columnist Jack Anderson. Moller's work as an investigative reporter led to reforms in Louisiana's nursing home regulation and uncovered ethics violations by city officials in Nevada.

STEVEN PROCOPIO is the policy director at the Public Affairs Research Council of Louisiana, where he guides PAR's research agenda. He previously served as chief of staff of the Louisiana Division of Administration, where he worked on transparency and fiscal issues. Prior to working at the Division of Administration, Procopio was the director of research and accountability for the Lieutenant Governor's Office and the Department of Culture, Recreation and Tourism. He is also the original director of the Louisiana State University Public Policy Research Lab, where he worked on a variety of policy issues for state agencies, nonprofits, and academic researchers.

ALBERT L. SAMUELS is a professor of political science and currently serves as the chair of the Department of Political Science and History at Southern

University. His research interests include American politics, Black politics, Louisiana politics, educational policy, and voting rights. Samuels has been frequently featured in media outlets as a commentator on local, state, and national political events.

ROBERT TRAVIS SCOTT is the president of the Public Affairs Research Council of Louisiana. He has forty years of experience dealing with public policy issues as a journalist, researcher, commentator, analyst, and nonprofit manager. He is an author of many PAR reports on state budgeting, taxes, economic development, open governance, ethics, and health care. His work has received national and regional recognition through awards for policy research, investigative reporting, business coverage, and writing. Prior to joining PAR, he was based in Baton Rouge for eight years as the capital bureau chief for the *Times-Picayune,* the New Orleans metropolitan newspaper.

JOSHUA P. STOCKLEY is the Lawson and Sharon Swearingen Endowed Professor of Political Science and the director of the University Honors Program at the University of Louisiana Monroe. Stockley's teaching and research cover campaigns and elections, southern politics, Louisiana politics, public policy, and public administration. His works have appeared in multiple journals and edited volumes, including the *Roads to Congress* series. Stockley has worked on grants and published technical reports for the Department of Interior, the Delta Regional Authority, and the Louisiana Governor's Office of Elderly Affairs.

RICK SWANSON is a professor of political science at the University of Louisiana at Lafayette and served as department chair from 2016 to 2019. He has written two textbooks plus book chapters, journal articles, and encyclopedia entries involving law and politics, including civil rights history. His current research explores the history of Black civil rights in Lafayette Parish and the rest of south-central Louisiana.

GARY WAGNER holds the Acadiana Business Economist Endowed Chair at the University of Louisiana at Lafayette. He has authored or coauthored more than sixty professional articles and reports and has delivered more than three hundred presentations to public audiences on national and regional economic conditions. His professional research has appeared in many leading economics journals, including the *Journal of Law and Economics, National Tax Journal, Economics and Politics, Regional Science and Urban Economics, Papers in Regional Science, Public Choice,* and *Public Finance Review.* He previously served as vice president and senior regional officer for the Federal Reserve Bank of Cleveland.

INDEX

Note: Page numbers in italics refer to figures and tables; those followed by "n" indicate chapter endnotes.